A GRAND BOOK
FOR THE BEDSIDE TABLE . . .
a serious, thought provoking work,
though it is often very humorous."*

To be a healthy-looking, more vital, more energetic person, you don't need to be a fitness fanatic or a health bore. You don't have to live by the rigid rules of the latest self-help fad or the harsh denials of the newest wonder diet.

goes beyond mere physical well-being—it is a blueprint for every facet of your life. With the gentle wit and solid medical advice of Dr. Donald Norfolk, you will be well on the way to a longer, more fulfilling life.

**Chattanooga Times*

THE HABITS OF HEALTH

DR. DONALD NORFOLK

AVON
PUBLISHERS OF BARD, CAMELOT AND DISCUS BOOKS

AVON BOOKS
A division of
The Hearst Corporation
959 Eighth Avenue
New York, New York 10019

Published by arrangement with St. Martin's Press.
Library of Congress Catalog Card Number: 76-17530
ISBN: 0-380-01935-3

First Avon Printing, May, 1978

Contents

Introduction

There is an old saying, "God sends the acute diseases, the chronic diseases we create ourselves." Over the past decades medicine has managed to control most of the world's major infectious diseases, but it is still powerless to alleviate the vast range of chronic ill-health, much of which is self-inflicted and stems from apathy and ignorance.

Professor H. Frederick Kilander of Wagner College, Staten Island, New York, has been carrying out a study of the health knowledge of large groups of children and adults. He finds that ignorance and superstition still abound. Nearly half the high school children he questioned, for example, still believe that fish is a particularly valuable "brain food." A similar study in Springfield, Virginia, showed that three quarters of adults think that vitamins provide vim and vigor, and over a third believe that sweating is a practical way of reducing weight.

A poll commissioned by the Blue Cross Association confirms that most Americans know far less about their health than they generally believe. Worse than their lack of knowledge is their failure to act on the knowledge they have. Thus the poll showed that while 81 percent of people appreciate the benefits of taking regular exercise, only 37 percent were putting this knowledge to practical use. Similarly, most people today appreciate the dangers of obesity and have a fairly accurate idea of how to lose weight, yet few take steps to keep themselves in trim. Why? Why this sad discrepancy between knowledge and rational conduct? Is our failure to protect our heritage of health due to laziness, lack of time, or the belief that keeping fit involves endless discipline and sacrifice?

In the past the road to health has often been made to seem a cheerless pilgrimage. When exercising, the masochistic maxim has been, "If it hurts, it must be doing you good." When dieting, the advice has been, "If it tastes good, spit it out." But asceticism has no part to play in the maintenance of health. Getting fit is, and should be, fun. It shouldn't involve hours of endless struggle, for health is the body's natural state.

The secret lies in the establishment of proper habits. That is the message of this book. By the age of twenty-five we are, according to psychologist William James, a "bundle of habits." If these habits are bad, our health will be poor. If our habits are sane, our health will be sound. We often excuse our behavioral quirks by saying that we are *creatures* of habit, overlooking the fact that we are also *creators* of habits. In the first place we make our habits, then forever afterward our habits make us. If we want to keep well–simply and surely, throughout our lives–we merely need to establish habits of health. We've got to eat, so why not train the body to eat well? Since we've got to walk, why not learn to move with elegance and grace? When we work, why not work with maximum efficiency? Why stand badly, when we can stand well?

This book analyzes every facet of our lives, from getting up in the morning to going to bed at night, from washing dishes to making love. It looks at the clothes we wear, the food we eat, the drugs we swallow, and the holidays we take, and offers the promise that if we order these simple daily activities aright, we will discover the simplest possible way of preserving health and happiness. There is no need to become a fitness fanatic or a health bore. If we get into the habit of health, without effort or fuss we will maintain our looks, life, and energy. Healthy habits of action will also improve other facets of our lives, for as psychologist Abraham Maslow has said, "All desirable traits in a human being correlate positively." This book, therefore, is not simply a manual of health: It is a blueprint for healthy living that offers in addition happiness, friendship, beauty, elegance, longevity, and success.

This way of life cannot be enforced. No public health measures, no legal reforms, no acts of Congress or Parliament will *make* us healthy. A million hospitals cannot create one healthy person, for the organization necessary for the treatment of the sick can never produce and maintain health. There are countless medicines aimed at relieving numerous specific diseases, but there is only one way to health: the correct use of the body. If we use our eyes badly, we suffer fatigue and strain. The remedy then is not to wear glasses, but to use the eyes correctly. Similarly, taking antacids or undergoing gastric surgery cannot "cure" the indigestion caused by faulty eating habits.

The urgent medical need today is not for improved drugs or more advanced surgical techniques, but for better application of our existing knowledge of health.

When people were living in a primitive state, they could safely rely on their instincts to order their behavior. When they became "civilized," they needed to acquire patterns of behavior more suited to their new environment and artificial urban way of life. These acquired patterns are handed down from generation to generation, but with the recent rapid changes in our way of life, we must expect that the habits we acquired from our parents will, in many cases, be sadly out of date. Hence the need for this book. It is written for teenagers (now is the time to establish sound habit patterns), parents (most bad habits are established in childhood), and adults (it's never too late to alter behavioral faults). In writing it I have tried to follow the advice given to authors by publisher Joseph Pulitzer: "Put it before them briefly so they will read it, clearly so they will appreciate it, picturesquely so they will remember it and, above all, accurately so they will be guided by it." Sections are arranged alphabetically for easy reference. The selection of material is necessarily idiosyncratic, for to publish a complete record of our present-day knowledge of health would, according to one estimate, require a continuous line of print stretching for 100 million miles.

I hope that it helps many to find their way to well-being and happiness. That so many suffer unnecessary ill health and invalidism distresses me. Why are people satisfied with so little? If we can be supple, why are we stiff? Why do we drag ourselves through life when we can be bubbling over with energy? If we can know the thrill of being fired with passion and enthusiasm, why do we settle for apathy and boredom? Death to me is not life's greatest calamity. "The tragedy of life," as Albert Schweitzer said, "is what dies inside a man while he lives."

We often indulge in the futile game of wishful thinking: "If only we weren't so fat." "If only we didn't get out of breath." "If only we had more energy." We highlight the problem with ease but don't go on to seek the cure. We don't look impotently at our cars and say, "If only the tires weren't flat" or "If only the engine were firing on all six cylinders." Once we spot the defect, we go out and seek the remedy. Why don't we do the same with our personal problems?

Now is the time to act, before physiological symptoms of disease produce pathological changes of disease which are less easy to correct. But if you're overweight, don't go on a crash diet; change to a steady diet that gets you slim and keeps you slim enjoyably (see *Obesity*). Don't push yourself to the point of complete mental and physical exhaustion and then rely on a fortnight's holiday to help you recover. Learn the secrets of relaxed living and make almost every day a holiday (see *Relaxation*).

Join the health revolution. Make a habit of health. Urge your friends and teach your children to do the same, for if character is habit of thought, health is habit of action.

Apathy

Apathy has been defined as "want of feeling, lack of passion, emotion or excitement." It is one of the endemic diseases of our age. People today tend to be tired, bored and indifferent; their lives an aching vacuum, an amorphous, colorless, purposeless void.

Psychologists explain that this all-pervading apathy stems from a greatly increased need for self-protection. To shield ourselves from the psychic stresses and strains of contemporary life, we are forced to cut off our feelings. To avoid experiencing emotional pain we develop the art of "playing it cool." To anesthetize ourselves against tragedy we alienate ourselves from the harsh and often brutal world around us. But this schizoid withdrawal is not without its dangers. If practiced too long it becomes an habitual set, an inflexible character trait that prevents our enjoying a full, vibrant, passionate life, for if we forever shield ourselves from feeling pain we must also deny ourselves the opportunity of experiencing pleasure.

Life can never be without risks, and we will never know happiness if we are not prepared to accept the possibility of suffering. There can be no pleasure without pain; no health without sickness; no mountain-top experiences without there being valleys of despair. To shake off the yoke of apathy, boredom and depression, we must have the courage to enter the maelstrom of life.

But the quest for happiness is not as hazardous as it might seem. We need as a first step only to recapture the simple pleasure of being alive–the *joie de vivre* we all know as children but often lose as adults. It is the birthright we squander with profligate lack of concern;

the basic delight of breathing, smelling, touching, tasting, feeling, growing and moving in a rich and exciting world.

California psychiatrist William C. Schutz, in his book *Joy*, speaks of the bodily joy which comes "not from an athletic body, but from one that functions smoothly, gracefully, without unnecessary strain; a body in which the joints move easily, the muscles are toned, the blood flows vigorously, the breathing is deep and full, food is digested well, the sexual apparatus is in good order, and the nervous system works effectively." Every single word in this book is dedicated to achieving this end, to obtaining the satisfaction and sheer delight of using the body as nature intended. One can never know freedom, happiness or peace of mind when one is functioning badly, is in poor physical condition, tired, weak or sick. The thesis of this book (and a major tenet of yogic philosophy) is that the path of liberation and the gateway of joy lies in the adoption of correct habits of bodily usage.

For centuries we have been taught to keep a tight rein on our emotions, to deny our bodily feelings and to shun the pleasures of the flesh. If we are to reintroduce now an element of ecstasy and passion into our lives, we must exchange anomie for bonhomie. We must throw off the inhibiting shackles of puritanism and learn once more to live, love and laugh.

To do this there is no need to go away for an encounter weekend, or enroll for a prolonged course of sensitivity training. Simply take this book in your hand and feel the smoothness of its pages, the hardness of its edge, the texture of its cover, the lightness of its leaves. This will improve your tactile sense. In the same way it is not necessary to take psychedelic drugs to become "switched on" to the wonderful colors and forms of the world around us. We merely need to open our eyes. To improve your color sense spend a day studying the color red. Notice how many shades there are of this one color, spot the infinite gradation of tones from vivid crimsons to delicate pinks, observe the frequent admixture of other colors, and discover how much green and yellow is reflected from what first appears to be a purely "red" apple or "red" tomato.

Start to explore the world around you with the curiosity of a child. Don't just eat an orange, but occasionally take it in your hands and observe its subtle coloring, its shape and myriad irregularities. Then with eyes closed feel the texture of its skin, the waxiness of its surface. Judge its weight and temperature and test its resilience to gentle pressure. Then slowly peel the skin, listening to the sound made as the skin is pared from the flesh. Finally, sample the juice and flesh of the fruit itself. With your senses honed and digestive juices flowing, no orange will ever have tasted quite so good! Do this with your other foods, roll them round your tongue, test their texture and savor their flavor for this will enhance your palate *and* improve your digestion.

Do the same thing when you are making love. Don't always hurry to the conclusion, but wallow instead in the sight, taste, touch and smell of the one you love. That will greatly increase your enjoyment of sex. In every aspect of life employ your senses to the full. Never be afraid to be a sensualist. Enhance moments of repose by meditating on the shape, texture and perfume of a flower, or the harmony, rhythm and tonal qualities of a favorite piece of music. In this way you will quicken your senses and banish boredom, for apathy literally means the absence of feeling (*a-pathos*). To escape its clutches we must re-establish contact with both our environment and our fellow man. We must no longer attempt to immure ourselves from the sufferings of others. In a competitive world we need once more to learn to care. Herein lies the salvation of society, and herein for us a rich source of inspiration and joy, for as psychoanalyst Rollo May says: "It is the mythos of care—and, I often believe, this mythos alone—which enables us to stand against the cynicism and apathy which are the psychological illnesses of our day."

Asepsis

In 1865, Joseph Lister became the first surgeon to carry out an operation using antiseptic techniques. An eleven-year-old boy had fractured his leg in a collision with a cart and the wound had penetrated the skin. In an attempt to prevent putrefaction, Lister took the revolutionary step of applying to the torn flesh a pad soaked in carbolic acid. The wound healed quickly and without infection. He repeated the procedure at subsequent operations and two years later was able to report to the British Medical Association that in nine months he had had "not a single instance of pyaemia, hospital gangrene or erysipelas," diseases that had previously killed up to 50 percent of patients undergoing surgery. (Lister chose carbolic acid because he remembered an incident in which an outbreak of cattle disease had been checked by treating the local sewage with a strong carbolic solution.)

In time, it was realized that carbolic acid was an unnecessarily caustic disinfectant for human skin, and gradually it was replaced by a succession of milder, more effective antiseptics such as iodine, surgical spirit, hydrogen peroxide, and formalin. These in turn have been superseded. In hospitals greater reliance now is placed on aseptic techniques–sterilizing instruments, "scrubbing up," and wearing protective clothing and masks–that prevent initial bacterial contamination of the wound. If infection occurs despite these precautions, it can normally be overcome today by appropriate antibiotic treatment.

A similar change has occurred in the recommended first-aid treatment of minor abrasions and cuts. It is realized now that antiseptics powerful enough to kill germs are also strong enough to kill human cells, including the white blood cells that combat infection and the young dermal cells responsible for the healing of skin wounds. Antiseptics, therefore, can easily do more harm than good. As Dr. Theodor Rosebury, Emeritus Professor of Bacteriology at Washington University in St. Louis, says, "The accepted treatment for minor skin wounds is to wash them clean and keep them dry and covered with gauze that lets air in and keeps dirt out." It is best to use special nonadherent dressings since the mass of tiny fibers projecting from the surface of even the smoothest piece of lint easily gets caught up in the healing wound.

Wounds should be washed with soap, running water, and a piece of gauze or soft nail brush until all particles of dirt and debris have been removed. Curiously enough, Lister's first attempts at wound-cleansing involved the use of cold water. At the time, it was believed that wound infection and the tarnishing of silver resulted from the action of poisonous gases or "miasmas" emanating from polluted cesspits and sewers. Lister conjectured that if frequent washing could prevent the tarnishing of silver cutlery, it might equally well check the putrefaction of surgical wounds. He followed the practice of washing wounds with cold water until Pasteur showed that wound-infection results from bacterial contamination rather than miasmic poisoning.

Zinc sulfate and boric acid ointments are mildly antiseptic and may be helpful in preventing the adherence of dressings to wounds, but their use is best avoided. It is part of the normal repair process for dead skin cells and bacteria to be cast off from the surface of a healing wound. Using ointments and wet, soggy dressings can only hamper this process of natural debridement and in addition is likely to trap dirt and germs around the wound.

Blood Pressure

It is believed that 23 million people in the United States are suffering from high blood pressure, a disease that is directly responsible for 60,000 American deaths each year and a major contributing factor in the cause of strokes, heart attacks, and kidney disease. Sadly, half the people with high blood pressure are totally unaware of their problem, which makes them four times as likely to succumb to a heart attack or stroke, and twice as likely to suffer kidney disease. What exactly is *high* blood pressure?

A certain pressure is needed to drive the twelve or more pints of blood around an arterial circuit, which measures somewhere in the region of 100,000 miles, and to make sure that an adequate supply of nourishment is distributed throughout the body from the furthermost parts of the toes to the very top of the head. This pressure was first demonstrated by an English clergyman, the Reverend Stephen Hales, in 1733. He inserted a narrow glass tube filled with water into the artery of a horse and watched the water rise to a height of nine feet. Since then the technique of measuring blood pressure has been considerably refined. Almost a century later a French scientist, Jean Louis Marie Poiseuille, hit on the idea of using a column of mercury instead of water to measure the pressure and so shortened the length of tube required. In 1896 an Italian, Riva-Rocci, showed that by placing an inflated cuff around the arm it was possible to measure blood pressure without having to penetrate an artery. And in 1905 a Russian physician called Korotkow introduced the use of a stethoscope, which made it possible to measure the blood pressure during the resting phase of the heart as well as when it was contracting.

So, by a concerted, cosmopolitan effort over a span of nearly two hundred years, the modern *sphygmomanometer*, "pulse pressure measurer," was developed. With its aid and with that of a stethoscope (a name inappropriately derived from the Greek words meaning an instrument for *looking* at the chest), doctors can quickly measure in millimeters of mercury the pressure of the blood during both phases of the heartbeat–a higher reading when the heart is contracting (*systolic pressure*) and a lower reading when the heart is relaxing (*diastolic pressure*). The standard measurement is usually given as 120/80 mm. of mercury, but it must be realized that this is an average reading for young adult males and not an ideal norm. Just as people vary in height, collar size, and color of hair, so they vary in what is for them a normal, healthy pressure of blood. Readings of 110/70 or 140/90 are almost certainly no more pathological and no more matters of concern than heights of 6 feet 2 inches or 4 feet 11 inches. Thus, when doctors measured the blood pressure of 742 healthy male students, they found that 75 of them had blood pressures which would be considered abnormally high, but they were not suffering from hypertension because for them these pressures were perfectly normal.

Blood pressure varies with our mood. Even the act of having it measured tends to push it up several points, which is why doctors generally place little reliance on single readings, preferring to take a second measurement when their patients are more relaxed. When we are excited, anxious, worried, or afraid, our blood pressure is automatically increased to insure that an adequate supply of blood reaches our muscles, heart, and brain in preparation for any physical action we need to take. When a crisis is over, the pressure automatically returns to its resting state. These fluctuations are perfectly natural and present no danger to health under normal circumstances, for even the relatively thin-walled arteries of the brain can withstand pressures ten to twenty times the normal resting blood pressure levels. Danger arises only when the arteries are diseased, or when the high pressures within them are unduly prolonged. Like hot water pipes, our arteries are built to withstand sudden surges of high pressure but are not designed to withstand sustained high pressures. When high pressures persist, the body does its best to compensate by strengthening and thickening the arterial walls, but this has the unfortunate side effect of increasing the resistance to the flow of blood and so raising the blood pressure still further. This tendency is aggravated by a resetting of the self-regulating mechanisms within the body that are responsible for the control of blood pressure, which become so accustomed to the higher pressures that they accept them as the new *base* level. This means that once started, hypertension tends to be a self-perpetuating disease. It can be treated by a whole range of antihypertensive drugs, but these can hardly be considered a cure and often produce unwelcome side effects such as impotence, dizziness, and drowsiness. More basic help is derived from reducing weight, eating less salt, and stopping smoking.

A Mayo Clinic study of 2,042 patients over the age of fifteen showed that blood pressure rises as weight increases, probably because it takes a mile of capillaries to feed each extra pound of fat, which means an increased volume of blood and an increased blood pressure. It was noted during World War II that people living on a sparse diet in occupied countries in Europe developed little fat and little hypertension.

Reducing salt intake is another sensible dietary precaution, since salt holds fluid within the body and so tends to increase the blood pressure. This risk was appreciated over four thousand years ago, and a Chinese medical text dating back to 2600 B.C. mentions that eating too much salt alters the pulse and causes a florid complexion (see *Salt*).

Quitting smoking helps reduce blood pressure because one of the direct pharmacological actions of nicotine is to increase pulse rate and blood pressure. Tests have shown that smoking only one cigarette increases the level of noradrenaline in the blood by 25 percent. Since the action of this stress hormone is to raise the blood pressure and constrict the blood vessels to prepare the body for "fight or flight," it would seem that even one cigarette is one too many for the hypertensive patient.

More important still is the development of a calm, relaxed approach to life. There is no doubt that the ideal way to escape hypertension is to avoid a hypertensive way of life. Dr. Ainslie Meares, an Australian psychiatrist, has found that most persons suffering from hypertension are typically ambitious, conscientious, and competitive. They suffer from frustration when they are held back from achieving their goals or maintaining their high, often inflexible, standards. Such persons wouldn't be true to themselves if they tried to adopt a lackadaisical approach to life. They must be encouraged to work and strive, says Meares, but at the same time helped "to develop a philosophy so that [they] can accept frustration without too great emotional disquiet." Even "relatively small changes in outlook may be sufficient to reduce anxiety below the threshold for psychosomatic disturbance," he finds.

At Harvard, Dr. Herbert Benson has helped patients to reduce their blood pressure by means of biofeedback techniques, rewarding them with five-second flashes of *Playboy* pinups whenever they relax enough to lower their blood pressure. But he too feels that these techniques need to be supported by an altered attitude toward life. Blood pressure may be reduced in the laboratory, he says, but "to keep blood pressure down at home and at the office may require some revision of behavior and even re-evaluation of life style."

Dr. William Brams of Chicago writes in his book *Your Blood Pressure and How to Live with It*, "If we doctors could prescribe domestic peace and a contented mind as easily as we prescribe pills, we could cure an impressive percentage of our patients tomorrow." We can obtain this treatment only by supplying it ourselves.

Breakfasts

The years have brought several changes in our pattern of eating, but none so great as the revolution that has overtaken our early morning meal. Breakfast was once a major repast. A typical breakfast menu of Clodius Albinus, the gluttonous Roman governor of Britain, was reported to be five hundred figs, a hundred peaches, ten melons, twenty pounds of grapes, and four hundred oysters (a hearty appetite, no doubt assisted by occasional visits to the vomitorium). In medieval Britain a suitable "braikfaste for my lorde and my ladie," according to the Northumberland Household Book, was two manchets of bread, a quart of beer, a quart of wine, two pieces of salt fish, and six baked herrings or sprats. By Edwardian times the early morning meal had grown in elaborateness and elegance. In his book *The Edwardians*, J. B. Priestley recalls a representative house-party breakfast of the time that was complete with porridge and cream, pots of coffee, China and India tea, and enormous sideboards groaning with cold meats, pressed beef, ham, tongue, and ptarmigan, accompanied by melons, peaches, nectarines, and raspberries, with scones, toast, marmalade, and jam to fill any remaining crevices. "Not since Imperial Rome can there have been so many signposts to gluttony," Priestley commented.

Then a change occurred. Gluttony was a vice, particularly abhorrent in an age encompassing distressing poverty among the newly emerged industrial working classes. Breakfasts had to become more utilitarian. Had not the early Christian ascetic, Saint Jerome, proscribed the eating of young cranes and steaming pheasants for breakfast? "Gluttony," claimed Saint Jerome, "is the mother of avarice." Even more pithily, he observed that too often "men's only God is their belly."

There was also the limiting factor of time. The occupants of Edwardian country houses could while away their ample leisure time breakfasting on chicken, woodcock, grilled trout, and steak, but the twentieth-century worker had work to do and a train to catch and so was forced to make do with a quick snack of boiled eggs, coffee, and toast. This trend has continued until the average breakfast today, if not completely overlooked, consists of little more than coffee, toast, and a bowl of cereal.

That great culinary heritage of the British people, the English breakfast, has been discarded in favor of the less nutritious, less sustaining, Continental snack. Its demise has been mourned by doctors, nutritionists, and educators alike. Sir Alan Herbert, the English poet, regrets that his countrymen are aping the "pale foreigners" who "must crawl through the morning on coffee and rolls." He rhapsodizes on the meal that built an empire:

Oh Breakfast, oh Breakfast, the meal of my heart,
Bring porridge, bring sausage, bring fish for a start.
Bring kidneys and mushrooms and partridges' legs
But let the foundation be bacon and eggs.

Certainly the modern breakfast is less nutritious than it was before. In 1970, a Consumer Subcommittee of the United States Senate conducted an inquiry into the flourishing breakfast-food industry and found that in tempting people to buy convenience foods, it was diverting consumer dollars away from more nutritious foods. Without their added vitamins, many packaged cereals were hardly more nutritious than the cartons they were packed in. "Puffed rice," reported one expert, "is five times as expensive as ordinary rice and yet provides smaller amounts of most nutrients." Analysis showed that the most popular brands of American breakfast cereals were the least nutritious. They "fatten but do little to prevent malnutrition." Their health claims in fact were just so much pap, cackle, and puff.

Eating a carbohydrate-rich breakfast of cereal, toast, and sweetened coffee is bad for the teeth. A leading British dentist reckons that feeding the family with a hearty breakfast of bacon and eggs could prevent hundreds of children's needing false teeth while they are still at school. It would also help to prevent fatigue. Schoolteachers report a lethargy and lack of concentration in many of their pupils during the final classes of the morning, which is probably due to an excessive lowering of blood sugar level. Surveys have shown that 50 percent of children in Britain have an inadequate evening meal and 25 percent go to school without a proper breakfast. This means that many youngsters go without food for eighteen hours, which leads to a lowering of blood sugar levels and consequent tiredness, irritability, and lack of concentration in the prelunch period. Charles Dickens observed the same phenomenon in adults and, when describing the case of *Bardell v. Pickwick* in *The Pickwick Papers*, stressed the importance of a good breakfast for jurymen. "A good contented, well-breakfasted juryman is a capital thing to get hold of. Discontented or hungry jurymen," he wrote, "always find for the plaintiff."

Many people skimp their breakfasts in the belief that this helps to keep them slim. In fact, the reverse is more often the case. Studies have shown that three quarters of the teenage girls who go without breakfast are overweight. This is because a falling blood sugar in the middle of the morning drives them to take calorie-rich snacks to boost their flagging energies.

It is important that the first meal of the day should be a true "break-fast." Continental breakfasts of cereal, toast, jam, and sweetened coffee provide plenty of calories at the start of the day, but their effect is short-lived. Carbohydrate foods like these are quickly absorbed, leading to a rapid drop in blood sugar level and a resultant feeling of fatigue and irritability. Protein foods such as eggs, milk, bacon, and sausage are less rapidly absorbed and so help to sustain energy levels during the morning. Proteins also increase the body's metabolic rate, which is why a breakfast of bacon and eggs makes such a warming start to a winter's day. (The actual heating of the food makes little difference. A piece of cold ham provides the body with as much heat as a slice of sizzling bacon of equivalent weight.)

Babe Ruth, the legendary American baseball player, started the day with a meal of porterhouse steak, four fried eggs, and a large portion of French fried potatoes, washed down with a pot of coffee and a pint of bourbon. Sir Winston Churchill preferred a lighter breakfast of grouse and caviar. In their different ways both men showed an appreciation of sound nutritional practice by insisting on starting the day with a sustaining meal rich in protein. As the South Americans say, "Eat breakfast like a king, lunch like a princess and dinner like a pauper."

Breast-Feeding

Despite the extravagant claims for many modern baby foods, there is little doubt that the finest food for growing babies is still mother's milk.

Breast-feeding is both simple and cheap. It requires no bottles, no sterilization of utensils, no warming to bring the milk to body temperature, and no laborious reconstitution of dried milk powders. More important, the formula of breast milk is always right. Cow's milk contains roughly three times as much salt as human milk, and twice the amount of protein. Drinking it can upset the osmotic pressure of the baby's blood and throw an undue strain upon the kidneys. Owing to the higher caloric content of cow's milk, bottle-fed babies are three times as likely to be overweight as breast-fed babies, and since 80 percent of overweight children remain obese in later life, British manufacturer's claim that a baby food "Builds Bonny Babies" might equally well read, "Creates Obese Adults." The early introduction of bottle-fed babies to the foreign proteins contained in cow's milk increases their risk of contracting allergies such as eczema and asthma, and their exposure to germs carried by feeding bottles and rubber nipples renders them prone to gastroenteritis. A survey carried out in Britain showed that over a third of the feeding bottles and nearly half the rubber nipples in use in private homes were not sterile. Further help in the infant's battle against infection is provided by the antibodies carried in its mother's milk and the early donation of white blood cells it receives in the colostrum, the rich yellow fluid secreted by the breasts immediately after childbirth. Bottle-fed babies also suffer in that the chemical composition of cow's milk favors the development within the intestine of potentially pathogenic bacteria of the coliform type, whereas breast milk encourages the growth of harmless lactic acid bacteria.

Breast-feeding for the mother is psychologically satisfying; it helps foster a good mother-child relationship and provides a stimulus that hastens the return of the womb to its prepregnant size. Mothers who breast-feed their babies are also less likely to develop breast cancer in later life, while those who suppress lactation with estrogen drugs treble their risk of getting a thrombosis.

The advantages of breast milk are such that ailing infants in hospital are often fed on milk expressed from donor mothers, and at one time it was a common practice for sick adults to employ a wet nurse. Dr. John Caius (1510-1573), the founder of Caius College, Cambridge, existed entirely on human milk during the last few years of his life and according to his biographer suffered wide swings of mood depending on the temperament of his current nurse. He was "peevish and full of frets when he sucked one woman . . . quiet and well when he sucked another of contrary disposition."

Many women doubt their ability to provide their babies with an adequate supply of milk, but generally these fears are unfounded. A study in Minneapolis showed that 96 percent of women exposed to an intensive breast-feeding promotional campaign were able to establish satisfactory feeding for at least two months, a figure considerably higher than the national average.

A mother will often express concern when her baby fails to show an immediate weight gain, taking this as a sign that she is supplying it with insufficient milk. In fact it is perfectly normal for babies during the first two days of their lives to lose anything up to 10 percent of their birth weight. This loss is generally made up within a fortnight, breast-fed babies tending to regain their birth weight slightly quicker than those who have been bottle-fed.

The amount of milk secreted varies from woman to

/oman and bears no relation to the size of her breasts. One woman is credited with supplying the needs of seven babies, producing ten pints of milk a day, one third of the output of an average dairy cow. There are any number of folk remedies for increasing the flow of milk, including eating powdered earthworms, dried goat udder, and boiled sea slugs. The only attested recipes are freedom from anxiety and the stimulus of suckling itself. The more a baby draws at the breast, the greater the flow of milk. In this way supply is adjusted to suit demand. When supplementary feeds are given, the baby's appetite is partially satisfied, sucking becomes less vigorous, and the supply of milk is reduced. Psychological factors also reduce the flow of milk. Adequate rest, contentment, and lack of haste stimulate lactation; anxiety, domestic worries, and feelings of inadequacy inhibit it. Certain drugs also reduce the flow of milk, notably birth control pills, antihistamine, and diuretics. In view of this, and of the fact that many pharmaceutical drugs are secreted in breast milk and can have an adverse effect on the child, they should be taken with care by nursing mothers and only under proper medical supervision.

The common problems encountered during breast-feeding are sore nipples and painful breasts. Both these conditions normally clear up in about four days. While a woman is breast-feeding, the nipples should be kept clean, but without excessive use of soap, which can destroy the protective mantle of fat covering the skin, leading to chapping and the development of painful cracks. Another protection is to place the breasts well into the baby's mouth during feeding and to remove the baby at the end of the feed by lowering its jaw to release its hold rather than drawing it away directly from the nipple.

Painful breasts often result when the breasts first fill with milk and become tense and tender. This tautness generally subsides when the babe starts feeding, but the pressure can be relieved where necessary by gentle manual expression of milk. When a tender lump appears in the breast, accompanied by feverish symptoms, it is advisable to consult a doctor, for this may be a sign of mastitis, a painful condition which often requires antibiotic treatment.

Breathing

From the moment of birth, when we take our first faltering gasp, to the twilight moment when we expel our final sigh, our lives are ruled by the air we breathe. We can go for weeks without food and days without water, but can survive for only minutes without air.

The ancients had no proper understanding of respiratory physiology, but they realized that it played a vital role in the maintenance of health. Breathing to them was a way of absorbing the mysterious life force that animated the world around them. The ancient Hebrews spoke of the "breath of life." Yogis, long before the discovery of oxygen, sought to gain control of *prana*, the vital force extracted from the air during breathing which, once absorbed into the system, brings health, vitality, and renewal to every organ of the body. The Romans shared the same belief and used a single word, *spiritus*, to describe both "breath" and "life force"; it is from this common root that we derive the words *spirit* and *inspiration* to describe the states of physical vitality and mental creativity which arise when we are bubbling over with the life force. (The word *expired*, used as a synonym for *died*, derives from the same source.)

Today we know far more about the physiology of respiration and yet, paradoxically, pay less attention than our forebears to the cultivation of proper breathing techniques. Two hundred years ago Voltaire said, "A good deal of human illness could be cured by breathing." In a sedentary age this is more than ever likely to be true.

The lungs consist of a mass of tiny air sacs called *alveoli*—approximately 300 million of them, joined together like an enormous bunch of grapes to provide an area over forty times the surface area of the body. Each alveolus is surrounded by a network of slender capillaries, which are just wide enough to allow the red blood corpuscles to pass by in single file. The corpuscles remain in contact with the alveolar wall for about three quarters of a minute, during which time they discharge their store of carbon dioxide waste and absorb oxygen, which they then transport throughout the body to nourish every individual body cell. The conscious practice of deep breathing exercises helps promote the oxygenation of the blood and the elimination of waste carbon dioxide.

To a yogi, breathing practices *(pranayama)* are just as important as the adoption of special postures (*asanas*). A favorite yoga exercise is the "healing breath," which is often used as a prelude to meditation, since it acts as both a tonic for the body and a sedative for the mind. It consists of a cycle of inbreathing (*puraka*), breath-holding (kumbhaka), and breathing out (*rechaka*), performed to a count which is always in the ratio of 1:4:2. If breathing in is carried on for a count of three, the breath is held for a count of twelve, and breathing out conducted to a count of six. The period of breath-holding must be maintained without tension and is of importance in that it aids the diffusion of air within the alveoli. The exercise should be repeated four or five times and performed once a day. According to the Shiva Sanhita, a classical Sanskrit text, the person who practices the healing breath "becomes healthy and likeable and emits a pleasant odour, and there will be good appetite and digestion, cheerfulness, a good figure, courage and enthusiasm and strength."

The discovery of the tonic effect of deep-breathing exercises was made independently by William Knowles, a young British merchant seaman who was sent to convalesce with his aunt in Montreal when he contracted tuberculosis. Here he came under the influence of Dr. Oz Ha-nish, a physician who combined the traditions of eastern and western medicine. The doctor noticed faults in the young man's pattern of breathing and suggested certain remedial exercises. These were to have a profound effect upon his life. They solved his immediate problem by helping cure his tuberculosis, but in time they did far more than this. Some years later, war broke out, and a young and inexperienced William Knowles found himself commanding a platoon of soldiers during the bloody battle of the Somme. His men had reached the point of complete collapse; burdened by the weight of their equipment and bowed down with fatigue, they were unable to lift themselves from the thick mud that lined the trenches. Captain Knowles knew it was useless to try and urge them on. They were far too exhausted to respond. But with a flash of inspiration he remembered the lessons he had learnt from Dr. Ha-nish and gave the command, "Breathe deeply." There, as they crouched in the trenches, the men started to breathe to Knowles's command: "In . . . out," "In . . . out." Gradually their tired muscle-fibers and exhausted brain-cells responded to the sudden surcharge of oxygen. Their energy returned. As if by a miracle, they found the stamina to continue their advance. Soon after, Captain Knowles was wounded by an exploding shell. While waiting for help to arrive, he found he could alleviate his pain by practicing deep, steady breathing. When army surgeons recommended the amputation of his gangrenous foot, Knowles declined their help and set about curing himself with the help of his special breathing exercises. When the war was over, Captain Knowles set out to proclaim the value of breath control. To his surprise and delight, a crowd of over a thousand people attended his first public meeting. Many more joined the Institute of Breathing which he formed in 1935. All were assured, "The way to better health is through better breathing."

Too many people are habitual shallow-breathers. At rest we use only a fraction of our total lung capacity—no more than a tenth when we are readying a book or writing a letter. If sedentary workers are to maintain the full efficiency of their lungs, they need to bring these dis-used areas into play by taking some brisk physical exercise every day, such as skipping, cycling, or running in place. This ventilates the little-used areas of the apex and bases of the lungs, increases the vital capacity of the lungs, and raises the rate of oxygen uptake from the alveoli. A useful exercise to improve lung function is to recite as much as possible of a poem or piece of Scripture with one breath, trying each day to increase the length of the passage repeated before drawing a second breath. This was a favorite exercise of Captain Knowles which can easily be fitted into odd moments of the day. When walking breathe in to a count of five or six strides, taking care to fill the lungs as fully as possible. Then for the next five or six strides, breath out, concentrating on expelling every particle of air from the lungs. Regular practice of this exercise will improve lung capacity, making it possible to increase the number of steps taken with each breath. A useful addition to this exercise, recommended by the poet Ella Wheeler Wilcox, is to repeat words suggestive of vitality and life while breathing in, and those evoking thoughts of rest and relaxation while breathing out. For example, while breathing in, mentally recite the words "Life . . . life . . . life . . . life . . . life" with every step taken. While breathing out, quietly repeat the words "Peace . . . peace . . . peace . . . peace . . ." The repetition of these words while breathing deeply can bring exhilaration to body and mind.

Another habit to be avoided is mouth-breathing. When we breathe through the nose, we warm and filter the inspired air. It has been estimated that we inhale 20 billion particles of foreign matter a day. When we breathe through the nose, most of these bits of dirt and dust are trapped in the sticky mucus-secretion that lines the airways. From there they are wafted harmlessly to the stomach by the cilia, the fine hairs that exert a constant sweeping action over the surface of the mucous membranes. Experimental animals have been given dirty air to breathe at temperatures ranging from 500° C. to -100° C., and in every case the air was cleaned and virtually warmed to body temperature before it entered the lungs. Such is the efficiency of the body's air-conditioning apparatus, providing it is not bypassed by breathing through the mouth. A further advantage of breathing through the nose is that it helps clear the sinuses. These drained easily when man walked on all four limbs, but the assumption of the upright posture has placed the opening of some of these sinuses above their bases, so they can no longer be drained by gravity. This makes it all the more important to breathe deeply through the nose, for this draws fluid from the sinuses in exactly the same way that the passage of a current of air sucks up paint in an aerosol paint spray. Because of this, an invaluable exercise for sinus-sufferers if deep alternate-nostril breathing.

Before performing any breathing exercise, it is advisable first to empty the lungs of stale air. Fishes are fortunate in that they receive a steady stream of oxygen in the water that flows constantly over their gills. We have to breathe out before we can take in a fresh supply of oxygen. Even then, only a sixth of the air in our lungs gets changed with every breath we take and this proportion is further reduced when we breathe shallowly. An ocean-going liner always empties its tanks before it takes on supplies of fresh water. In the same way, we should occasionally clear the lungs of stale air by breathing out forcibly, so that we can make way for a draft of fresh air.

One of the great values of work songs was that they encouraged deep expiration. They also helped induce a state of relaxation. When we are tense, we breathe in a rapid, shallow fashion. This removes carbon dioxide from the blood and leads to changes in the chemistry of the blood which in turn produce the classical symptoms of anxiety, dizziness, muscular cramps, faintness, increased heart rate, and anxiety feelings. This can be controlled by consciously reducing the rate of respiration, a process we perform unconsciously when we yawn or sigh. A group of ninety-five student nurses was given a battery of psychological tests designed to measure their level of anxiety. They were then asked to lie down, relax, and listen to an amplified recording of their own breathing sounds. As they listened their breathing became smoother, more regular, and more relaxed. Afterwards they were tested again and it was found that their anxiety scores had been reduced by their steady breathing. There can be few better relaxants than deep, regular breathing. If you have to perform in public, sing a song, or give an after-dinner speech, and you can feel your heart pounding and the muscles in your throat knotting up, take a few seconds off and make a point of breathing slowly, deeply, and rhythmically. Concentrate in particular on breathing out. Imagine you are a hot-air balloon slowly collapsing to the ground as you exhale. Automatically the tension disappears. If you should still find worry thoughts scurrying through your mind, focus attention on your nose, feel the nostrils flare when you breathe in, and observe the coolness of the inspired air, compared to the gentle warmth of the air as it leaves the lungs. Alternatively, hum gently and feel the vibration of the nose and lips as you slowly exhale. This has a marked sedative effect and is infinitely safer before a driving examination than the dangerous practice of taking tranquilizers.

The best way of curbing anxiety and controlling tension is to "get it off your chest." Most emotional states are associated with changes in our pattern of respiration. We catch our breath when we are afraid, sigh "like a furnace" when we are suffering from unrequited love, yawn when we are bored, grunt when we make love. Laughing, crying, and screaming are all modified forms of breathing. It follows that when we hide our emotions or suppress our feelings, we keep a tight check on our breathing. As psychiatrist Wilhelm Reich observed, "it has become clear that the inhibition of respiration was the physiological mechanism for the suppression and repression of emotion, and consequently, the basic mechanism of neurosis." He found that many of his neurotic patients felt a tight band around their chests. As they found it impossible to let go of their breath, he often placed his hand on their abdomens and gently pressed to coax full expiration. This helped them relax and often improved their sexual performance, for as Reich found, "Deep expiration brings about spontaneously the attitude of [sexual] surrender."

Psychologist William Schultz, a pioneer of encounter

group therapy, finds it valuable to get people to release their repressed screams. He invites them to howl with anguish or bellow to give vent to their long-suppressed rage. If they find difficulty in doing this in public, he suggests they do it in the shower or while driving a car on the open road—anything to reduce tension and to restore a relaxed pattern of respiration.

It is unfortunate that we can exert so much control over the process of respiration, for as Captain Knowles remarked, "What man can control, man can abuse." But we can in time learn to do unconsciously well, what we now do unconsciously badly, and with this improvement we can add enormously to our vitality and health.

Bust Development

The female breasts are sex symbols, which explains the importance attached to their size and shape. Their role as milk-producing mammary glands seems to be of secondary importance today. Many modern women deny themselves the satisfaction of breast-feeding their offspring for fear of losing what some consider their "feminine charms."

The criteria by which these charms are judged show considerable cultural variation. Two anthropologists studied the preferences shown by thirteen different races and found that eleven preferred large breasts, two favored breasts that were upright and hemispherical, and two—both in East Africa—admired breasts that were long and pendulous. These two groups encouraged young girls to pull down their breasts in order to develop a fashionable droop. In general it is found that races favoring youth strive for breasts that have the fullness and height of late adolescence, while those stressing woman's maternal role admire breasts that have the sag of the more mature, fertile woman.

Corseting is the commonest method of achieving the full, high bust favored in the West. This was perhaps so even in the Middle Ages. When King Henry VII sent his three envoys to examine the Queen of Naples, he asked them particularly to mark her breasts and paps whether they be large or small." The ambassadors reported that "the said Queen's breasts be somewhat great and . . . trussed somewhat high after the manner of the country."

A number of attempts have been made to increase the actual size of the female breast. The earliest method was to apply to them various unguents and lotions. An ancient Indian love manual assured its readers that "continous treatment with antimony and rice water will cause the breasts of a young girl to become large and prominent so that they will steal the heart of a connoisseur as a robber steals gold." Mae West reported in her autobiography that as a young girl she massaged her breasts with cocoa butter and afterwards bathed them in cold water in order to preserve their firmness and shape.

It is doubtful that these methods produced any worthwhile results. The recent use of breast-developing creams containing large quantities of synthetic sex hormones has been more successful, but it has been outlawed, since it can interfere with the menstrual cycle and predispose to cancer. As one doctor said, "Better be flat than foolish." The practice of injecting silicone into the breasts, a method favored by some models and "topless" waitresses, has been similarly discouraged as it can lead to mastitis and disfiguring fibrosis of the breasts. (The silicone *implants* offered by plastic surgeons are, or should be, chemically inert. Here, the hazards of major surgery should be weighed before electing mammaplasty.) Water massagers can produce a temporary increase in size by augmenting the flow of blood to the breasts, but even this method is not without its risks, for as a professor of medicine has said, "An increased blood supply to the breasts is the last thing a women with an undetected tumor wants."

The British Consumer Council carried out a survey of all these various breast-development techniques and concluded, "We do not say that none of these things will work. What we do say is that in some cases they may be dangerous, in other cases they may not be worth the money, and that in all cases you should consult a doctor."

Exercise aimed at developing the pectoral muscles covering the chest will often increase breast size but makes little difference to the volume of glandular tissue contained by the breasts. A survey of the development of top-class women tennis players, published in a medical journal under the title "Aspects of Muscular Development of Women in Sport and Industry," showed that almost without exception "the right breast was measurably larger than the left due entirely to the constant vigorous wielding of the arm holding the racket both laterally and, more especially, vertically when serving." In industry a similar effect was observed among typists, although here it was the left breast which was more highly developed, owing to the repeated manual operation of the typewriter carriage. It was estimated that this action was performed 1,200 times a day, and "this sustained exercising of the muscles contiguent (sic) to the left breast cannot help but have the effect of enlarging it and giving it added firmness."

Fortunately it is not necessary to become a full-time typist or engage in top-class tennis in order to develop the pectoral muscles. They can be strengthened by a simple exercise called the "Cossack Squeeze." The instructions for this exercise are quite simple. Fold the arms and grip each arm with the opposite hand. Raise the arms to shoulder level in the fashion of a Cossack dancer and then squeeze the arms together. Relax and repeat several times a day. This will strengthen the pectoral muscles, which form the base and major support for the breasts.

The development of the glandular tissue of the breast is less easily achieved. This is under hormonal control and is little affected by exercise or massage. It can, however, be influenced by emotional stimulation, by overcoming sexual frustrations, or achieving greater fulfillment and contentment in life. Psychiatrist Arthur Janov, in his book *The Primal Scream*, notes that approximately a third of the flat-chested women he treats have independently reported an increase in the growth of their breasts. "When they went shopping," he writes, "they were surprised to discover that they needed new brassiere sizes." In one case the growth was so great that the patient's husband was convinced his wife was receiving hormone injections. "I have had many of these women measured by their physicians to verify the growth," Janov writes, and "in every case it has been corroborated."

Sagging breasts are not so easy to treat. According to Dr. John Wulsin of the University of Cincinnati College of Medicine, the problem is one of gravity. "The fibrous attachments which support the breast stretch under the influence of gravity," he writes, and "once lengthened by tension these fibrous connections do not resume youthful dimensions, and despite hopeful legend, no amount of exercise will restore their pristine mammary profile." Postural improvement will help, but the only cure for sagging breasts that he recognizes is the wearing of a "satisfactory brassiere." He sees no harm, however, in going braless.

Café Coronaries

It is estimated that in America 1,400 people a year die in restaurants from what are popularly known as "café coronaries." They are eating and drinking happily with friends, and then they suddenly collapse at the table, unable to speak or breathe. The tragedy has all the outward appearance of a coronary attack but in fact is due to suffocation brought on by bolting a large portion of food that has lodged at the back of the throat and blocked the windpipe.

The condition must be treated as an absolute emergency. There is rarely time to take the victim to hospital, for death will ensue if the airway is not cleared within minutes. Some restaurants now keep long-handled pincers, called Kelly clamps, expressly for this purpose. Alternatively a finger or a handle of a spoon can be used to hook free the lodged particle of food.

A more effective way of clearing the windpipe, endorsed now by both the American Medical Association and American Red Cross, has been devised by Dr. Henry Heimlich of the Jewish Hospital in Cincinnati. Known as the "Heimlich Maneuver," it mimics the action of a cough, forcing food out of the windpipe by a sudden expulsion of air from the lungs. This is achieved, if the victim is lying supine, by kneeling astride his body, placing one hand on top of the other between his rib cage and navel, and giving a quick, upward thrust with the heel of the lower hand. This raises the diaphragm and sharply and forcibly compresses the lungs. The same effect can be obtained in the erect or sitting positions by standing behind the victim with arms clasped around his waist and the fist of one hand reinforced by the palm of the other pressed into his abdomen between rib cage and navel. A sharp upward thrust is now given and repeated until the impacted food is expelled. It is advisable to seek medical aid once the choking has been relieved.

It is suggested that if a person collapses suddenly in a restaurant the chances are fifty to one that he or she is choking on food rather than suffering a coronary attack.

Café coronaries can be prevented by making it a habit to take smaller bites of food and to chew thoroughly before swallowing (see *Mastication*).

Change

Variety is the spice of life. Without it we become irritable, lethargic, and depressed. The monotonous routine imposed on sailors living for months on end in nuclear submarines frequently leads to symptoms of psychic distress; and from submariner to secretary, much of the fatigue we experience today stems from boredom rather than prolonged physical work. In these instances a change is likely to prove more beneficial than a rest; a new hat or an excitingly different hair style is a better tonic than a month's supply of vitamin pills.

Adeline Reynolds enjoyed a new lease of life at the age of seventy when she abandoned her role as a housewife and embarked on an acting career. She found the preparation for her new work exhilarating, taking lessons in swimming, tap dancing, riding, and fencing. In her eighties she was still bubbling over with *joie de vivre*. "I keep myself limber," she said, "by always learning something." If we are to grow, we must accept a change. To remain young we must retain the curiosity of youth and be willing to embrace new experience.

Before the Industrial Revolution people were exposed to constant variety in their lives. They were kept in close touch with nature and inevitably experienced its ceaseless ebb and flow, the gradual transition of the seasons, the regular passage of night into day. To exist they had to turn their hands to many crafts. One day they might act as hunters, the next as masons, carpenters, herdsmen, or vets. No two days were alike. Their lives had no fixed pattern but consisted in doing what necessity demanded and the day allowed. Life for modern workers has become far less flexible, each working day being a mirror image of the one before: set hours, humdrum conditions, routine work; permitted hours of repetitive play following scheduled days of repetitive work. To remain sane, industrial men and women need to break free from this stultifying routine. As in the Roman Saturnalia, they need to experience the fun of occasionally exchanging roles. Once in a while masters should become servants, breadwinners become breadmakers, and the meek take on the mantle of the bold and become decision-makers. From time to time, rigid disciplinarians should let their hair down and spend a night carousing with friends, and rugged sportsmen find time to develop and express the more tender side of their personalities. This is the way of re-freshment, the way to climb out of the rut and extend our personalities. Only in this way can we hope to achieve our full potential.

But while the stimulus of change is good, too much change can be harmful. Sickness frequently results from failure to adapt to violent change. As Hippocrates said two thousand years ago, "It is changes that are chiefly responsible for diseases, especially the greatest changes." René Dubos, editor of the *Journal of Experimental Medicine*, confirms that "in Europe and America, all periods of social upheaval have been accompanied by a marked increase in the incidence of disease." This was apparent in Europe towards the end of the nineteenth century and formed the basis of Max Nordau's book *Degeneration* (1895). Nordau spoke then of "the vertigo and whirl of our frenzied life." In fifty years the length of railways in Europe had increased from 3,000 to 218,000 kilometers and the number of travelers grown from 2.5 million to 614 million. During the same time the volume of letters distributed in Britain had increased fivefold and the number of books produced in Germany risen seventeenfold. "Its own new discoveries and progress have taken civilized humanity by surprise," Nordau wrote. "It has had no time to adapt itself to its changed conditions of life."

Since then the rate of change has quickened, placing

still greater strains on man's powers of adaptation. As Alvin Toffler demonstrated in *Future Shock* (1970), we have been subject to "dizzying disorientation brought on by the premature arrival of the future." Until the nineteenth century man was unable to travel faster than a horse. Then came the development of the steam locomotive, which in 1825 permitted a top speed of 13 miles per hour but by the turn of the century was achieving speeds of 100 miles per hour. The invention of the airplane led to speeds of 400 miles per hour by 1938. Since then, in a matter of years, we have moved on to supersonic flight and men hurtling through space at 18,000 miles per hour. Revolutionary developments like these have meant a revolution in our way of life. We no longer spend our days in the comfort and security of one small community. The average American now moves to a new home about fourteen times during his or her life. Each move provides a stimulus, but it also entails a loss. We may gain a better job and a home with parquet floors, extra bedrooms, and a luxury kitchen, but we leave behind a neighborhood where we feel at home, friends we've grown to love, and the garden we've tended with infinite care. Changes like these can damage our health.

Dr. Thomas Holmes, professor of psychiatry at the University of Washington in Seattle, has made a detailed study of the effects of change on our physical and mental well-being. He has assigned a point system that helps evaluate the amount of stress likely to result from changes in our lives (see Table) and has found that people who score more than 300 points of change on this scale in any one year have an 80 percent chance of suffering heart attacks, depression, or other serious illness. When the total of points lies in the 150—300 range the risk falls to 53 percent, and it falls to 33 percent when the total is under 150.

A measure of change is necessary for the maintenance of health, but too much change is damaging. For each of us there is an optimum level of stimulation; a level that varies from time to time according to our total life situation and that depends on our basic disposition. Those who are anxious by nature are more easily threatened by strange experiences and unfamiliar environments. Success lies in striking the right balance between the stimulus of change and the security and stability of maintaining the status quo. As Dr. John Fuller of the Jackson Laboratory Biomedical Research Center in Bar Harbor, Maine, says, "Some people achieve a certain sense of serenity, even in the midst of turmoil, not because they are immune to emotion, but because they have found ways to get just the 'right' amount of change in their lives."

When boredom strikes, we need to introduce change, but when we find ourselves overwhelmed by constant change we need to emphasize the permanent elements of our lives, to strengthen what Toffler has described as our "stability zones." These vary for each individual. For one person it may mean establishing closer links with the unchanging world of nature; for another, forging more intimate bonds with family and friends. Some find comfort in history or religion, others in the performance of time-honored rituals or familiar routines. Children upset by sudden upheaval may turn to hugging a favorite toy, while their parents may don old clothes and spend a day pottering round the garden. We all need to find our own fixed reference points, foxholes to retreat into when the emotional hurly-burly grows too fierce.

TABLE

STRESS VALUE OF LIFE CHANGES

Event	*Score*
Death of spouse	100
Divorce	73
Marital separation	65
Jail term	63
Death of close member of family	63
Personal injury or illness	53
Marriage	50
Fired from job	47
Marital reconciliation	45
Retirement	45
Change in health in member of family	44

Event	*Score*
Pregnancy	40
Sex difficulties	39
Gain of new family member	39
Change in financial state	38
Death of close friend	37
Change to different type of work	36
Change in number of arguments with spouse	35
Mortgage over $10,000	31
Foreclosure of mortgage or loan	30
Change in responsibility at work	29
Son or daughter leaves home	29
Trouble with in-laws	29
Spouse beginning or stopping work	29
Outstanding personal achievement	28
Beginning or ending school	26
Revision of personal habits	24
Trouble with boss	23
Change in hours or conditions of work	20
Change in residence	20
Change in schools	20
Change in recreation	19
Change in social activities	18
Mortgage or loan less than $10,000	17
Change in sleeping habits	16
Change in number of family get-togethers	15
Change in eating habits	15
Vacation	13
Minor violations of the law	11

Circumcision

Circumcision is probably the oldest operation known to man. Murals some four thousand years old, discovered in Egyptian tombs, show young boys, standing, having their foreskins removed by priests while assistants pinion their arms behind their backs. Anthologists believe that since certain tribes in recent years have carried out the rite using a scalpel of sharpened stone in preference to a metal knife, the ritual probably dates back earlier still to the Paleolithic Age. Among the early Egyptians circumcision formed an essential part of the initiation into the priesthood and ruling class, a practice that apparently continued for several millennia, for Pythagoras, the great Greek scholar, was not allowed to study in the Egyptian temples until he had been circumcised.

Various attempts have been made to explain the ubiquity and primitive appeal of the circumcision rite. Some see it as a blood offering to the gods, the sacrifice of a part to insure the welfare of the whole, a fertility rite, an act of atonement for incestuous desires, or a pact of dedication. Occasionally it was used as a means of identification of slaves or the members of a tribe so that they could be differentiated more easily from strangers, spies, and possible enemies. Whatever its early significance, the practice of circumcision was adopted by the Egyptians and later became an integral part of the Jewish and Muslim faiths. The Egyptians possibly saw a symbolic link between the penis and the sacred serpent. The snake achieved immortality, they believed, by shedding its skin, so possibly they sought to extend their own lives by robbing their penis of its protective skin. To the Jews circumcision represents an essential part of the pact between Abraham and God. It is in no way obligatory for Christians, and yet the Christian calendar–which records time from the year of Jesus's birth–starts not from the day of his birth but from January 1, the day of his circumcision, a day still celebrated within the Christian Church as the Day of Circumcision. Abraham did not have his foreskin removed until he was ninety-nine, but today the Jewish male is normally circumcised when he is seven days old. In other cultures the operation is performed at puberty, and among certain Arab tribes it formed an important part of the prenuptial rites. The circumcision of the Arab male provided a severe test of endurance, for it involved an extreme form of body mutilation, which has recently been outlawed by the Saudi Arabian government. In the presence of his bride-to-be, an Arab had to submit to an operation that, as one source has it, consisted of "cutting off the skin across the stomach below the navel and thence down the thighs, after which it is peeled off, leaving the stomach, the pelvis, the scrotum and the inner legs uncovered and flayed." If he flinched or showed undue distress, his betrothed could refuse to go through with the arranged marriage.

But circumcision must not be considered a purely masculine rite. Many tribes have practiced female circumcision, consisting of the removal of the clitoris and some or all of the external female genitalia. In fact, it has been suggested that female circumcision predated circumcision of the male. One aborigine group in Australia removed the clitoris and labia of young girls at puberty, a ritual followed by ceremonial intercourse with numerous male members of the tribe.

Apart from its value as an initiation rite, it is possible that circumcision was seen by primitive people as a way of enhancing the difference between the male and female sex organs. It removed from the female the clitoris, which is the analogue of the male penis, and took from the male the foreskin, which not only resembled the female labia but also hid the male organ in all its rampant, rosy glory.

In Victorian times, female circumcision was advocated

to prevent or curtail masturbation and to cure a variety of female maladies, a belief that persisted well into the present century, particularly in America. In 1912, an American textbook stated that "circumcision for the girl or woman of any age is as necessary as for the boy or man"; and as recently as 1936, another American textbook, Holt's *Diseases of Infancy and Childhood*, was recommending circumcision for boys and was "not averse to circumcision in girls or cauterization of the clitoris." This despite the fact that removal of the female clitoris is totally unlike the amputation of the male foreskin in that it seriously interferes with sexual responsiveness and can never be justified on medical grounds.

But then are there any grounds for continuing the primitive ritual of male circumcision, described by some doctors as the "rape of the phallus"? The operation is certainly being performed less frequently than it was, but in Britain it is estimated that a quarter of male children are still being circumcised and in America, the figure is believed to be as high as 80 percent. Yet such is the mystery surrounding the operation that many adult American males cannot say for certain whether or not they have been circumcised. A medical survey carried out a short while ago in Buffalo, New York, showed that a third of the men who claimed to be circumcised were actually intact, while an equal number who thought they had retained their foreskins had in fact been circumcised.

Apart from its use in phimosis, a very rare condition in which an excessively tight foreskin blocks the flow of urine, is there any medical reason for submitting male infants to the pain and possible psychological trauma of an operation that can cause infection, hemorrhage, painful urination, and in some cases even death?

At one time circumcision was advocated as a means of reducing the sensitivity of the tip of the penis. It was thought this would reduce the desire to masturbate and also delay the male orgasm, prolonging the sex act and increasing the pleasure of the female partner. Dr. H. H. Van de Velde, one of the earliest writers on sex technique, gave currency to these particular theories, telling of women who had sought in vain to "match their sexual gratification with their sexual desires" and had finally turned for satisfaction to members of the circumcised races. He also quoted one Fehlinger, who in his study of the *Sexual Life of Primitive People* had said, "The purpose of circumcision is probably the prolongation of coitus, as the exposed glans takes longer to reach the summit of stimulation than the covered." There is in fact no basis for this particular piece of folklore, for the work of sex researchers has shown that there is no difference between the sensitivity of the penis of circumcised and uncircumcised males. The operation therefore will not enhance copulatory pleasures or decrease onanistic desires.

Others recommend circumcision on hygienic grounds, a far more convincing argument, for it is undoubtedly more difficult to keep the uncircumcised penis clean. The undersurface of the foreskin contains glands that secrete smegma, a waxlike substance that helps to lubricate the tip of the penis. This is a useful function, but unless the smegma is removed by regular washing it undergoes bacterial breakdown that not only produces an unpleasant odor but also creates irritation and may cause balanitis, a painful inflammatory condition affecting the penile tip. It is even possible that if prolonged, this chronic irritation can predispose to cancer of the penis, a rare condition but one that is undoubtedly more common in uncircumcised males. In the same way it has been found that cancer of the cervix is more common in women married to uncircumcised men, possibly because during intercourse they are brought into repeated contact with smegma that has undergone bacterial breakdown. Cervical cancer is rare among Jewish women, and in the Subcontinent it is less common among Muslim women, whose husbands are circumcised, than in Hindus, whose husbands retain their foreskins. On the other hand cervical cancer is more frequent among lower-class Muslim women, whose husbands, though circumcised, maintain relatively low standards of personal hygiene, but is rare among high-caste Parsi wives whose husbands, though uncircumcised, can be expected to maintain high standards of personal hygiene. This evidence should not be taken as an argument in favor of circumcision but as a warning of the dangers of low standards of personal cleanliness. As an editorial in a recent issue of the *British Medical Journal* says, "There is no case for recommending circumcision rather than hygienic measures to adults as a means of preventing cervical cancer." For all but the ignorant, indolent, or mentally defective, who are unlikely to wash their genitals adequately, the discomfort and dangers of the operation outweigh the possible benefits.

As a pediatrician writing in the *Journal of the American Medical Association* has put it, "If a child can be taught to tie his shoes or brush his teeth or wash behind his ears, he can also be taught to wash beneath his foreskin."

Climate

Few people realize how much they are influenced by the weather. We know that climatic changes affect our mood—on bright days our disposition is "sunny," on dull days our spirits are "under a cloud," and on humid days we feel "under the weather"—but the influence of climatic change extends further than this.

In 1931, when Britain was passing through a grave economic crisis, S. F. Markham, then parliamentary secretary to Prime Minister Ramsay MacDonald, set out to study the factors that make a nation great. He analyzed such possible conditioning factors as the location of mineral resources, diet, language, endemic disease, and the presence of eminent leaders, but he came to the conclusion that the most important prerequisite for national success was the possession of an equable climate. In his book *Climate and Energy of Nations* he points out that all the major civilizations of the past—Egypt, Persia, East China, Babylon, Carthage, Mexico, Sumeria—have developed in maritime countries with a mean average temperature of 70°.

Professor Clarence Mills, when professor of experimental medicine at the University of Cincinnati, made a detailed study of the effect of climatic change on human health and behavior. He concluded, "Climatic factors in life play a startling and dominating role in all we do. . . . They affect man's rate of growth, speed of development, resistance to infection, fertility of mind and body, and the amount of energy available for thought or action." He conducted animal experiments showing that rats brought up in a cool environment fared much better than those reared in tropical heat: They were more active, matured quicker, began their sexual cycles earlier, were more resistant to infection and quicker to solve maze puzzles. He attributed these marked differences to the enervating effect of heat, which makes it more difficult to dissipate body heat and so necessitates a gearing down of bodily activity. But Professor Mills also noted that rats brought up in hot environments lived longer than they did when reared in cooler rooms, despite their greater susceptibility to infection. This, he felt, was because they lived calmer lives and did not burn themselves up with senseless activity. He sees in this a warning for the hard-driving, restless businessmen in the world's temperate zones. "Certain real dangers accompany this more dynamic, cool-climate existence," he writes, "dangers of early exhaustion or breakdown of body machinery." To compensate for this he recommends that active people living in temperate climates should make a point of taking lazy holidays in the sun and reducing the pace of their work during the summer months. He also suggests taking a rest after lunch, which he feels is more important for workers in temperate zones than for the inhabitants of hot countries who regularly take an afternoon siesta (see *Siesta*). This is particularly true of the North American businessman: "Nowhere else is the climate quite as driving in its effects or as upsetting with its frequent storm changes." Americans, says Professor Mills, "need more rest instead of less, but their energy and restlessness keep pushing them on at a rapid pace until the collapse comes."

Exposure to high temperatures during the early stages of pregnancy may also affect brain development. Some researchers have found that children conceived in the summer months have generally lower I.Q.s than children conceived in the winter.

Experiments conducted by Dr. Marshall Edwards of Sydney, Australia, have shown that when pregnant guinea pigs are exposed to high temperatures, they are prone to give birth to offspring with poorly developed brains. In view of this finding, expectant mothers are advised to keep cool during the early stages of their pregnancies. They should avoid excessively hot baths and saunas which, Dr. Edwards warns, may be "a possible cause of human sporadic abortions, stillbirths, and congenital malformations."

"Keeping our cool" also helps to curb the aggressive feelings which tend to arise during hot weather. More murders are committed in July and August than at any other time, and surveys have shown that crimes of sex and violence are twice as high in the South of Italy and France as in the cooler North. An eight-year study of forty thousand cases of violent assault in New York showed that the crime curve closely follows the temperature graph, being at its lowest in the coldest month, January, and rising to a peak in the hottest month, July. In warm weather we obviously need to take particular care to control our tempers and to make extra allowances for the irritability of those around us.

The ideal climate, as well as affording an equable temperature, should also provide a comfortable humidity, preferably within the range of 40-50 percent. Higher humidities than this lead to listlessness, lower humidities to increased irritability. At the turn of the century a British doctor, E. G. Dexter, made a study of the behavior of people in schools, prisons, and banks, and reported that low humidity was associated with "excessive restlessness of mind," nervous tension, insomnia, and "peculiarities of conduct." Excessively low humidity also dries out the skin and mucous membranes of the nose and throat and probably increases our susceptibility to respiratory infections. The lungs like to receive air as hot and as moist as is found in a tropical forest, but the air in many American homes during the winter months is often drier than it is in the desert. (The humidity in the Sahara Desert is about 20-25 percent; in some American homes in the winter, as little as 3-5 percent.) To insure comfort during the winter, it is therefore advisable to keep the air in living rooms moist by placing containers of water in front of radiators and fires, or by using a humidifier controlled by a humidistat, which releases moisture whenever the humidity in the room falls below a preset level. This also helps to protect furniture from cracking and developing loose joints.

Our bodies also react to quite small changes in atmospheric pressure. The earth is surrounded by 5 quadrillion tons of air which at sea level exerts a pressure of 14.73 pounds per square inch. This means that an average-sized man with a surface area of 20 square feet has to withstand a continual pressure of nearly 19 tons of air! Moreover, a change in atmospheric pressure of only 0.01 pounds per square inch will increase the pressure on the body by as much as 28 pounds, which is quite enough for us to feel. When atmospheric pressure falls, the body tissues swell, which explains why so many people can foretell approaching storms by the onset of headaches and rheumatic aches and pains. Frank Brown, Morrison Professor of Biology at Northwestern University, Evanston, Illinois, has cultured a number of animals under carefully controlled climatic conditions. He has shown how sensitive all living creatures are to impending changes in barometric pressure. "Every living thing studied in our laboratory during the past three years," he writes, "from carrots to seaweed, and from crabs and oysters to rats—has shown this capacity to predict very safely beyond chance the barometric pressure changes usually two days in advance."

When barometric pressure rises, we tend to become slower in our reactions and more prone to accident. Studies have shown that on high-pressure days, deaths increase 20 percent, accidents at work 20–40 percent, and traffic accidents 40–70 percent. This means that high barometric pressure is a more important cause of automobile accidents than such more-recognized weather hazards as fog and ice. A road-accident study in Hamburg showed that frost increased accidents by only 5.2 percent and glazed frost by 6.4 percent, whereas the arrival of a high-pressure front caused accidents to soar 40 percent. As the World Meteorological Organization, a United Nations agency, points out, "It is most noteworthy that all researchers have been able to show that the so-called trivial weather dangers to traffic—fog, slippery roads, glazed frost, etc.—played an appreciably smaller part in causing the accidents than the simultaneous disturbance to the human body caused by the direct onset of the weather stimulus." It is better in fact to fit our cars with barometers, than ice detectors, and just as necessary to take additional care when the barometer is rising rapidly as when fog descends.

Research workers in the field of bioclimatology have also discovered that we are extremely responsive to changes in atmospheric electricity. The air around us normally contains millions of electrically charged particles called *ions*, which have a stimulating effect on the activity of the body. City life, unfortunately, takes many of these ions out of circulation. As Dr. Albert Krueger, professor of bacteriology at the University of California, says, "People traveling to work in polluted air, spending hours a day in offices or factories, and living their leisure hours in urban dwellings, inescapably breathe ion-depleted air for substantial portions of their lives. There is increasing evidence that this ion-depletion leads to discomfort, enervation and lassitude, and loss of mental and physical efficiency." This is particularly so when there is a change in the balance between positive and negative ions. Normally there is a slight excess of positive over negative ions in the ratio 1.2 to 1. When there is an increase in the number of positively charged ions—as there is before a storm or in dry, centrally heated rooms—we tend to feel stuffy, depressed, and irritable. When there is a preponderance of negative ions—as there is after a storm, or at the top of a mountain—our intake of oxygen is increased and we feel exhilarated. The Chinese have shown their appreciation of the euphoric effects of high negative-ion concentrations by their predilection for living near waterfalls, which generate many negatively charged particles.

In recent years a range of simple machines has been developed which generate and release into the atmosphere a stream of negative ions. When introduced into Philadelphia's Northeastern Hospital, they showed the ability of eliminating or drastically reducing postoperative pain in 57 percent of cases. When used in the Catholic University of Buenos Aires, they allayed tension and produced favorable results in 80 percent of people suffering from anxiety syndromes. A test at a Swiss bank showed that negative ions also help to reduce the risk of respiratory infection. Over three hundred of the bank's employees volunteered to work in environments where the air was invigorated by a booster charge of negative ions. At the end of thirty weeks, their sickness record was compared with a similar group who had continued to work in normal, untreated rooms. An amazing difference was found: The group working in the treated rooms had had only one day off work with respiratory illness for every sixteen taken by the control group! This is partly due to the stimulating effect that negative ions have on the nasal mucous membrane. Normally the cilia, the fine hairs that line the respiratory tract, waft to and fro at the rate of 900 beats a minute, sweeping the airways clear of dirt, dust, and microorganisms. When there is an excess of negative ions in the atmosphere, this rate may be increased to 1,200 beats a minute; when there is a preponderance of positive ions, the flow of mucus is reduced, and the rate of ciliary beat is slowed to 600 beats per minute—lower still if cigarette smoke is present. This helps to explain the high rates of sinusitis and catarrh among city workers, for enclosed environments often become supercharged with positive ions when dry air circulates over radiators or through air-conditioning systems consisting of metal filters, ducts, and fans. To give ourselves an energy boost, to shake off lethargy, and to clear stuffed heads and blocked sinuses, we need to fling wide the windows from time to time, sit by waterfalls and raging seas, climb to the top of hills and mountains, and at every possible opportunity, get out into the country and breathe the good, fresh air. This revitalizes us by bombarding our bodies with negative ions and by bringing us into contact with the additional stimulus of rapidly changing currents of air.

A generation ago doctors in Europe made great use of climatic therapy, sending patients to convalesce in resorts chosen according to their basic qualities. Some resorts were recognized to be bracing, other relaxing. Thus patients in Britain needing to rest were sent to Bournemouth or Bath, while those in need of a tonic were sent to Skegness or Brighton. Analysis showed that the relaxing resorts were generally set in sheltered sites where there was little movement of air; the bracing resorts, on slopes traversed by constant currents of air. In the static air conditions that often prevail in centrally heated offices and homes, we feel a degree of enervation that can be quickly and simply alleviated by opening a window or operating a fan. This was less necessary when homes were warmed by open fires, for burning fires always create their own drafts and currents of air.

Seaside resorts are bracing because of the constant movement of onshore and offshore winds. The presence of minute quantities of ozone in the air contributes little or nothing to this tonic effect, and it is a mistake, condemned by doctors throughout the world, to try to mimic the health properties of seaside air by introducing ozone-generators into the home. They may reduce odors, probably by deadening the sense of smell, but do nothing to "freshen" the air. Ozone is a highly toxic gas and one of the principal irritants in the photochemical smog encountered over Los Angeles. At low concentrations it causes irritation of the nose and throat, and at higher concentrations, coughing, choking, and fatigue. As it reduces resistance to chest infections, it is a particular hazard to elderly people or infants. If it is necessary to remove odors and freshen the air within a room, this should never be done with an ozonizer; an open window is much safer and far more effective.

But not all winds are equally efficacious. The *khamsin* in the Middle East is an example of an ill wind which blows no one any good. Experiments in Israel show that 50 percent of people living in Jerusalem suffer khamsin-related symptoms–tension, headaches, and increased irritability–during the days when this dry, warm wind is blowing. Professor Felix Sulman, of the Hebrew University department of applied pharmacology in Jerusalem, has shown that the presence of excess positive ions in the atmosphere during this time stimulates the secretion of serotonin, a hormone that has a direct effect on the nervous system. He has found that the use of negative ion generators helps to lessen the severity of khamsin-related symptoms.

Other countries experience similar noxious winds. Italy has the *sirocco*, France the *mistral*, and Germany the *föhn*; chinook winds blow each winter in the Rocky Mountains, and Santa Ana winds in California. In each case these winds bring with them a quickening of tempers and an increase in crime rates and traffic accidents.

As a general rule, when currents of air travel for long distances over land masses, they carry with them a preponderance of positive ions. This is because the surface of the earth bears a positive charge, which tends to repel large numbers of negative ions. When air is drawn downward from the upper layers of the atmosphere, as happens more often in temperate zones than in the tropics, it normally carries with it large numbers of negative ions. The turbulent movement of large masses of air that occurs before a storm generates large quantities of positive ions, which helps explain the lethargy and increased irritability generally experienced before a storm. Professor Frank Brown of Illinois has shown that even simple animals, such as snails and planarium worms, respond to tiny changes in the electrostatic fields around them. "The sensitivity which has been proven," he writes, "indicates the living thing to have more than 100 times the sensitivity which would be required, for instance, to 'perceive' the electrical field created by a thundercloud rising miles away on the horizon." Farm animals generally become increasingly restless when a storm is brewing, and humans also sense the change, which tends to produce stormy scenes arising from tempestuous feelings.

Professor Richard Lynn, professor of psychology at the Institute of Economics and Social Research in Dublin, has found that the amount of anxiety a nation experiences is related to its climate, the closest correlation being between the level of anxiety and the number of storms that occur within the country. He finds that countries experiencing relatively few thunderstorms (Britain, Canada, Ireland, and Holland) have low anxiety rates, as measured by the incidence of suicides, smoking, alcoholism, heart attacks, and road accidents. Countries that have frequent thunderstorms (Japan, Italy, and France) also show the highest anxiety rates.

We may not be able to avoid ill winds, storms, and tempests, but we can be aware of the effect they have upon our health, can make better use of brief vacations and longer holidays to derive the benefit of climatic change, and can take steps to provide, within our own offices and homes, a much better climatic environment.

The Central Health Resort and Physiotherapy Institute of Russia has established for the benefit of workers in Moscow a chamber in which any desired climatic conditions can be mimicked. "The air we use in treatment is made up according to prescriptions based on a study of the climatic features of many health resorts in the Caucasus, the Crimea, and the countryside," says the Institute's head, Dr. Yuri Danilov. "Twenty or twenty-five minutes in the air treatment chambers fills healthy people with vim and vigor and increases their resitance to disease germs," he claims.

With a little thought and care, we could provide a similar therapeutic climate in our homes. As it is, with the current emphasis on hermeticaly sealed windows and dry, centrally heated air, few homes today approach this ideal.

Clothing

Clothing is worn for decoration, defense, and decency. Physiological necessity forces us to protect our bodies from the cold; society demands we cover our sex organs and erogenous zones; while vanity impels us to adorn our bodies according to the prevailing fashion, if not with clothes, at least with tattoos and body paints. Frequently these needs conflict. While trying to obey the fluctuating demands of fashion and meet the purely arbitrary sexual mores of the day, we often interfere with the normal physiology of the body.

Toward the end of the eighteenth century, a number of doctors in Europe sponsored a book that attacked the wearing of tight stays and corsets, which they held responsible for over ninety-seven separate diseases in women, ranging from sleepiness, apoplexy, and whooping cough to consumption and epilepsy. Somewhat later, in 1868, the Council of German Women held a congress in Stuttgart at which they sought to overthrow the "tyranny and vagaries of fashion" and start a dress-reform movement that would encourage women to shun clothing "injurious to health" and wear only garments that met "the demands of taste and suitability." This reform is still needed, for even now we dress according to the dictates of fashion rather than the demands of health and suitability.

Ideally we should wear as little clothing as possible. The body needs to be bathed in light and air if the skin is to perform its essential functions efficiently (see *Sunbathing*). One of the major activities of the skin is to act as a heat-regulating mechanism to help keep the body temperature at a constant level. In hot climates the blood vessels in the skin dilate so that more blood is brought to the surface for cooling. At the same time, the production of sweat is increased, and this cools the body as it evaporates. This process is hampered if too many clothes are worn. As Dr. O. G. Edholm, Head of the Department of Human Physiology at the National Institute for Medical Research in London, has said, "In these circumstances, any clothing is a barrier to heat exchange; so in theory complete nudity is the answer." He realizes there are esthetic and moral objections to total nudity, together with such difficulties as the lack of protection against insects and thorns, so he suggests that as a compromise in warm weather we should wear "the practical minimum of clothing."

In colder weather we need to protect ourselves from excessive heat loss. This means insulating the body by surrounding it with a cocoon of warm, dry air. Normally our clothes hold somewhere in the region of fifty pints of air. The more air we trap around our body, the better the insulation we provide. For this reason, two layers of thin underclothing give better protection than one thicker layer, particularly if they have an open weave. Natural fibers are generally better insulators than the denser synthetic fibers, because they trap more air around the body. This is particularly true of wool, which, unlike cotton, has a natural resilience that makes it resist compression. Wearing a mink coat, the ultimate in winter luxury, is merely an expensive way of surrounding the body with air.

Since we lose heat fairly evenly from the body surface, it is important in winter to cover all areas of exposed skin (see *Hats*). The legs account for about a third of the surface area of the body (the same proportion as the back and front of the trunk), and it is vital that they should be properly covered in the winter. A woman who goes out in mid-January in a miniskirt is likely to feel almost as cold as if she were wearing a topless trouser suit. Keeping fingers and toes warm is a problem, for although their volume is small, since they consist of a series of narrow cylinders, they have a disproportionately high surface area. To maintain their warmth they need to be particularly well covered.

Dr. Gustave Jaeger, founder of the famous chain of shops and pioneer of the dress-reform movement, believed that good health came from encasing the body in wool, not just to provide warmth, but also to insure the equal distribution of blood throughout the body. (He believed that men developed potbellies and spindly legs because they overheat their stomachs while neglecting to protect their legs.) Dr. Jaeger advocated the wearing of sanitary woolen shirts, sanitary woolen body-belts, and sanitary woolen one-piece undergarments. This tradition that only wool should be worn next to the skin dates back far earlier than this. The perfect Jewish wife, according to the Moffatt translation of Proverbs 31: 21, "fears not snow for her household for they all wear scarlet wool." Today, however, there are many admirable substitutes for wool, and there is little benefit to be derived now from wearing *red* flannel next to the skin. The vegetable extract originally used to dye cloth red had strong counter-irritant properties, so that placing red woolen cloth next to the skin warmed the body. Now that synthetic dyes are used, this property is lost.

To maintain intact the covering of air trapped around the body, it is necessary to wear outerclothes that are windproof and waterproof: windproof to stop the convection of heat away from the body, and waterproof since air conducts heat better when it is damp. (Clothes lose nearly half their insulating value when they are wet.)

Ideally our clothing should be more flexible than it generally is, for the amount of insulation our clothes provide should be regulated according to the outside temperature and the amount of heat generated within the body. Thus, the clothing that is sufficient to keep a man comfortable while working in an office at 68° F. (20° C.) is also sufficient to keep him warm while walking in a corridor at 50° F. (10° C.) or running outside when the temperature is down to freezing point. The only way to achieve this degree of flexibility is to wear several layers of outer clothing that can be removed as required.

In the hot weather it is advisable to wear outer clothes that are light in color in order to reflect the sun's heat rays. Wearing darker clothes in the winter has the reverse effect and helps to keep the body warm. A horrible demonstration of this phenomenon was seen after the atomic bomb explosion at Hiroshima when victims of the holocaust wearing patterned dresses had designs etched into their flesh. Where the pattern was dark they suffered the deepest burns; over the lighter areas, which reflected the heat, they suffered less severe damage.

In hot climates many natives wear dark clothes, but this is for practical reasons because they show the dirt less. The wealthy in these areas generally wear white.

Ideally we should not overclothe the body either in summer or in winter. The small blood vessels within the skin need to be subjected to variations in temperature if they are to maintain the responsiveness that our health depends on. The less clothing we wear the more exercise they get. During the summer, in the home and on the beach, we should wear the minimum of clothing and let our bodies breathe. In 1930 the psychologist John Carl Flugel looked back on the misplaced prudery of Victorian holidaymakers who concealed their bodies under ankle-length bathing dresses and behind bathing machines, which were horse-drawn vehicles pulled into the sea so that bathers could slip into the water without exposing their bodies. We regard them "with astonishment mingled with disgust," he wrote. Yet perhaps future generations will feel the same way about us and our insistence on wearing clothes (however scanty) when we go for a dip in the sea. As Flugel wrote, "We should be able to tolerate nakedness where it is obviously called for, as on the bathing beach."

Our bodies need to be free to move. Amelia Bloomer of New York realized this when she discarded the cumbersome hooped petticoats of her day and started wearing loose pantaloons, later nicknamed "bloomers" after her. Despite this brave lead, most of her countrywomen continued to encase themselves in steel-reinforced corsets, which three generations earlier had been condemned by John Bulwer in *The Artificial Changeling* as opening "a door to Consumptions and a withering rottenness." When these were given up by American women in World War I, it was estimated that 28,000 tons of steel were saved, enough to build two battleships. Today steel corsets have largely been replaced by girdles, but even these can have a harmful effect. There is evidence that tight underclothes increase the incidence of varicose veins. Doctors working at the London School of Hygiene and Tropical Medicine made a detailed study of over five hundred women working in the cotton mills of northern England and found that varicose veins occurred in 45 percent of the women wearing corsets and in 30 percent of those wearing girdles but in only 18 percent of those wearing no restrictive undergarments.

Tight bras are another source of discomfort and pain. The pressure of tight bra-straps can cause neuritis in the arms and fibrositis of the shoulders and between the shoulder blades. While it is possible to dispense with a bra (see *Bust Development*), most women feel more comfortable when wearing some form of breast support. They should choose a bra with a cup size sufficient to hold the breast without compression and with supports that do not cut into their flesh. Shoulder straps should be wide enough to distribute the weight of the breasts evenly without grooving the skin. Like shoes, bras should be tried on before being bought, and ideally should be purchased in the premenstrual phase, when breasts may be enlarged by fluid retention. A good test is to make sure they permit the unhampered taking of a deep breath.

The wearing of tight gloves and socks deprives the hands and feet of the blood they need to keep them warm, and predisposes to chilblains. For comfort and health, clothing needs to be loose.

At the beginning of the century, patients suffering from nervous exhaustion were advised to wear light, loose clothing to cut down the excessive stimulation of the fine nerve endings in the skin. This argument may have been false, but the basic principle was sound, for loose clothing has always been associated with relaxation and tight clothing with discipline and tension.

We slip into a loose housecoat to relax, but "gird up our loins" to prepare for battle. Soldiers are dressed in tight jackets and boots to keep them alert. The city businessman wears a close-fitting jacket, collar, and tie during the working week, but when he wants to unwind on the weekend, he wears a sloppy sweater and open-necked shirt. A tight grip around an animal's neck will make it tense, as every snake-charmer knows. Possibly the grip of a tight collar has the same effect on a soldier or clerk.

Loose clothing, on the other hand, has a soothing effect. Dr. Andrew Combe, an Edinburgh physician, wrote a book on dress reform that was in its fourteenth edition by the time that Mrs. Bloomer introduced her famous pantaloons. In it he recommended the wearing of loose clothing so that "every movement of the body gives a gentle stimulus to the cutaneous vessels and nerves, which assists their actions and maintains their function and health." Desmond Morris, in his book *Intimate Behavior*, refers to the "body reward" of wearing soft underclothes. This is the sales point that advertisers emphasize when they stress the silky, soft, caressing nature of their merchandise. Wearing soft, loose clothes is comforting.

Clothes, in addition to being light and loose, need to be permeable. Even at rest we lose about a pint of fluid a day from the surface of the body. Unless the clothing we wear is pervious, this moisture collects around the body and cannot evaporate. Cotton and wool make admirable materials for underclothes since they transmit this moisture by a process of wicking. The early nylon shirts and underclothes were uncomfortable to wear because they were impervious. Now that they are mixed with natural fibers and given a more open weave, they have overcome this early disadvantage. (A greater disadvantage of wearing synthetic fibers is that they generate static electricity. A charge of up to 10,000 volts per square centimeter can be developed that, though it has little current behind it, can produce a very hot spark that can jump a sizable gap and has been known to set off explosives.)

Dr. Jaeger believed that his sanitary woolen shirts needed to be washed only every six or eight weeks but, like all other garments, woolen underclothes collect germs and need to be cleaned regularly. One of the disadvantages of men's clothing is that it is not easily washed. Bacteria collect around the collars of jackets and waist bands of trousers and, since these sites are subjected to repeated friction, this can easily lead to crops of infected spots and boils. Clothes must be kept clean. This particularly applies to the socks of men suffering from athlete's foot and the pants of women with cystitis (inflammation of the bladder), although as a basic rule stockings, socks, and underclothes should be washed and changed every day.

Color

We often fail to appreciate the enormous effect of color on our lives. We recognize the difference between a drab existence and a "colorful" life but rarely attempt to brighten our lives by the judicious introduction of color. Yet our ability to see life in all its myriad hues is one of our proudest possessions, which few other animals share. Sheep, mice, and rabbits are completely color-blind. So too are bulls, which react with equal violence whether annoyed by the waving of rags red, green, pink, or blue.

At one time it was thought that diseases could be cured by bathing the body in different-colored light. During the smallpox pandemic of A.D. 980, the Japanese introduced the idea of segregating patients in special isolation hospitals in wards draped with red cloth. This "red treatment" for smallpox was introduced into Britain in the fourteenth century and was revived again in recent times by Niels Finsen, the Danish pioneer of artificial sunlight therapy (see *Sunbathing*). There appears to be little scientific evidence that color therapy such as this has any direct physical effect on the body.

The appropriate use of color, however, does play an important part in the prevention of accidents. Some colors are more visible than others. Tests have shown that bright orange/yellow is one of the most easily detected colors, being seen four times faster than red. This makes it an admirable color for cars. An analysis of car accidents in Britain confirms that blue and green are the most dangerous colors for cars, bright orange the safest. This is also the color that should be worn by cyclists, particularly at night. In approximately 60 percent of accidents involving cars and motorcycles, the drivers of the cars have complained that they did not see the motorcyclists until it was too late. If they had been dressed in bright orange jackets instead of the customary suits of khaki or brown, these accidents might have been avoided.

Color, though it has little direct physical action on the body, does affect us psychologically. This we acknowledge in our traditional color symbolism. We recognize that pink is the color of health when we refer to the fit, happy person as being "in the pink of good health" and "seeing the world through rose-colored glasses." Green stands for simplicity and lack of sophistication, which is why we call inexperienced people "greeners" or "greenhorns." Black we associate with evil and badness, and so we derive the terms black magic, black looks, black despair, black sheep, and blackguards. Blue stands for depression, which we acknowledge when we talk of suffering the "blues" and "blue streaks"; red is for violent action, "seeing red," and "painting the town red"; and yellow the color of cowardice and low behavior, hence "yellow streaks" and "yellow press." (Yellow is also traditionally the color of the robe Judas wore and, before the Revolution, the symbol for prostitution in Russia.)

Laboratory experiments have shown that red has a stimulating effect on the nervous system, increasing blood pressure and quickening the pulse and respiratory rates. Blue has the reverse action, an effect that was put to practical use by an American football coach who painted the room in which he gave his team its prematch pep-talk a stimulating red, and the room where they relaxed after the match a sedative blue. This is an example of the intelligent use of color. If we are going to paint our rooms, it costs no more to paint them the right color than the wrong color. This also applies to lecture halls. An American psychologist arranged for a lecturer to give the same twenty-minute lecture to two student audiences, one gathered in a red lecture hall, the other in a blue room. When interviewed afterward, the students in the blue room complained that they had been rather bored by the lecture, which they thought had lasted longer than twenty minutes. The group in the red room, on the other hand, found the lecture more interesting and judged its length to be less than twenty minutes.

In Munich, Henner Ertel, director of the Society for Rational Psychology, has been studying the effect of color on the mental development of children. He and his co-workers have found that children prefer rooms painted light blue, yellow, yellow-green, and orange. In these rooms they are more alert, lively, and creative than in rooms painted in what they consider "ugly" colors (white, brown, and black). Merely moving them from room to room can affect their performance on I.Q. tests. When a random sample of nearly five hundred children were moved to color-coordinated rooms, their I.Q. ratings rose on average twelve points; when tested in drab surroundings, they fell fourteen points. That this is not just a temporary effect is shown by the fact that a group of children educated in carefully chosen color environments showed a fifteen-point I.Q. lead over a control group matched by age and I.Q. after six months, and a twenty-five-point lead after eighteen months. Their social behavior was also enhanced. In a warm orange room their positive social reactions (smiles and friendly words) increased 53 percent, while their negative reactions (shows of hostility and irritability) decreased 12 percent.

Dr. Max Lüscher, professor of psychology at Basle University, has made a twenty-year study of the psychological effects of color and believes that the color preferences we show give some indication of our underlying personalities. He finds that people who favor yellow, the color of sunlight (the time of day for action and hunting), are active, spontaneous, adaptable, and creative. Those who choose dark blue, the color of twilight (when people retreat to the safety of their homes), are likely to be passive, relaxed, tender, and affectionate. People choosing red, the color associated with excitability, tend to be impulsive, competitive, revolutionary, and erotic; those choosing green (the complementary color of red) are frequently the reverse: stubborn, tenacious, and resistant to change. Dr. Lüscher finds violet popular among preadolescents, emotionally immature adults, and homosexuals. Since violet has artistic and mystical associations, it is often chosen by people who want to glamorize themselves and impress others. Brown is preferred by people who feel lonely and need physical comfort and companionship and was a frequent choice of displaced persons after World War II.

Color has a powerful influence on our behavior. Advertisers know that a well-chosen color advertisement can have fifteen times the pulling power of the same display in black and white. Changing the color of packaging can also have a dramatic effect on sales. Housewives given a certain detergent in a yellow packet reported that it was too strong; when offered the same powder in a blue packet, they complained that it left their clothes looking dirty; when presented the powder in a color-coordinated package of blue and yellow, they found the powder "wonderful." In the catering industry, care is often taken to insure that food is served on correctly colored plates. A salad served on a blue plate looks dead; served on a cool pink plate it looks fresh and green, because pink is a tone of red, the complementary color of green, and so emphasizes the greenness of the salad. The pharmaceutical industry is also coming to appreciate the importance of color when preparing drugs. Tests were made at the University of Newcastle-upon-Tyne, England, to discover the effect of dispensing the same drug as tablets of three different colors: red, yellow, and green. It was found that patients suffering from anxiety benefited most when their tablets were colored green, while patients with depression showed maximum improvement when their tablets were yellow.

The same care should be taken when choosing colors for the home. If we want our rooms to look warm, we need to choose colors at the red end of the spectrum. If we want them to feel cool, we should color them blue. Similarly, if we want to be cheered up, we need to select warm colors; if we want to be relaxed, cool colors.

As Louis Cheskin, President of the American Institute

of Color Research, reports, "The cool colors have a sedative effect, and being in an environment of cool colors has proved to be very calming to highly nervous people." But this effect can easily be overdone. It can be overstimulating to live in a room of pure red, and too depressing to remain for long in a completely blue room.

Children, members of primitive societies, and country-dwellers tolerate strong primary colors better than adults living in towns, who are already subjected to a high level of sensory stimulation and so respond better to more muted colors. Selecting the right color for a room is not easy for there is a great difference between the effect of warm reds, (red and yellow) and cool reds (red and blue). Variety also has to be introduced. It is possible to select a harmonious color scheme involving different shades of blue, but this generally provides insufficient visual stimulus and tends to be dull and lifeless. We need both sedatives and stimulants. Rooms that are predominantly yellow need to be highlighted by splashes of blue (the complement of yellow); green rooms cry out for accents of its complement, red. By following these complementary pairings, we follow basic physiological principles and are sure of striking a harmonious chord that can have a profound effect upon our psychological well-being.

Defecation

Deeply entrenched in folk mythology is the belief that a regular daily emptying of the bowels is essential for the maintenance of vitality and health. "A man whose bowels move regularly and normally will live very long," said Herodicus, the Greek philosopher. The hieroglyphic inscription on the tomb of an Egyptian physican shows that this preoccupation with regular bowel function dates back at least 4,500 years, for the tablet lists the physician's official title as "Guardian of the Royal Bowel."

But the human bowels were not intended to work with such clockwork regularity. If left alone they empty automatically but erratically, as the need arises and the opportunity affords. Some people may naturally pass three movements a day; for others the natural habit is a movement every second or third day. The frequency is also subject to emotional variation, being reduced when we're fearful or depressed, increased when we're beset by preexamination nerves. There is even a case on medical record of a man who went from June 18, 1900, to June 21, 1901, without passing a movement and felt perfectly fit until the end of the period.

It is wrong to make "A Movement a Day" a slogan of health. Obsessive adherence to this rite has led in the past to the widespread abuse of purgatives.

There has never been a shortage of laxative drugs. The world abounds with plant extracts—senna, cascara, jalap, aloes, and rhubarb—that exert a strong cathartic action. These were the mainstay of the ancient physician's pharmacopeia, for in an age of largely ineffectual medicine, they possessed the singular advantage that they so obviously worked. Later, pills of metallic antimony were also used. They exerted a purgative action by irritating the gut wall, and since antimony was currently being used by alchemists to refine precious metals, it seemed reasonable to believe that it would also help to rid the body of its dross. As Paracelsus said, "Just as antimony purifies gold and leaves no slag in it, in the same shape and form it purifies the human body." Antimony pills were expensive to buy but economical to use, for being made of metal they passed unchanged through the body and with a little care could be recovered, washed, and used again. They were known, in fact, as "perpetual pills," and were sometimes handed down from generation to generation as family heirlooms.

The taking of artificial aperients, though common, is not without risk. Purgatives like cascara and senna can prove too irritating for the intestinal walls and their use can lead to griping pains and an excessive loss of body fluid and salts due to the frequent passage of large quantities of watery stools. Mineral oils like liquid paraffin can impair the absorption of vitamins A and D and may themselves be absorbed and deposited in the liver and spleen. Moreover, all purgatives, taken regularly, carry the risk of habituation. The more we take them, the greater our dependence on their artificial aid and the weaker we make our body's natural response. The clumsy artifice of man can never replace the art of natural body function. The realization of this is leading to a gradual decline in the sale and use of aperients, although the pharmacies of America still stock over seven hundred different proprietary laxative preparations. Regular purgation is rarely necessary and should be undertaken only on medical advice.

Just as we overemphasize the value of regularity of bowel function, so we overstress the dangers of costiveness. Constipation—"the white man's burden"—has been blamed for everything from debility to sterility. In the early part of the twentieth century it was held responsible for "autointoxication," a sinister process of slow self-poisoning through the absorption of toxins from an overloaded, sluggish bowel. Inner cleanliness was the watchword of the day; constipation, public enemy number one. But toxins are not readily absorbed from the large intestines. Moreover, the classical symptoms of constipation—headache, lethargy, and irritability—arise from the overdistention of the lower bowel, not from the absorption of toxins. They can be artificially produced by stuffing the rectum with cotton wool and can be relieved by evacuating the rectum of accumulated fecal material.

The commonest cause of constipation is the abuse of purgatives and the repeated denial of the natural "call to stool." An infant generally evacuates its bowels immediately after a meal. This is because the presence of food in the stomach initiates a reflex that brings about the powerful contraction of the muscles of the colon (the so-called gastro-colic reflex). This reflex response is often less noticeable in adults. A rushed schedule leaves no time for bathroom calls after breakfast or lunch; and who wants to break up the party for so mundane a chore after dining with friends? So the promptings of nature are ignored and in time become less urgently felt. This is the background for most chronic constipation, which should be treated, not with purgatives, but by restoring normal bowel action, by answering the call to stool, by taking additional exercise to restore the tone to drooping muscles and by switching to a diet rich in roughage (see *Roughage*).

Our obsession with the mechanics of defecation has possibly made us neglectful of its more important hygienic aspects. A wide variety of diseases—typhoid, poliomyelitis, dysentery, and salmonella infections—are spread by fecal contamination. Human feces contain countless bacteria, which form a third to a half of its total solid mass. Fortunately most of these bacteria are dead, and many of the living are nonpathogenic, but it takes very few virulent organisms to create an epidemic. It is practically impossible to evacuate the bowels without suffering some bacterial contamination of the fingers and nails, so to prevent the spread of enteric infection, the hands must be washed after every visit to the toilet.

Ideally, flush toilets should be foot-operated to prevent the spread of infection to flush handles, and every w.c. should have its own wash basin to avoid infecting door handles when moving from room to room. Lavatory seats are another common source of disease spread. A survey showed that in homes carrying cases of dysentery, a third of the lavatory seats were infected. This could be obviated by returning to the old-fashioned seatless latrines, where the subject squats over an open hole. This arrangement has the added advantage of getting the body into a position during defecation in which the abdomen is supported by the thighs. This reduces the risk of hernias and insures that bearing-down pressures are focused on expelling the abdominal contents rather than on ballooning out the abdomen.

When toilets are flushed, a certain number of germs are also dispersed in an aerosol spray which may spread up to three feet from the lavatory basin. To check this additional method of germ-dissemination, it is advisable to make a habit of lowering the lid of the toilet before operating the flush.

The perineal area naturally requires cleansing after defecation, and a variety of techniques have been employed to carry out this essential ablutionary process. Rabelais tells how Gargantua experimented with every conceivable form of "rump-wiper" and eventually settled on the neck of a goose. Strict Muslims at one time performed the initial cleansing with a lump of earth and carried with them suitable sods wrapped up in their turbans. Social historian Reginald Reynolds reports in *Cleanliness and Godliness* that medieval man made use of tiny bundles of hay known as mempiria, or wiped himself with a curved stick—which he suggests is the origin of the expression "getting hold of the wrong end of the stick." Archeologists working at Vindolanda, a Roman site in Northumberland, England, have unearthed an ancient latrine surrounded by discarded strips of cloth which were most probably the precursors of modern toilet paper.

When carrying out this essential debridement, women

and girls must make a point of wiping from front to rear, rather than in the reverse direction. Having shorter, more exposed urethral passages than men, they must take care not to carry germs forward into their genitalia and so into their bladders, where they can proliferate rapidly and so give rise to painful bouts of cystitis.

After this initial cleansing, the perineal area should, if possible, be thoroughly washed. The Romans equipped many of their public latrines with buckets of salt water containing a sponge tied to a stick. With this device "the passer by cleansed his person, and then replaced the stick in the tub," according to J. G. Bourke in *Scatological Rites of the Nations* (1891). For the Muslims, cleansing the body after evacuation is a religious ritual. Originally, it consisted of three spearate processes: *istinjah* ("removal"), *istinkah* ("ablution"), and *istibra* ("drying"). The first process was performed with a clod of earth, the ablution, by washing with water at least twice, and drying, with a piece of linen a yard in length. There is no doubt that washing is the finest way of cleansing the body after defecation, and it is to be hoped that before long every bathroom will be equipped with a bidet for this express purpose.

The disposal of fecal waste today is largely the responsibility of the public health authorities. At one time householders tipped their overflowing chamberpots into the street below.

Nowadays we are more careful of the way in which we dispose of our excrement, although we still empty large quantities of untreated sewage into the sea, which may present a health hazard to swimmers. Nobody, however, seems sure of the extent of the risk. Authorities in New York City allow swimming when the coliform count is as high as 2,400 organisms per ml., but on Long Island swimming is banned when contamination reaches a tenth of this level. In Britain the Public Health Laboratory Service has expressed the opinion that "bathing in sewage-polluted seawater carries only a negligible risk to health, even on beaches that are aesthetically very unsatisfactory." On the other hand W. Brumfitt, professor of microbiology at the Royal Free Hospital, London, believes that people who swim in the Mediterranean Sea during the crowded summer months have a one-in-seven chance of contracting a virus disease directly related to sewage contamination, such as conjunctivitis, laryngitis, sinusitis, enteritis, or hepatitis. While the risks are still unknown, it pays to avoid swimming in contaminated waters. When there is an element of doubt, swim, but keep the mouth closed. If water is polluted, bathe in it—don't drink it.

Dentures

Over half the population of Great Britain above the age of forty-five have lost all their teeth. This mass mutilation is the result of physical delinquency. It shows a crass lack of care producing a self-inflicted illness which in its pandemic proportions has no equal anywhere else in the world today.

When first introduced, false teeth were fashioned from blocks of ivory, patiently carved to resemble natural teeth and held together by heavy metal springs. They were clumsy contraptions that would often clatter to the floor if the wearer gave an unguarded cough or sneeze.

George Washington was one of the first Americans to wear these teeth, and his historic set of "sea horses"–the uppers carved from walrus tusk, the lower set from elephant ivory–were a popular exhibit at the 1939 New York World's Fair. But Washington, like most of his contemporaries, found these teeth uncomfortable to wear; they pained his gums and caused his lips to bulge, as can easily be seen in the portrait chosen to decorate dollar bills. He frequently had to send the teeth back for alteration, and on one occasion received them back with a note reprimanding him for not giving them adequate care. Ivory is a porous substance easily stained by coffee, tobacco, and tea, and his teeth were "very black, occasioned," his dentist didn't doubt, "either by your soaking them in port wine, or by your drinking it."

At a later date false teeth were made from celluloid, a material that was easier to clean but had other limitations. Novelist Sir Compton Mackenzie tells of a friend who fell asleep in an armchair in the Savile Club with a cigarette between his lips. He awoke some minutes later with fumes pouring from his mouth—the cigarette had set fire to his teeth.

From whatever material they are made, false teeth require regular cleaning, for tartar forms on them just as it does on natural teeth. Food débris must be removed from teeth natural and artificial within twenty-four hours, otherwise it forms a hard plaque that cannot be removed by simple brushing. These plaques irritate the gums and can lead in time to inflammation of the inside of the mouth, an uncomfortable condition known as "denture stomatitis." They can also interfere with the normal fit of the teeth, a matter of some importance, since the comfort and security of modern dentures depend to a very large extent on the accuracy of their fit.

The early dentures were constantly slipping out of place, much to the discomfiture of the wearer, who frequently had to pause in midsentence to manipulate them back into place. Disraeli once taunted Lord Palmerston in the House of Commons that his false teeth "would fall out of his mouth when speaking if he did not hesitate and halt so in his talk." False teeth then were a simple horseshoe-shaped row of teeth set in a matrix molded to fit the upper and lower jaws. The lower set was held in place by gravity, aided occasionally by weighting the teeth with lead. The upper set was attached to the lower by a metal spring which, hopefully, kept the teeth in contact with the upper jaw when the mouth was opened.

Modern dentures are much more securely fastened. The lower set is splayed out at its base so that it is held in place not only by gravity but also by the pressure applied by the tongue and cheek muscles. The upper set is held to the roof of the mouth by suction, which can exert a pressure of up to fourteen pounds. For this to happen effectively, the teeth must fit accurately and must include a plate that covers as wide an area as the wearer can tolerate. This wide area of contact and close approximation to the palate and gums makes it more than ever important to keep the teeth clean.

Some dentists believe that denture-cleansing is best

done by regular daily brushing with soap and water, using a soft nail brush. Others prefer soaking the teeth each night in a safe alkaline peroxide cleaner. All agree that false teeth must be removed for cleaning and should be cleaned at least once a day on all surfaces.

Ideally, dentures should be left off during the night to give the gums a periodic relief from pressure and to allow a freer flow of blood through the delicate tissues lining the mouth. This also provides an opportunity to strengthen the gums by finger massage, gentle brushing, or chewing on gum or special dental chewing bags.

It is particularly important to remove partial dentures for their daily cleaning, for food débris tends to collect in the recesses where the retention clasps are attached. This also permits the cleansing of the undersurface of the saddle plate and so prevents "saddle sores." The fewer the natural teeth remaining in the mouth, the greater the attention they require.

With the passage of time, both full and partial dentures tend to work loose. This is not because of wear in the plate, but because of the natural shrinkage with age of the underlying jaw tissues and the attrition caused by constant pressure on the gums. It is possible to compensate for a slight loss of fit by using dental fixatives. These special powders are generally made from natural plant extracts, such as tragacanth and acacia, which swell when moistened by saliva to form a mucilaginous gel that fills out the slight inaccuracies and helps the teeth adhere to the mouth. Greater inaccuracies of fit necessitate relining the teeth with plastic polymers, which can be hardened at mouth temperature. These mold relines, although not as tough as the matrix of the dentures themselves, will generally last for several years.

Dishwashing

Prewar textbooks of domestic science and family hygiene laid down an elaborate routine for washing plates and dishes. They advocated the use of two enamel bowls (one for washing, the other for rinsing), rubber gloves sprinkled with talc, a mop, a sprinkling of washing soda, and at least *three* large dishtowels so that one could be used for china, one for silver, and the other for glass. Unfortunately, this time-honored kitchen-sink drill often leaves dishes less sterile after washing than they were before, because of the transmission of bacteria from contaminated dish towels. A survey a short while ago showed that ordinary, innocent-looking dishcloths and dishtowels can carry as many as three billion bacteria, particularly if they are allowed to remain damp between washes.

To avoid this particular form of germ-dispersion, dishes should be washed in water as hot as the hands can stand, using a dishcloth that in between meals is washed, dried, and thoroughly aired, as well as being given an occasional boil. The dishes should then be rinsed and left in a rack to dry. There is no need to dry them with a towel; this is a waste of time and a potential source of bacterial spread.

Better results still are obtained with a dishwasher. This employs repeated rinsings, and stronger detergents and hotter water than the hands can stand, so it gets dishes that much more sterile. It has been found that with even the most careful hand-washing, the number of bacteria on a tea cup can be reduced only to about five thousand. Using a dishwasher, the count is down to well under a hundred.

Drafts

It's an old belief that cold winds cause disease. Stiff necks are believed to come from sitting in front of an open window, backache from working outdoors in damp clothes, and colds from getting chilled after taking a bath or washing one's hair. In fact, there is no medical evidence that drafts cause either rheumatic or infectious disease.

The early symptoms of an impending cold or chest infection often include a feeling of coldness accompanied by fits of shivering, and it is tempting to conclude from this that the infection has come as a result of getting chilled. But experiments at the Common Cold Research Unit in England have shown that you can inoculate human volunteers with one of the common cold viruses, dress them in damp clothes, and put them in a tunnel exposed to blasts of cold air without their showing any increased tendency to develop a cold. What evidence there is in fact suggests that in the presence of cold viruses, respiratory infections are more likely to develop from prolonged exposure to dry heat than to damp cold. It has been found, for example, that soldiers billeted out of doors in tents suffer less respiratory infection than those housed in centrally heated barrack blocks, and a cheese factory in Wales has reported that employees working in heated offices have on average twice as many colds a year as those working in the factory food-refrigeration rooms. So keeping warm and away from drafts is no protection from the common cold.

Another widely held belief is that children suffering from fevers need to be kept warm. Children with a sore throat or infected ear shiver, and this is taken as a sign that they are feeling cold and need to be kept warm in jerseys, extra blankets and hot water bottles. In fact the reverse is the case. The child shivers because he has a fever and his temperature needs to be reduced, not raised. This is best done by removing bedding and clothing and allowing the naked body to cool down by the normal process of air-conduction. If this fails to bring the temperature down sufficiently, the child's body should be sponged with cold water, for in these feverish states cooling drafts are to be welcomed rather than discouraged.

Similarly, there is no evidence that cold winds give rise to rheumatic disease. Gardeners with bad backs and office workers with stiff necks may blame their trouble on exposure to real or imaginary drafts, but while their aches and pains are invariably improved by heat, they are unlikely to be caused by exposure to cold. A mobile research unit compared the incidence of rheumatoid arthritis in Britain and Jamaica, and found that the disease occurred with equal frequency in the two countries, but that the Jamaicans complained less, possibly because of the milder weather.

Drugs

Drugs are being used to an ever-increasing extent to manipulate and control human behavior. From a "twilight" birth to a narcotized death, we subject our lives to chemical control. Advertisements assure us that for every ailment there exists a sovereign remedy. If our bowels fail to react according to schedule, we are encouraged to swallow a laxative; if we wake with the early morning sniffles, we are urged to take a patent cold cure; or if we suffer twinges of lumbago after an afternoon's gardening, the recommended remedy now is not a hot mustard bath, but a muscle-relaxant drug. So it is that every day in Britain half the adults and nearly a third of the children take some form of medication. In America the per capita consumption of drugs is probably higher still. Millions of dollars' worth of drugs are being poured down the national gullet: drugs to relieve pain, induce pleasure, suppress appetite, counteract fatigue, and promote sleep. Steroids are being used to increase the bulk of male athletes, hormones to delay the periods of girl swimmers, sedatives to calm hyperactive schoolchildren, and estrogen to prolong the youth of menopausal women. No wonder this has been called the "great stoned age," such is our primitive reliance on magic potions and wonder-working pills.

Some drugs are undoubtedly life-savers, but the great majority prescribed today are both unnecessary and undesirable. Professor T. Higuchi, Regents Professor of Pharmaceutical Chemistry at the University of Kansas, estimates that 90 percent of drugs administered today are unnecessary. This widespread use of drugs promotes disease rather than health. Andrew Lwoff, French Nobel Prize-winner, estimates that 30 percent of illness in France today is caused by abuse of drugs.

Whole textbooks are now devoted to the subject of iatrogenic disease, the disorders caused by modern medication. Unlike the relatively harmless placebos of yesteryear, today's drugs are powerful agents, and any drug that is a power for good can equally well be a power for ill. As Sir Derrick Dunlop, chairman of the British Safety of Drugs Committee, points out, "There is no such thing as a completely safe and effective medicine. Most medicines are given to modify or repress some biological process. Without this capability they will be useless in treatment; with it, they are bound to cause adverse effects from time to time."

This applies to even the most simple remedies. Many people abuse their digestive apparatus. The resulting indigestion is intended as a warning signal and a gentle goad to encourage them to change their faulty eating habits, possibly to eat a more wholesome diet, to reduce the size of their meals, or to eat in a more leisurely fashion. Swallowing large quantities of antacids may suppress the symptoms of indigestion but cannot relieve its underlying cause. Moreover, the consumption of antacids leads to a compensatory increase in the secretion of hydrochloric acid within the stomach, which means that further antacids have to be taken to prevent this "acid rebound" effect. Habitual dosage on this scale can lead to alkalosis, a potentially serious alteration in the chemistry of the blood. Similarly, constipation can be treated in one of two ways: by switching to diet rich in roughage (see *Roughage*) and by reestablishing natural bowel habits (see *Defecation*), or by taking laxative drugs. There can be no doubt about the superiority of the first approach, which leads to permanent cure, while the other affords only temporary palliation. The one remedy produces as a by-product the improvement of general health, the other introduces the risk of numerous unfortunate side-effects. (All purgatives depress the natural defecatory reflex. Prolonged use of irritative laxatives can cause chronic irritation of the bowel, while purgatives such as liquid paraffin tend to inhibit the absorption of fat-soluble vitamins.)

The body is intended to be self-regulating and should produce within itself all the chemicals necessary for optimum function; consequently the extraneous administration of drugs in cases of indigestion or constipation only serves to disturb normal homeostasis. As Dr. Andrew Malleson says in his book *Need Your Doctor Be So Useless?* "Most of the standard treatments prescribed in general practice for minor physical illnesses not only confound the principles of scientific medicine, but they are even contrary to common sense. They are just silly. The therapeutic attack is delivered not against the cause of the disease, but against the symptoms that the disease causes; and these symptoms are often the body's defence mechanisms against the disease causing agent. Recovery takes place, not because of, but in spite of, treatment."

The Thalidomide tragedy drew attention to the dangers of taking certain drugs during pregnancy, and subsequent research has shown the widespread distribution of this risk. A study at the School of Public Health, University of California, Berkeley, has shown that mothers who take tranquilizers such as Librium during the early stages of pregnancy are four times as likely to give birth to children with severe congenital abnormalities. Similar research at Edinburgh University has shown that this risk extends even to everyday remedies such as indigestion tablets and aspirin which, when taken during the first twenty-eight days of pregnancy, can lead to congenital anomalies such as heart defects and limb deformities.

In view of this, it is wise to assume that all drugs are dangerous until proved otherwise. Familiarity with drugs should never breed contempt, for the most frequently used drugs are also the most commonly abused. This is certainly true of aspirin. Every day the people of America consume twenty-five tons of aspirin, enough to provide every man, woman, and child with two and one fourth tablets a day. Most of these are taken to relieve simple pains which often cry out for more specific treatment: the toothache that requires a visit to the dentist, the postural backache that signals a change of chair, and the fibrositis that comes from working with undue tension. Pain is a distress signal that should not be ignored. Taking analgesics can never produce a cure; it can only provide temporary relief for warning symptoms that may stem in some cases from serious pathological conditions that require immediate attention, and in others from minor functional disturbances that with a little care can be easily corrected. Despite the bland assurances of their advertisers, analgesic drugs are not as harmless as sweets. Each has its own particular side effect: Codeine produces constipation; phenacetin may harm the kidneys; paracetamol in large quantities damages the liver; and aspirin in even small doses can cause gastrointestinal bleeding. Two thirds of the people who take three to four aspirin tablets a day suffer loss of blood from the stomach, and one doctor has estimated that the one million aspirin addicts in Britain lose enough blood among them to fill a domestic swimming pool every three days.

Equally abused are the wide range of psychotrophic drugs which we take in ever-increasing quantities to control our moods—to provide calmness when we are anxious, energy when we are tired, sleep when we are wakeful, and happiness when we are sad. But anxieties and tensions, like pain, are warning signs that should not be suppressed with drugs. They should stimulate us to modify our life situation—to overcome frustrations, to avoid unnecessary stress, and to satisfy our basic emotional needs. A life without fluctuating moods would be too dull to be tolerable, and if we use drugs to suppress the experience of emotional pain, we bar ourselves also from experiencing moments of elation and joy. When we are depressed, two verses of poetry or Scripture are likely to do more permanent good than thrice-daily doses of phenelzine, and when we are anxious meditation offers more hope than medication for long-term relief.

Tranquilizers and sedatives, like analgesics, can also produce serious side-effects. One study of 7,500 people taking tranquilizing drugs brought to light 96 cases of allergy, general toxic effects in 78, habituation in 72, severe liver disturbance in 31, "other severe symptoms" in 97, 2 suicides, and 2 deaths from other causes. Added to this, in 1,700 cases serious emotional problems were created in essentially normal people, and existing emotional illness aggravated in a further 827 instances. Hardly a recommendation for the chemotherapeutic management of tension states!

Often psychotrophic drugs need to be taken in pairs, a second drug being necessary to counteract the imbalance caused by the first. For example, the sedative effects of sleeping pills taken late at night often persist well into the following morning, so it often becomes necessary to wake up with the aid of stimulant pills or strong black coffee. Norman Mailer tells the tragic story of Marilyn Monroe's growing dependence on sleeping pills. Unable to sleep without pills, she came to take more and more until the night when, even with their aid, sleep eluded her. "Does she splurge for a few more and get a couple of hours' sleep, thereby to stagger forth in drastic stupor for a working day," asks Mailer, "or should she pass into morning without sleep and try the job on stimulants." Judy Garland became similarly hooked on drugs; toward the end of her life she was taking amphetamines in the morning to wake her up, minor stimulants during the day to keep her going, a morphine injection before her evening engagements, and sleeping pills last thing at night to put her to sleep. This is the slippery slope many people find themselves on when they become dependent on drugs, and it is estimated that for every five people hooked on heroin, marijuana, and LSD, there are 1,200 addicted to medically prescribed sedatives. But happiness can't be dispensed over a druggist's counter. Pills cannot solve personal problems, and no amount of antidepressant drugs will turn rain into sunshine or gloom into joy. Doctors do their patients a disservice when they offer them "happiness" pills. In pharmacological terms there is precious little difference between a doctor's prescribing for an unhappy patient five milligrams of Valium three times a day and ordering him a thrice daily measure of Scotch. Neither drug will cure his underlying problems. As Dr. Colin Brewer, lecturer on psychiatry at Birmingham University, has pointed out, "By making misery a medical problem, we take away the patient's responsibility for solving his own problems."

Neither happiness nor health can be found by taking pills. If we value our well-being we must kick the drug habit, for we do ourselves only harm when we fly to the bottle for every tiny physical ache or psychic pain.

Sir William Osler, the great Canadian physician, once said, "One of the first duties of the physician is to educate the masses not to take drugs." That lesson has still to be learned.

Exercise

We all need a certain minimum level of exercise to keep ourselves fit. Without it, we suffer disuse atrophy; we become obese, breathless on the slightest exertion, permanently tired, and prone to varicose veins, arteriosclerosis, heart disease, and a wide range of rheumatic aches and pains. As Hippocrates, the father of medicine, observed, "That which is used develops. That which is not used wastes away."

Over the years our lives have become less and less active. At work, horsepower has replaced musclepower, and in the home, a variety of labor-saving gadgets has relieved us of the need to wash and polish floors, brush carpets, and clean dishes. As a result the daily exercise levels of many people now fall below the minimum necessary to preserve optimum bodily function.

Underexercised muscles grow weak and flabby. Dr. E. A. Mueller of the Max Planck Institute in Germany has shown that if an arm is immobilized in a plaster cast, it loses 30 percent of its power within one week. Insufficient use also leads to a weakening of the texture of the bones, which means that fractures occur more readily. Underexercised joints become stiff, and this, together with lowered muscle tone, leads to stiff necks, weak ankles, and bad backs. Specialists at Bellevue Hospital in New York estimate that fully 60 percent of back pains stem from muscle weakness and fatigue, both products of lack of exercise.

Stiffness, often caused by sheer lack of mobility, also has an aging effect. As Princess Luciana Pignatelli says in *The Beautiful People's Beauty Book*, "Few defects give age away quicker than rigidity. . . . A body that cannot move and bend freely, no matter how slender and pampered, no longer looks young."

But doctors currently are most concerned about the effect of lack of exercise on the heart. Coronary disease now accounts for a third of deaths among middle-aged males, and it is known that men with sedentary jobs are twice as likely to suffer heart attacks as those who perform more active work. The heart, after all, is only an elaborate muscular pump, and like every other muscle in the body, it needs regular exercise to keep it in trim.

Regular exercise also helps to keep us slim, and nutritional studies have shown that overweight is often caused by underexercising rather than by overeating (see *Obesity*). Exercise also helps to work off some of the tensions and frustrations of life. Doctors attached to the West Point Military Academy have noted that psychiatric disorders are less commonly found among athletes than among cadets with low physical-fitness ratings. This accords with the findings of Dr. Hans Selye, the world's foremost authority on stress, who has shown in laboratory experiments that rats trained to a high degree of physical fitness are able to withstand a level of stress—from shocks, noise, bright lights, and pain—that is enough to kill untrained animals.

Exercise, then, is a perfect conditioner for the healthy and a valuable cure for the sick. The list of diseases that can be wholly or partly attributed to exercise deficiency is growing, and weighty medical tomes are now being written on the "hypokinetic diseases"—the diseases that result from lack of exercise. As Dr. Thomas Sydenham, one of Britain's most eminent seventeenth-century physicians, said, "If only one knew the benefits of exercise and could keep his knowledge secret, he might easily make a fortune." Many governments have tried to foster national health by encouraging their people to take more exercise. In Russia over 9 million workers now take part in "break gymnastics," substituting a schedule of keep-fit exercises for the usual mid-morning cup of coffee. It is claimed that the introduction of these gymnastic sessions has made workers feel better, less irritable, and less prone to back pains, and in some cases has led to an increase in production of up to 25 percent. In China everyone who is not sick is obliged to get up at 6:00 A.M. to do half-an-hour's exercise to help keep the nation fit.

Volvo, Sweden's largest car-manufacturer, insists that every executive, from the managing director downward, must take thirty minutes' strenuous exercise every week, either in the firm's gymnasium or over a specially designed cross-country course. Mussolini, Italy's wartime leader, also recognized the importance of managerial fitness. He staged athletic contests for senior members of his government that included an obstacle race involving vaulting over a live horse, jumping a hedge of bayonets, and leaping through a hoop of fire.

But the real therapeutic benefits of exercise come not from staged activities such as these, but from the reintroduction of more vigor in our everyday lives. Wherever possible, we should shun the use of machines. Self-drive golf carts, electric shoepolishers, elevators and escalators, and automatic egg-whisks should be banned. Cars should be saved for only the most essential long-distance journeys. All other trips should be taken on foot or by bike. On weekends a walk in the country or a family game of tennis should replace the usual Sunday drive. Television-viewing should be cut by a third and the time saved spent on gardening, carpentry, table tennis, or other active pursuits. The day should start with a routine stretch and limber-up. After an early-morning shower enjoy a vigorous rubdown followed by a few moments running in place. Balance on one leg while putting on socks and shoes, perform a dozen half-knee bends every time you visit the toilet, and take every flight of stairs you meet at a steady trot. Get into the habit of leading a more active life. As former heavyweight boxing champion Gene Tunney recommends, "Take *regular* exercise—not violent week-ends of golf, or sporadic bursts of squash, but a daily drill that becomes as much a part of your life as cleaning your teeth."

Find time also during the week for a spell of at least

twenty minutes' vigorous exercise such as running, swimming, tennis, or squash, for it is necessary to indulge in exercise strong enough to raise the heart rate to near-maximum levels to improve cardiovascular function and protect the heart. Exercise at this level will also reduce the tendency of the blood to form clots and as a bonus will temporarily increase the output of sex hormones (which is doubled when top-class athletes swim flat out for eight hundred meters). Many people fear that exercise at this level will place an undue strain upon the heart, but there is little risk of this if the exercise is carefully graduated. Over a period of twenty years, Dr. Thomas Cureton, as head of the fitness research laboratory at the University of Illinois, designed and supervised the exercise schedules of over fifty thousand businessmen and has yet to encounter a heart attack caused by taking too much exercise.

The safest reconditioning exercises are rhythmical activities such as walking, cycling, swimming, dancing, and jogging, which can easily be graded according to one's age and physical condition. Exercises involving sustained tension and strain—such as heavy weight-lifting, wrestling, pushups, isometric muscle contractions, and tug-of-war contests—are best avoided in the early stages of rehabilitation, since they tend to increase the blood pressure.

People with a history of high blood pressure, arteriosclerosis, or coronary disease *need* exercise but should take it only under medical supervision. Exercise is an invaluable aid in the recovery from heart attacks, and most doctors today encourage patients to strengthen their hearts after a coronary attack by taking graduated exercise, starting with gentle walking on the flat and then progressing in easy stages to brisker walking, cycling, jogging, and often full running.

A short while ago an executive of a well-known firm consulted his doctor complaining of fatigue, breathlessness, and general loss of joie-de-vivre. The doctor examined him thoroughly but could find no evidence of organic disease apart from slight obesity and a trace of hypertension. So he wrote out a prescription and handed it to the executive. It read, "Exercise mildly today, exercise more tomorrow, continue until directed to stop." That is the finest tonic available for any sedentary worker who feels a few degrees below par.

Eye Baths

It is remarkable that the eyes, although among the most delicate organs in the human body and constantly exposed to smoke, dust, and acrid fumes, are so seldom affected by disease. When they do give trouble, the natural tendency is to doctor them with ointments, drops, and lotions, which often do more harm than good. Popular remedies in the past were applying drops of castor oil, dried hen's dung, or milk boiled with a white poppy. In the eighteenth century Lord Stafford, when suffering from weak eyesight, was advised by his physician to "abstain from all conjugal intercourse with his wife" for a period of twelve months. He followed the cure faithfully but with scant reward. After a year of total celibacy his sight was no better, and his wife pregnant.

If it is ever necessary to bathe the eyes, it is best to avoid using an eye bath. Dust and germs, when they linger in the region of the eyes, tend to collect in the folds at the base of the eyelids. When an eye bath is pressed against the eye, these crevices are sealed off and cannot be reached by the bathing fluid. A better technique of eye-bathing is to tip the head back, turn it slightly to one side, and then pour a weak saline solution (one level teaspoonful of salt in a pint of warm water) onto the open eye, catching the overflow in a bowl pressed against the cheek, with a towel held in readiness to mop up any excess. If an acid or alkali enters the eye, the eye should be bathed immediately in cold tap water for ten to fifteen minutes. This is an emergency situation and there is neither the need nor the time to prepare a warm saline solution.

At other times the finest solution to bathe the eye with is human tears. This, after all, is a natural saline solution produced by the lachrymal glands tucked away in the upper, outer corner of the eyes. Every time we blink—six to thirty times a minute—the eyelids carry a thin film of tears across the eye, and it is this windshield-wiper action which helps to keep the eyes free from dust and dirt. If a particle of grit gets trapped under one lid or the other, the eyes immediately water more freely, and this normally flushes the particle away. If this natural cleansing action fails, the best first-aid treatment is to blink rapidly for a few seconds or gently pull one lid over the other. It is safe to try to remove loose particles of débris with the corner of a clean handkerchief, but never wise to remove particles that are firmly embedded on the eye or that lie directly over the pupil. These need skilled medical attention. And never rub the eyes, for this can only aggravate matters.

When it comes to bathing the eyes, tears have another definite advantage over artificially prepared saline solutions in that they are bactericidal in their action. Some years before he discovered penicillin, Sir Alexander Fleming demonstrated the remarkable germ-killing properties of human tears. He had been impressed by the fact that the eye, although one of the most sensitive structures of the body and constantly surrounded by floating germs, so rarely became infected. He started to investigate. He squeezed lemon juice into the eyes of some of his students, sucked up their tears with a fountain-pen filler, and dropped them onto a culture dish which contained a flourishing growth of bacteria. Within a short while the bacteria disappeared, dissolved by a substance in the tears which he later isolated and named *lysozyme* from the Greek *lysis*, "dissolving." It is this substance which keeps the eyes among the most sterile parts of the surface of the human body.

In Babylonian days the treatment of inflammation of the surface of the eye, or conjunctivitis, was to "disembowel a yellow frog, mix its gall in curd and apply to the eye." This could have done little to benefit either frog or man. But the accompanying instruction–to cut up a raw onion and drink it with beer–had some validity, for this would cause the healing tears to flow and so help to check the infection.

Today episodes of conjunctivitis or "pink eye" are commonly treated with antibiotics, for while the inflammation can arise from the mechanical irritation of wind, smoke, and chemical fumes, it is more commonly caused by bacterial or viral infection. This is generally highly contagious and can easily be spread by contact with infected fingers or towels. Excessive bathing of the eyes is to be avoided in these cases, for it can spread the infection and also dilute the tears and so weaken their normal protective bactericidal action.

Eyesight

For nearly eighteen months during his childhood, novelist Aldous Huxley was almost completely blind and could read only Braille. He recovered his sight partially but afterward always suffered strain and fatigue even when reading with the aid of the powerful glasses prescribed for him. Then in 1939 his vision suddenly deteriorated. He wondered how he could cope with his work if, as now seemed possible, he went completely blind. Why is it that the human eyes are so peculiarly vulnerable to damage? he pondered. Other organs are protected by a self-healing mechanism; why not the eyes? Broken bones mend automatically, torn skin is repaired, and shed blood cells replaced. Did this *vis medicatrix naturae* not apply to the eyes?

At this point Huxley heard of the method of visual reeducation pioneered by Dr. W. H. Bates, a New York oculist. He took up the technique and faithfully practiced the exercises with the result that, as he reported, "Within a couple of months I was reading without spectacles and, what was better still, without strain and fatigue. The chronic tensions and the occasional spells of complete exhaustion were things of the past."

Many others have been able to improve their eyesight and dispense with glasses after following the Bates method. Its success lies in the appreciation that visual defects are frequently functional in origin. This means that they are open to cure, rather than mere palliation. The orthodox approach to eye disorders, on which the entire ophthalmic industry is based, is that organic change precedes functional breakdown. Spectacles are prescribed to correct refractive errors which are held to lead to eye strain.

Bates said that this sequence of events is frequently reversed. He found that strain is often the cause rather than the result of visual defects. The cure therefore lay in the elimination of strain rather than in the prescription of glasses, which at best could act as no more than a crutch on which the user would come to rely. Reeducation in the proper use of the eyes would eliminate strain, prevent damage to the delicate mechanism of the eyes, and help the body overcome existing visual defects.

The proof of this theory came from the thousands of people who benefited from its application. In Germany numerous "seeing-schools" were opened, and in 1934 a German army surgeon reported that the vision of many army recruits had improved following eyesight training. Their marksmanship, he found, was sharper when they left off glasses and had instruction at a seeing-school, and he recommended that people with failing sight should not immediately resort to wearing glasses but first take a course in visual reeducation.

Most people today would also benefit from learning how to use their eyes efficiently. Too many bring to the act of seeing unnecessary tension and strain. Relaxation is the open sesame to better sight, as it is to other psychomotor skills such as gymnastics, singing, and golf. The more effort we employ, the more tension we engender and the poorer our performance becomes. In extreme cases, if we allow ourselves to become screwed up with anger, we can become almost "blind with rage." We must *allow* the eyes to see, rather than employ any effort to *make* them see. In an art gallery, don't strain forward to see a picture; stand back and let the picture come to you. Follow the advice of Lao-Tzu: "Don't push the river, let it flow." You defeat your object when you try too hard.

Staring never helps. To see clearly we need to keep our eyes on the move. If our eyes become fixed on an object for too long, our perception grows dim, in the same way that if we keep our fingers resting on a table we cease to register contact with it after a while. In these cases movement of the fingers or eyes immediately quickens our awareness.

There is another important reason for keeping the eyes mobile. We see with the aid of over 130 million light-sensitive receptor cells (rods and cones), which are not uniformly distributed over the eye. On the outside of the retina there is a preponderance of rods, the cells that respond best to dim light, so to see clearly at night we need to make use of our "peripheral vision" by looking slightly to the side of the object we want to view. Toward the middle of the retina there is an increased concentration of cones, the cells responsible for daylight vision. Sharpest vision is obtained when we focus light on the macula lutea, the small yellow spot at the back of the retina where there is the densest concentration of cones and a total absence of rods. In some parts of the retina, a nerve fiber connects with up to 100 separate rods and cones, but at the macula lutea each cone has its own nerve fiber. This means that when we focus on the macula we transmit the most detailed picture possible to the brain. To see clearly we need to develop the art of macular vision. We cannot take in an entire scene with one fixed gaze but need to build up a composite picture in the same way that a television picture is developed from a series of dots or petit-point impressions. Staring is self-defeating, for it produces tension and prevents this free-scanning movement of the eyes. A rigid gaze reduces the acuity of vision with the inevitable result that we try harder, stare more fixedly, and so suffer more tension and strain.

As Aldous Huxley writes in *The Art of Seeing*, "A stare always defeats its own object; for, instead of seeing more, a person who has immobilised his sensing apparatus (an act which also immobilises his closely correlated attention) thereby automatically lowers his power of seeing." The role of the eyes in seeing is largely passive; the active work is reserved for the brain, which has to carry out the intricate task of interpreting the sensory data presented to it.

Unfortunately, many of the visual tasks we have to perform today encourage the development of a fixed stare. When we drive a car, watch television, use precision instruments, do fine needlework, add columns of figures, or read a book, we are forced to use the eyes in an unphysiological way which leads to tension, fatigue, and visual strain. Muscles always complain if they are held for too long in a state of sustained contraction, which is why it hurts to grip a pen, carry a suitcase, or bend over for hours on end in the garden. Natural activities like walking, swimming, and dancing produce little strain because they involve the alternate contraction and relaxation of muscle groups. This alternation is, in fact, the ideal way to use the muscles of trunk, limbs, heart, or eyes.

The movement of the eyeballs is controlled by six muscles. If we hold a fixed gaze for too long, we develop in these muscles a state akin to writer's cramp. To avoid this, we need to keep our eyes on the move or failing this, make a point of breaking up periods of prolonged study or concentration on close visual tasks with moments devoted to conscious movement of the eyes. The same applies to the ciliary muscles inside the eyes which control the curvature and therefore the focal power of the lens. The longer we focus on close objects, the more we tense these muscles.

Primitive man was constantly shifting his attention, focusing first on the bushes in front of him and then gazing away into the distance. In this way he rested and provided gymnastics for his ciliary muscles. We, on the other hand, concentrate on a book or television set for hours on end and so suffer visual strain. To prevent this we need to look up from our work from time to time and focus on a distant object. Similarly, when driving, we should not focus constantly on the road in front but should occasionally lift our eyes and look at the horizon, before quickly returning our attention to the road ahead.

Playing ball games involves a constant alteration of focus that provides valuable exercise for the eyes. This may explain why sportsmen seem to preserve their eyesight better than bookworms.

Another bad visual habit is the maintenance of a wide-eyed stare. This again is a sign of tension, for whenever an element of effort is introduced into the process of seeing, we tend to cut down our natural rate of blinking. This is unfortunate, for blinking is a protective act that serves several important functions: It lubricates the surface of the eye, sweeps it clean of dirt and dust, and provides it with regular periods of rest. A blink lasts for about three tenths of a second. This means that with an average blink rate of twenty per minute (slightly higher for men than for women), we shield our eyes from the light for 10 percent of the waking day. This provides much-needed rest for the light-sensitive retinal cells. The temptation is to reduce the rate of blinking when we concentrate, but anyone carrying out intricate work should avoid this tendency to stare and make a point of blinking regularly.

Nature, unfortunately, has not provided us with ear flaps to cut out unwanted sound, but it has provided us with eyelids to block out unwanted light, and these should be used whenever possible. There is no point staring into space, or worse still, puckering the brows, while thinking, for this is no aid to creative thought.

When the eyes are not in use, they should be closed. Conversely, when the eyes are open, they should be employed to the full. We can improve our vision by improving our powers of observation. Sight depends on the interpretation provided by the brain, and this relies as much on stored visual memories as on current visual stimuli. Read the simple sentence, "John walked though the door," and the brain will assume the missing *r* and read the words as "John walked th*r*ough the door." An experienced proofreader, on the other hand, will immediately spot the missing letter for, in many ways, we see what we want to see and are trained to see. An editorial in the British *Daily Express* made the point most cogently: "Few people see things. They look at them, but they do not see them. They carry away no impression, they form no mental picture. Their brains are asleep even if their eyes are open. Be one of the few who use the gift of sight intelligently with alert faculties, not like an owl or codfish." People who do this will enhance their visual faculties and increase their enjoyment of life.

If through faulty habits the eyes become strained, or if they grow tired through use in conditions of poor illumination or excessive glare, never rub them. Try instead the following techniques, which should be performed without glasses. Rest the eyes by covering them with the palms of the hands. Relax and, for a few seconds, imagine you are in a warm, dark, velvet-lined room. Then open the eyes and blink rapidly and evenly, trying to develop the lightest possible butterfly wink. Mobilize the muscles in and around the eyes. Exercise the facial muscles surrounding the eyes by first screwing up the eyes and puckering the brows and then relaxing them. Repeat several times. To relieve tension in the six orbital muscles, keep the head still and move the eyeballs in their sockets in first a clockwise and then a counterclockwise direction. Repeat several times. Finally, hold one finger eight inches away from the eyes, gaze at its tip, and then look into the distance. Repeat several times. This will ease tension in the ciliary muscles. If massage is to be used to relieve visual fatigue, it should be applied to the temples and neck—never to the eyeballs themselves. People with a tendency to eye strain or suffering from refractive errors of the eyes can benefit from practicing these simple exercises every day.

Fasting

Fasts have been undertaken for a variety of reasons, most of them completely unrelated to questions of health. Mystics have ventured them to induce hallucinations; political activists, as a dramatic form of social protest. They were performed by primitive man as an act of self-denial or penitence to try to propitiate angry gods. Even as recently as the seventeenth century, the British government ordered days of national fasting when, according to the famous diarist Samuel Pepys, the people were enjoined to "pray for more seasonable weather." Fasting has also played an important part in the religious lives of Hindus, Buddhists, Christians, Jews, and Muslims, though this is now declining. The six annual fast days once observed by the Jews are now, for all but the most orthodox, reduced to a one-day fast on the Day of Atonement. Among Christians, fasting is generally limited to a mere token abstention from certain luxury foods during the period of Lent, but all good Muslims, unless they are children or idiots, are still required to abstain from all food and drink from sunrise to sunset during the forty days of Ramadan, the exact length of the fasts of Moses, Elijah, and Christ.

Under natural conditions, both animals and children show a marked loss of appetite when they are ill, and this has led to the common belief that fasting should be employed during the early stages of an illness. As the often-misquoted English proverb puts it, "Starve a cold, nor feed a fever." This, so the story goes, enables the body to concentrate its energies on combating the underlying disease. To nature-cure practitioners, "fasting is the body-cleanser supreme." They regard the symptoms of malaise which often accompany fasting—the headache, nausea, coated tongue, and bad breath—as sure signs that the body is engaged in the process of eliminating waste products. But in fact these symptoms are due to the breakdown and release into the bloodstream of body fats and are similar in origin to the symptoms experienced after overindulgence in a rich, fatty meal. Sometimes an "eliminative" fast is prescribed, with the recommendation that it be continued until the tongue and breath are clear. This advice is not only based on a fallacy, it is also extremely dangerous. As Dr. Henry Lindlahr, one of the pioneers of nature-cure therapy pointed out, had he followed this principle when fasting his patients, "it seemed doubtful whether breath and tongue would clear up before the patient was ready for the undertaker."

There is no need to abstain from food during the early stages of a fever. The need then is for a light, nutritious, easily assimilated diet rich in vitamins and minerals, accompanied by plenty of fluids. But while there is no need to fast, there is equally no need to force-feed in the mistaken belief that this is necessary to keep up one's strength. The appetite, which naturally lessens, provides an accurate guide.

Fasting is currently being used in hospitals as a method of rapid weight-reduction. The fast is generally limited to seven to ten days, during which time the average person will lose somewhere in the region of sixteen pounds. Little hunger is felt after the first one or two days, and the losses in weight are well maintained, probably because appetites tend to become permanently reduced during the fast. A followup study made at a hospital in Glasgow, Scotland, showed that one third of the obese patients who had lost weight in this way had maintained their entire weight loss after an interval of three years.

Fasts of this length need to be taken under strict medical supervision, but fasts of two or three days can safely be undertaken by individuals acting on their own provided they are basically healthy and not prone to gout or suffering from diabetes, high blood pressure, or coronary disease. Most of us eat too much, and an occasional weekend fast can prove beneficial. Experiments with laboratory animals show that mice fed for two days and starved on the third increase their life span by 40 percent. Others fast because of the feeling of well-being it induces.

Sir Francis Chichester, who set the world speed record for a solo round-the-world navigation at the incredible age of sixty-six, kept fit by indulging in a variety of sports, yoga, breathing exercises, and careful dieting. In his book *How to Keep Fit* he describes these various methods, but adds that "for me fasting is the most beneficial treatment I have ever experienced." Whenever he needed a tonic, he took a two or three-day fast, during which he drank only apple juice and at the end always felt stronger, happier, and much more full of energy.

Fasts like these can often be taken without disturbing one's normal routine; one of Dr. Lindlahr's patients, who followed a forty-nine-day fast, took long walks every day and felt fitter and stronger at the end of the fast than he did at the beginning.

Flies

In the words of one expert, flies are "one of the most dangerous insects associated with man." In one village in the Middle East, half the inhabitants have been made blind in one or both eyes by trachoma, a disease transmitted by flies. Elsewhere in the world they are responsible for carrying dysentery, typhoid fever, cholera, and food poisoning.

The ancients obviously recognized that flies were carriers of disease, for both Nergal and Beelzebub, the disease gods of Babylon and Phoenicia, had as their symbol the fly.

Troubles stem from the fly's appalling eating habits. A fly will eat anything. It cheerfully alternates between kitchen refuse, animal dung, rotting vegetation in compost heaps, and human food. It tramples over its food, sampling as it goes, for its six feet are organs of taste as well as locomotion. As it cannot cope with solid food, it is forced to liquefy everything before it sucks it up through its trunklike proboscis, which it does by regurgitating onto the food some of the contents of its last meal. So, as it travels from horse manure to pork pie, it spreads disease by its feet, vomit, and excreta. An examination of a fly's track will clearly show numerous light and dark spots. The light smears are vomit spots, the dark spots patches of excreta. (One researcher counted 1,102 of these spots on a six-inch square of glass.)

Flies live for only thirty days or so in the summer and up to three months in the winter. To make up for his short life, they breed prolifically. An undisturbed female will lay 100-150 eggs in one day and repeat this process several times during her short life. These eggs hatch into maggots within eight to forty-eight hours and shortly after are converted to pupae and then to fully developed adult flies. This brief maturation period means that a female fly laying an average-size batch of eggs on April 1 could be responsible for the production of over 5 trillion adult flies by the middle of September. (It is estimated that a single pair of flies could produce enough progeny in the course of a single summer to cover the entire land mass of Germany to a depth of forty-seven feet). Fortunately, conditions have never been favorable for quite this explosive rate of growth, and as the fly is both stupid and slow, traveling at no more than four and a half miles an hour, it makes a ready prey for frogs, lizards, snakes, spiders, and birds. But enough survive to present a sizable health hazard, particularly during warm weather.

It may not be possible to exterminate the fly, but it should be possible to eliminate the filth on which it feeds and breeds. To do this, wastebaskets and garbage pails should be sprayed with insecticides and kept clean and covered, drains cleared, refuse burnt, animal shelters and runs regularly cleaned, animal excreta buried, and compost heaps covered with a layer of earth. Inside the house, food must be kept covered and cupboard doors closed at all times.

Gums

Most people make an attempt to clean their teeth, but few pay adequate attention to the health of their gums. As a result, according to the World Health Organization, "Periodontal disease is one of the most widespread diseases of mankind. No area of the world is free from it. And in most areas it has a high prevalence, affecting in some degree half the child population and almost the entire adult population." Yet this common disease, which in adulthood is responsible for the loss of far more teeth than dental decay, is essentially preventable.

Care of the gums should form an integral part of the daily routine of oral hygiene.

In a state of health our teeth are surrounded by a tight collar of gingival tissue. This ends in a sharp fringe, similar to the cuticle at the bed of a nail, which seals the tooth and protects the tooth socket from the entry of food particles, bacteria, and dirt. If the gums are allowed to become diseased, they change from being firm and tight to being swollen, soft and tender. This weakens the seal around the teeth and permits the development of small pockets in the gums where food débris can lodge and germs multiply. This secondary infection can lead to a condition known as pyorrhea, which literally means a "flow of pus." If left untreated, gum disease leads to a permanent loss of gum tissue and a gradual working loose of remaining teeth.

With the passage of time we become "long in the tooth," not because our teeth grow but because periodontal disease makes our gums recede, a fact utilized by farmers when they assess the age of a horse by examining the state of its teeth. Similarly, when plantation owners judged the health of slaves by peering into their mouths, they were guided by the health of their gums than by the presence or absence of dental disease. This was a reasonable precaution to take before buying a slave for, according to a paper delivered at a recent dental congress, "beside destroying gum tissue, the bacteria and toxins from gum infection may be absorbed into the blood stream and even the gastrointestinal tract, where they are thought to be a significant contributory factor in a variety of disorders." The rot may start in the mouth but doesn't necessarily end there.

A major cause of gum disease is the formation of deposits of food at the base of the teeth. These hard plaques irritate the gums and cause gingivitis, the first step in the cycle of periodontal disease. They can be prevented by thorough cleansing of the teeth (see *Teeth Cleaning*). If allowed to remain, these plaques become hardened by the deposition of calcium and other mineral salts to form calculus or tartar, which can only be removed by scaling, administered by a dentist or dental hygienist. The value of this procedure has been recognized for over nine hundred years, but it is still too little used today. Albucasis (1050–1122), an Arabian surgeon and one of the earliest dental practitioners, described fourteen dental scrapers in his book *De Chiurgia* and explained the process by which "on the surface of the teeth, both inside and outside, are deposited rough, ugly-looking scales, black, green and yellow; this corruption is communicated to the gums, and the teeth are in the process of time denuded." He recommended, "Lay the patient's head on your lap and scrape the teeth and molars." Regular scaling is still the only effective treatment for removing the accumulation of unwanted tartar. Ideally it should be carried out at least twice a year.

Massage is the other way of protecting the health of the gums. Animals existing on a fibrous diet of fruit, vegetables, and raw meat, get adequate massage for their gums as they chew their food, but civilized man living on a regime of soft, cooked meals almost certainly needs to supplement this natural stimulus by a little additional friction. This can be applied by lightly brushing the gums, rubbing them with a rough cloth, or massaging them with salt. All three of these methods are of considerable antiquity.

Antony van Leeuwenhoek, the Dutch draper whom historians have largely overlooked, pioneered the development of the microscope and with its aid became the first man to recognize the existence of bacteria. He discovered the vast population of organisms, both benign and pathogenic, which inhabit the human mouth. "All the people living in our United Netherlands," he wrote, "are not as many as the animals I carry in my own mouth." This caused him to pay great attention to dental hygiene. In 1683, at the age of fifty-one, he wrote, in a letter to Francis Aston, secretary of the Royal Society, "Tis my wont of a morning to rub my teeth with salt, and then swill my mouth out with water: and often after eating, to clean my back teeth with a toothpick, as well as rubbing them hard with a cloth; wherefore my teeth, back and front, remain as clean and white as falleth the lot of few men of my years, and my gums (no matter how hard the salt be that I rub them with) never start bleeding."

This prophylactic treatment can hardly be bettered today: daily frictional massage of the gums with a rough cloth or towel, judicious use of a soft toothpick to dislodge impacted particles of food, with the additional support of frictional finger massage of the gums with ordinary table salt if they show the slightest sign of becoming inflamed, swollen, tender, or prone to bleed.

Total extraction of the teeth is another way of "curing" periodontal disease, but as Theodor Rosebury, emeritus professor of bacteriology at Washington University, points out, this is rather like using a guillotine to cure a headache.

Hangovers

A hangover is basically the result of alcohol poisoning. It is characterized by throbbing headaches, dizziness, and lethargy. Some people and certain races are more prone to suffer these symptoms than others. A major Swiss drug company carried out research on alcohol tolerance and found that Americans suffered fewer unfortunate side effects than Chinese, Japanese, Koreans, and other Asians. This was confirmed by research conducted at the University of California that showed that while Americans remained relaxed, alert, and happy on a measured dose of alcohol, Orientals experienced anxiety, throbbing pain in the head, dizziness, and often a facial flush a few minutes after drinking that was rarely observed in the Americans.

Considering that our forefathers drank wine and beer as we now drink coffee, tea, and Coke, it is amazing that they handed down to us so few hangover cures. The Roman patricians tried to ward off the ill effect of drinking by wearing around their heads garlands of flowers and herbs. More effective is the age-old "hair of the dog that bit you" approach. Some of the ill effects experienced after a bout of drinking are withdrawal symptoms that can be staved off for a while at least by drinking more alcohol. The popular barman's hangover cure contains the alcoholic drink Fernet Branca laced with a gastric stimulant such as peppermint or Worcester sauce. Ava Gardner's favorite recipe is more potent: Take a large balloon glass; half-fill it with ice; add twisted orange peel, a measure of gin, and a half measure of brandy; and top it with champagne.

Since two of the effects of alcohol poisoning are dehydration and a lowered blood-sugar level, it pays to take plenty of fluids, preferably sweet fluids, after going on a drinking spree. Samuel Pepys, the seventeenth-century English diarist, was advised by his brother-in-law to take plenty of fresh orange juice after a bout of heavy drinking, a cure which has much to recommend it, for orange juice contains fruit sugar, or fructose, which helps the body burn up alcohol.

Not all hangover symptoms, however, result simply from alcohol intoxication. Scientists attached to the Institute of Pharmacology at the University of Florence believe that some of the effects, and particularly the throbbing headaches, stem from histamine poisoning. They recommend that people prone to hangover headaches should avoid red wines, which are particularly rich in histamine, or switch to drinking Chianti Classico, which is one of the few wines in the world that do not contain free histamine. Alternatively, they suggest taking an antihistamine tablet *before* drinking, for this they find often prevents the hangover that comes from drinking quantities of red wine.

Alcoholic drinks also contain aromatic substances called congener constituents, which give them their unique properties and delightful individual flavors, but which can also produce unfortunate toxic effects. This explains why drinks with few congener constituents, like vodka and gin, produce far fewer hangovers than those rich in congeners like brandy and whisky. At the University of California sixty students were given equal doses of alcohol in the form of either six double whiskies or six double vodkas. The next morning two thirds of the whisky-drinkers complained of a hangover, but only one third of the vodka-drinkers, with hangover headaches ten times as common among the whisky-drinkers.

Mixing drinks is harmful, not because it mixes different sources of alcohol, but because it brings together a variety of different congener constituents.

Plum brandies such as slivovitz are notorious producers of hangovers because they contain the congener methanol. Sherry, another potent tipple, suffers because it contains large quantities of acetaldehyde. Eating the fruit of the persimmon tree is a popular hangover cure in Japan, and recent research has shown that this fruit contains an ingredient that reduces the level of acetaldehyde in the blood of rabbits by as much as two thirds. Work is now going on to identify and isolate the active agent contained in persimmon juice in the hope that it can be offered as an effective hangover cure.

Coffee, the favorite standby of heavy drinkers, helps to stimulate the nervous system when it has been depressed by taking too much alcohol and can also slow down the rate of absorption of alcohol from the stomach. To produce this last effect requires at least two to three cups of strong black coffee taken *before* the alcohol leaves the stomach.

Food also slows down the rate of alcohol-absorption. A formal dinner starting with a double whisky, two glasses of wine during the meal, a glass of port with the cheese, and a large brandy afterward will raise the blood-alcohol level to a comfortable 60 milligrams at the end of an hour. Taking the same amount of alcohol at a cocktail party without any accompanying food, as say four double gins, will make the blood alcohol level soar to 140 milligrams, which is enough to produce symptoms of gross intoxication in most people. Eating after the party will do little to lessen these effects, for by this time most of the alcohol will have left the stomach.

Aspirin and aspirin-based remedies such as Alka-Seltzer are best avoided as hangover cures because they tend to irritate the stomach, which may already be inflamed by taking too much alcohol.

Hats

Hats are worn primarily as a form of personal adornment but occasionally serve as symbols of status and rank. The king's crown, the sultan's fez, and the bishop's miter all proclaim the eminence of the men who wear them. Hats are also worn as a mark of respect. In the presence of Jehovah the Jewish male covers his head in keeping with the Old Testament tradition and law, but when the Christian stands before his God he bares his head, a paradoxical reversal of behavior for which there is no easy explanation. Hats are also used for signaling, being doffed in respectful greeting, tossed in the air as a sign of elation, thrown to the ground as a gesture of despair, or wrung in the hands as an expression of grief.

The wearing of special reinforced hats or helmets can save lives and should be a routine practice of those whose occupation entails the risk of head injury, such as horseback riders, security guards, demolition contractors, and motorcyclists. Protective headdress enclosing the hair should also be worn by workers engaged in the preparation of food, to prevent the spread of infection; and by those operating machinery, to prevent accidents resulting from the trapping and tearing away of long hair.

In most other instances there is little real need to wear hats. Given an average head of hair, there is no need to protect the head from sunshine, heat, rain, or all but extreme cold. The hair and scalp provide an adequate covering for the head. Hair is impermeable to rain and yet allows the evaporation of sweat; it protects against the excessive loss of heat unless slicked down with too much grease or hair oil; and it guards the skin against sunburn.

Only hairless infants and baldheaded men need to wear hats to protect themselves from the sun's ultraviolet rays.

Many people wear panama and white linen hats in summer in the belief that doing so helps prevent "sunstroke," a physiological disaster that was once said to result from the direct action of sunlight on the brain. Blacks were thought to be spared the catastrophe of cerebral overheating by the greater thickness of their skulls. The only hope for Caucasian travelers in the tropics was to cover the head with a pith helmet and the nape of the neck with either a spinal pad, as issued to British troops on tropical service in the 1939–1945 war, or a neck drape as worn by members of the French Foreign Legion. But neither of these measures is necessary, for it is now known that the sun's rays cannot penetrate the cranium and there is no difference at all in the thickness of Negroid and Caucasian skulls. Heatstroke arises from a total breakdown of the body's heat regulation mechanism and is not directly related to overheating of the skull, nor can it be prevented by wearing a tropical hat.

In the depth of winter the wearing of a hat, though it can do nothing to prevent catching a cold, can add considerably to comfort. We lost heat fairly evenly from the surface of the body. The more skin we expose, the more heat we lose. Experiments have shown that about 20 percent of the heat of the naked body is lost through the head, so going hatless on an icy day is rather like centrally heating a house and then leaving the front door open.

Holidays

Dr. Beric Wright, medical adviser to Britain's Institute of Directors, has said, "A holiday is probably the most valuable insurance policy of all against stress, disease and fatigue." But what makes a successful holiday? Is it sunshine, rest, activity, relaxation, stimulus, or change?

The little medical research which has been done on the subject suggests that thousands of people today are choosing vacations that are not wholly appropriate to their needs. Professor Pierre Delbarre, dean of the faculty of medicine at the Cochin Port Royal Hospital in Paris, has studied the subject in detail. He suggests that when planning holidays, we should pay more attention to correcting the "biological disequilibria" of our lives and less to acquiring a tan or rushing off to visit faraway places. He believes, for example, that most people would benefit by taking more short breaks rather than one long annual holiday. "Biological imperatives," he suggests, demand that we should take two or three periods of eight to ten days' holiday a year, since this helps prevent the buildup of tension and fatigue (see *Rest Pauses*). He also recommends that holidays should be taken in the spring and fall when we are most likely to feel fatigued. In July and August our metabolism and ability to work are at a peak, which makes the summer, in his opinion, the least appropriate time of the year to take a holiday.

Holidays originally were holydays, the days of the calendar set aside for the celebration of pagan or religious rites. They were essentially carefree days when entire communities forgot their routine work and gave themselves over completely to pleasure and play. Dancing in the streets and on the village greens played an important part in these festivities; in fact, the Old Testament word for holiday carries the secondary meaning "dancing in a circle," a link so well established that in 1577 the English poet Barnabe Googe said, "Do you not know that it is a holiday, a day to dance in?"

Public holidays still exist throughout the world to mark various religious festivals and secular events such as Labor Day, Thanksgiving Day, and the days of national independence. Their number varies from state to state and country to country. Italy has seventeen; Canada eleven to eighteen; Denmark eleven; France and Belgium ten each; the United States of America nine to fifteen, and Britain seven. Only rarely today are these public holidays made the occasion for public celebration. instead of communal singing, feasting, and dancing, they now provide opportunities for individuals, or at best families, to visit friends, parks, and stately homes, or simply to paint the house or tend the garden. So the holydays celebrated by entire communities have become the vacations taken by individuals or families alone, and in the process they have lost much of their communal merriment and cathartic play.

In recent years increasing leisure and improved methods of transport have led to greater opportunities for overseas travel. The word *travel* comes from the same French root as *travail* and means "to work or labor," and no doubt to begin with, with no established travel trade to smooth the way and only primitive forms of transport, travel was an exceedingly laborious affair. But it did bring people into intimate contact with the foreign environments they visited. Today it is possible to travel widely but experience little. Coach tours are often more likely to broaden the seat than the mind.

The nineteenth-century traveler embarked on a Grand Tour of Europe that often lasted two or three years and came back with a richer sense of history and a deeper appreciation of the arts. His twentieth-century counterpart is whisked by coach through eighteen cities in fifteen days and suffers from cultural indigestion, often bringing back little more than a reeling head or an upset stomach. The first form of travel lead to the Enlightenment, the second to the great disillusionment.

The contemporary holidaymaker is not a traveler in the old sense of the word but a tourist, a modern word derived from the Latin *tornus*, "a person carried around in a circle." The early travelers came into direct contact with the native population, ate their food, observed their customs, shopped in their local bazaars, and often adopted their dress. The modern tourist travels by jet, eats steak and French fries in an international hotel of standard international design, shops in a supermarket that could as easily be in Iowa as in Istanbul, and wears not the native costume but the routine tourist uniform of slacks and open-neck shirt adorned not with a string of beads but a strap festooned with Leica camera, lenses, and exposure meter. He or she is encapsulated in a carefully prepared protective cocoon and is often less likely to experience excitement, liberation, or change by taking a packaged holiday in Morocco than by staying at home, slipping on a caftan, barbecueing shish kebab, sitting on cushions, and enjoying a candlelit alfresco supper.

Holidays can help correct the "biological disequilibria" of our lives only if they are chosen with care. On holiday we need to find ourselves, not lose ourselves. The middle-aged executive conscious of his declining youth and virility would probably benefit more by going mountain-climbing, which would give his ego a boost, than by taking a beach holiday and exposing his pallid paunch to unfortunate comparison with the lithe torsos of tanned young water-skiers. And the middle-aged woman whose family have fled the nest and who feels surplus to requirements would probably gain more satisfaction taking a party of Girl Scouts on a camping expedition than trailing round as a suprenumerary on one of her husband's Far Eastern business trips, for above all else she needs recognition of her value as an individual. Holidays in this way can replace the missing elements in our lives and provide opportunities for self-discovery and growth. They can inject excitement into dull, routine lives; provide an opportunity for consumers to become creators; enable town-dwellers to rediscover their grass roots; the lonely to find company, and the repressed to let off steam.

But if holidays are to be truly re-creational they need to be prescribed with as much care and individual attention as a doctor shows when prescribing treatment for his patients.

Kissing

Apart from the sex organs, the most sensitive areas of the human body are the fingers, lips, and tongue. In view of this, it is not surprising that when humans meet they generally make initial contact with either hands or mouth. With a touch or a kiss we can convey a multitude of messages. With our hands we can exchange a formal handshake, a friendly embrace, a soothing stroke, or an erotic caress. With our lips the possibilites are equally great. As a form of greeting we kiss friends on the cheek, infants on the top of the head, and lovers on the lips. When we kiss a person to show respect, we choose a site in keeping with our relative status. As Desmond Morris points out in *Intimate Behaviour*, we choose "the cheek, for friendly equality; the hand, for deep respect; the knee for humble submission; and the foot, for grovelling servility." When we wish to abase ourselves completely we "bite the dust" or become a servile "boot-licker."

Since we cannot contact God directly, when we wish to evoke the aid of the Almighty we kiss a sacred symbol, a holy relic, the Bible, or the bishop's ring. We spit when we curse, but kiss when we grant a benediction. We kiss an injured part to make it better and at Las Vegas kiss the dice before we throw to bring good luck.

Then there is the lover's kiss, that delicious sensory cocktail of taste, touch, and smell, but never sound. (It is interesting to note that when adults kiss children on the mouth they generally make a smacking sound that precludes prolonged erotic contact and signifies to all in earshot that this is not to be mistaken for a sensual kiss.) Kissing normally forms an integral part of precopulatory arousal. The Kama Sutra of Vatsyayana suggests that during the early stages of sexual congress kisses should be exchanged on "the forehead, the eyes, the cheeks, the throat, the bosom, the breasts, the lips and the interior of the mouth." At a later stage, it recommends "fighting with the tongue" and "pressing the teeth of one against the mouth of the other."

The term *maraichinage* is often given to the deep lover's kiss, where a couple "sometimes for hours, mutually explore and caress the inside of each other's mouths with their tongues as profoundly as possible" (Van de Velde, *Ideal Marriage*). The term stems from the maraichins, the inhabitants of part of the Vendee of Brittany, with whom it is a popular local pastime and, according to a local mayor, "a real antidote against depopulation."

This prolonged stimulation helps to prepare the sexual organs for coitus, a process that generally takes significantly longer in the female than the male. It is a process often omitted, generally to the detriment of one party, when the sex act is performed between prostitutes and their clients, or uncaring, jaded husbands and their wives.

Lovers also exchange genital kisses. Many people expressed shocked surprise when the sex researches of Dr. Alfred Kinsey revealed that practically half the American adults studied indulged in genital kissing, applying the lips to the female genitalia (cunnilingus) in 54 percent of the cases and to the penis (fellatio) in 49 percent of the cases. These practices are condemned by both the Jewish and Christian religions and are legally banned in every state in the U.S.A. apart from Kentucky and South Carolina. (Illinois, Wisconsin, Mississippi, and Ohio maintain the odd inconsistency that cunnilingus is acceptable but fellatio a felony.) But, as Kinsey pointed out, it is hardly surprising "that the two parts of the body that are the most sensitive erotically, namely the mouth and the sexual organs, should be brought into contact with one another so often." Moreover, for some women cunnilingus is the most reliable way of achieving an orgasm. It is a method that doesn't demand potency in the male and can be indefinitely sustained without making the male orgasmically satiated (see *Orgasm*).

Doubts are occasionally raised about the hygienic aspects of kissing. In Tudor times the kiss was a more popular form of greeting than the handshake and this, in the opinion of Dr. Frederick Cartwright, head of the department of the History of Medicine at King's College Hospital, London, contributed significantly to the rapid spread of syphilis in medieval Britain. The same is probably true of the transmission among students of glandular fever (infectious mononucleosis), which is often referred to as the "kissing disease." Reviewing the situation, Dr. Theodor Rosebury, emeritus professor of Bacteriology at Washington University, St. Louis, says that all respiratory diseases can be transmitted by mouth-to-mouth kissing, as can syphilis in its active secondary stage and, under certain circumstances, herpes simplex (cold sores) and glandular fever. But he estimates the risk of transmitting disease in this way is equivalent to the "chance of being hit with a golf ball as you walk through the park." Despite this, he feels it is good manners to avoid kissing people when you have a cold, and to refrain from kissing babies at all times. Bacteriologist Dr. John Drew, in *Man, Microbe and Malady*, makes a similar assessment of the risk. Speaking as a bacteriologist, he finds kissing a "fundamentally insanitary habit" and, among schoolchildren in particular, "a fertile method of distributing infections of the human respiratory tract." But speaking as a man, he is forced to agree that "the risk is, in most cases, worth while."

Laughter

A sense of humor is an invaluable possession. If we want to lead a long, joyful life we should cultivate the habit of laughter, which Aristotle described over two thousand years ago as "a bodily exercise precious to health." This is one of the secrets of longevity: a cure for tension and a remedy for stress. He who laughs, lasts.

Dr. John Kellogg ran a sanatorium at Battle Creek, Michigan, where he helped restore the health of a steady stream of rich and famous patients. He employed the usual range of diets, exercises, and thereapeutic baths, but one of his most popular and successful rejuvenation cures was a series of "laughing sessions" held in the sanatorium gymnasium. Here the tired and the tense were helped to laugh their troubles away. A similar technique is employed by Dr. Vachet of the Paris Institute of Psychology. He encourages students to dispel their tensions and dissolve their anxieties by indulging in uninhibited, rollicking laughter. Better a belly laugh, he feels, than a constant bellyache.

Many philosophers and psychiatrists have written learned treatises on the psychology of laughter, from Plato and Aristotle to Kant, Bergson, Freud, Huxley, and Koestler. All agree that the physical act of laughter is characterized by a sudden release of tension. Part of the art of the comedian, in fact, is to build up a degree of tension, then release it in a sudden outburst of laughter. Alfred Hitchcock does this in his thriller films. A couple hiding in a room are convinced that an assailant is closing in on them. The anxiety mounts, aided by spine-chilling incidental music. Then, slowly, the door to the room swings open.

The cinema audience gasps. Tension is at its peak. Then a cat walks slowly into the room. The audience collapses into a sudden outburst of laughter and relief. The same occurs when we set out to make children laugh. We create an atmosphere of tension by playing anxiety-provoking games such as peek-a-boo and hide-and-seek. If we overdo the stress, the baby cries, but if we judge things correctly, it laughs from the sheer relief of discovering that its fears have been unfounded.

Relief from tension is always pleasurable, whether the tension is caused by hunger, sex, anger, or anxiety. Normally we get relief by taking some form of purposeful activity: We eat, copulate, fight or run. When these outlets are denied us, we can often find release through laughter. As early as 1863 the English philosopher Herbert Spencer pointed out that when emotional energy cannot find release in one direction, it may sometimes erupt as laughter. When it does the energy is spent, for in these circumstances, as Arthur Koestler suggests, "laughter prevents the satisfaction of biological drives, it makes a man equally incapable of killing or copulating; it deflates anger, apprehension and pride." This helps us lead a civilized life and makes it easier for us to live peacefully in closely confined communities. But despite all our attempts to play the part of rational, civilized beings, we are still basically animals. As Aldous Huxley says in discussing the role of laughter, "We carry around with us a glandular system which was admirably well adapted to life in the Paleolithic times, but is not very well adapted to life now. Thus we tend to produce more adrenaline than is good for us, and we either suppress ourselves and turn destructive energies inwards or else we do not suppress ourselves and we start hitting people." As an alternative, we can laugh. In this way we can give vent to repressed anger, embarrassment, anxiety, or lust.

Freud believed that laughter springs from the constant conflict between our strong animal drives (id) and the restraints superimposed by our conscience (ego and superego). We try desperately to be cultured creatures, but every now and then the mask slips and we lose our hard-won dignity and composure. We laugh modestly when the window-cleaner loses his trousers and uproariously when the pompous judge trips over a step while solemnly entering court, or when a decorous society hostess gives out an unintended belch. For a few moments the mask slips; we stop pretending that we are model citizens and are content to be our honest-to-goodness animal selves. Laughter of this kind comes when our pent-up animal energies find a way around the inhibiting barrier erected by our conscience. This stops us from taking life too seriously or becoming too obsessed with our own importance. Laughter helps preserve our mental health. As one psychiatrist observed, "I've seldom been called upon to help a person who had a sense of the ridiculous, and I've *never* had to treat anyone who could really laugh at himself."

This is the value of both satire and mildly self-deprecating humor, which with their pointed barbs help to prick the balloon of puffed-up arrogance and inflated self-righteousness. Laughter is a safety valve and probably the only way of giving vent to all our pent-up animal energies of which society wholly approves.

Laughter also exerts a powerful socializing force, for it is a form of nonverbal communication akin to the warning signals of birds and the appeasement gestures of monkeys. When a bird spots danger, it gives out a distress cry that is immediately taken up and relayed by the rest of the flock. Similarly, a macaque monkey, meeting a tribe of strangers on neutral ground, signals his peaceful intentions by baring his teeth, smacking his lips, and rolling his head from side to side, looking as he does so like a little old man chuckling over a *New Yorker* cartoon. We use similar methods of nonverbal communication. When we greet strangers with a smile, we give an assurance that our intentions are wholly peaceful. When we laugh we signal to those around that all is well and there is no danger on the horizon, so it is safe for the members of the group to relax, let their hair down, and enjoy themselves in a carefree, uninhibited way. This explains why laughter is so infectious. "Laugh and the world laughs with you," the saying goes, and by its very nature laughter helps break down the barriers between people and encourages feelings of group unity. You can't be sure that a barking dog won't bite, but you can be pretty sure that a laughing man won't turn and stab you in the back. So you relax and feel at ease in his company. As Victor Borge says, "Laughter is the shortest distance between two people."

Laughter also helps us cope during times of stress. In the good times we laugh from pleasure, in the bad times from sheer necessity. That's why some of the finest humor arises during times of national disaster. Whenever the harsh realities of life are too grim to face head on, it helps to convert them into a joke. The ghettos have always produced their own brand of humor. In time of famine, we try to double up with laughter rather than hunger. During the London blitz, a shared sense of humor helped to maintain public morale, and in the 1914-1918 war, British frontline troops even made fun of the sight of the corpses strung out like washing on the barbed wire entanglements. The soldiers laughed to protect themselves from being consumed by horror and grief, and because crying could do no good, could never bring the dead back to life. As Henri Bergson, the French philosopher, put it, at times like these laughter provides a "momentary anaesthesia of the heart."

Abraham Lincoln is usually pictured as a dour, unsmiling individual, but in fact he had a sparkling wit that stood him in good stead in his early days as a circuit lawyer and helped support him later in his life when, as President, he had to face the horrors of the American Civil War. On one occasion, when the war was at its height, he insisted on prefacing a meeting of his War Cabinet by reading a humorous skit by Artemus Ward. The Cabinet was incensed by his seeming frivolity. Secretary of War Edwin Stanton admitted afterwards that he was on the point of quitting the meeting in utter disgust, but Lincoln read on. When the sketch was finished he said, "Gentlemen, why don't you laugh? With the fearful strain that is upon me night and day if I did not laugh I should die and you need the medicine as much as me." The President was undoubtedly right. We all need the medicine of laughter, and particularly so when times are hard, for it's when we've got least to laugh about that we most need to laugh.

Laughter is also a probable aid to creative thought. Arthur Koestler, in his masterful analysis of inventive genius, outlined in *The Act of Creation*, points out that there are several close parallels between the sudden act of creation and the spontaneous eruption of laughter. Seeing the joke is, in many ways, similar to solving the problem. "We all know," he writes, "that there is only one step from the sublime to the ridiculous; the more surprising that psychology has not considered the possible gains that could result from the reversal of that step." It is possible, he feels, that the practice of laughter may enhance our powers of creative thought. Others go further and suggest that the liberating effect of laughter is little short of a religious experience. Novelist G. K. Chesterton believed that the religion of the future would be based on a more highly developed, subtle form of laughter, and Havelock Ellis has said, "Even the momentary expansion of the soul in laughter is, to however slight an extent, a religious exercise."

Few activities can produce such widespread beneficial effects. Laughter aids digestion by increasing glandular secretion, relaxes the muscles, dilates the arterioles, and brings a blush to the skin and a sparkle to the eyes. Even the plainest face becomes attractive when wreathed with a smile. German anthropologist Hans Hass, who has made a detailed study of human behavior with the aid of concealed movie cameras, has been much impressed by the beautifying effects of laughter. In his book *The Human Animal* he tells how he filmed a Chinese woman during a fit of fury when her face looked positively repulsive. Ten minutes later she was smiling and her face, while not classically beautiful, was positively attractive. "This signal beautifies any face," writes Hass. Why then is laughter—the all-purpose youth-promoting, tension-relieving, life-preserving tonic—so little used today? Does our neglect date back to the teaching of the early Puritan fathers, who thought that laughter was an unseemly frivolity that the cultured man should seek to suppress? The Earl of Chesterfield captured the feeling of the time when he said, "Nothing is so illiberal and so ill-bred as audible laughter." This powerful influence undoubtedly lingers on today, for many people still find it necessary to stifle their chuckles behind discreetly raised hands and would feel it improper to indulge in a really hearty belly laugh. (According to his biographers, Hitler always covered his face when he laughed.) But these inhibitions must go if we are to preserve our health and mental poise. We take life far too seriously these days. Laughter must be encouraged. We would be much more effective if we used laughter rather than drugs as a means of escape from anxiety and tension, and we'd stand a far better chance of furthering the brotherhood of man if we transmitted round the world peals of laughter rather than posses of earnest diplomats. The world would be a much more peaceful place if we took to throwing custard pies instead of Molotov cocktails.

Longevity

The average mammal achieves a life span that is roughly seven and a half times its age at maturity. This suggests for man a lifespan of approximately 120 years, a figure that many physiologists believe to be well within our capabilities.

At the beginning of the century, the average American male could expect to live to be forty-seven. By 1950, his expectation of life had increased to sixty-seven. If we could eliminate the two major killing diseases in the civilized world—cancer and coronary disease—the average life expectancy would be increased by five years. Halving the toll of automobile and other accidents would add a further six months to our lives. But far more could be done by changing our way of life. Pavlov, the great Russian physiologist, maintained that everyone could and should live to be a hundred. Failure to do this, he said, was due to "intemperance, lack of regularity, and their own criminal attitude towards their bodies."

Most nations can recall folk heroes who in the latter stages of their lives have performed prodigious feats of physical endurance. Russia produced George Hackenschmidt, the world wrestling champion, who kept fit at the age of eighty-five by jumping over the back of a chair fifty times. Yugoslavia gave birth to Fanny Copeland, a remarkable woman who at the age of eighty-eight was still able to climb the country's highest mountain, the 9,400-foot Triglav in the Slovenian Alps. And America has had the recent example of Larry Lewis, the San Francisco waiter who was performing a full day's work at the age of 105 and also jogging the nearly seven miles to work each day. Are these people to be regarded as freaks, or is this level of performance within the reach of all of us? A detailed study of over five thousand American centenarians showed "that the people who survive are not 'biological accidents' as has been claimed, but people who in their daily living have made exceptional adjustments to life situations." The secrets of a long and healthy life are few. One of the earliest textbooks of gerontology–*Medicina Gerocomica: The Galenic Art of Preserving Old Men's Health* (1724)–listed them as fresh air, regular diet, temperance, and above all else exercise. "Every man is a fool or becomes a physician when he arrives at 40 or 50 years of age," said the author, Sir John Floyer, who lived to be 85. Recent studies confirm the importance of regular exercise.

The director of the Georgian Gerontology Center in Russia made a special study of the centenarians living in the Caucasian mountains and reported that he found not a single idler among them. "Their entire lives," he said, "consist of rationally organised cycles of outdoor work, rest and play." Similarly, gerontologists who have studied the centenarians living in Vilcabamba, a large valley in Ecuador, report that most of them carry on some kind of work until the day they die. As the Soviet Institute of Gerontology concludes, "a man could live longer if he were allowed to work longer." As it is, more than six times as many women as men live to be a hundred, partly, no doubt, because they rarely retire from active work.

Peace of mind also appears to contribute to longevity. Many centenarians stress the importance of regular habits, and while they do not claim to be always happy, they often speak of the basic contentment of their lives. It was noticeable that there was not a single bachelor among the Caucasian centenarians, one of whom emphasized the importance of a happy marriage. "My first six wives were all wonderful women," he said. "If a man has a good and kind wife he can easily live to a hundred years." Unfortunately, his seventh wife was an angry woman, and he claimed to "have aged at least ten years since marrying her."

The right mental attitude to life is also important. We must take care to live until the day we die. As Dylan Thomas wrote, "Old age should burn and rave at close of day." Many people quit the stage of life not at the final curtain but after the second act. Sixty for many people is a time for giving up, but at sixty-seven Tolstoy learned to ride a bicycle and at about the same age Gandhi started his campaign for independence in India, Sarah Bernhardt played the part of the nineteen-year-old Joan of Arc, Catherine the Great took a new lover, and Enoch begat Methuselah. Anyone wanting to remain young should follow Jung's advice, given when he himself was seventy-six: "Live each day as if you'll be here for another 100 years. Then you really will *live* to the end."

Medicated survival is not enough. We must strive not only to add years to life, but also to add life to years.

Mantras

Mantras have been described as words or sentences "having some influence when recited with meaning." This wide-ranging definition applies equally well to the use of words as curses, prayers, incantations, and oaths, for words are only symbols that, when repeated purposefully, will produce mood changes and trigger off chains of associated actions and ideas as surely as Pavlov's dogs learned to salivate at the ringing of a bell.

Psychologist William James points out in his study of *The Varieties of Religious Experience* that the repetition of devotional phrases has been used within many religious disciplines to induce the transcendental state of mystic vision (see *Meditation*). Yogis meditate with the aid of mantras that refer to some aspect of the godhead, the most commonly employed being the single syllable *om*, which represents God in all his fullness and power. When repeated, these mantras help to create a feeling of "oneness," a sense of cosmic unity, a glorious merging of the self with the infinite. But they also have certain direct physiological effects. The repetition of a mantra can act as an aid to concentration; provide a soothing, repetitive stimulus, like the rocking of a cradle or the crooning of a lullaby; and help direct attention away from obsessive doubts and anxieties, in the way that a person beset by sudden tragedy will sometimes hold on to sanity by repeatedly mumbling an often meaningless word or phrase.

Brian Josephson, Nobel prizewinner in physics, speaking at a symposium on transcendental meditation with the Maharishi Mahesh Yogi, suggested that the value of reciting a mantra is that it prevents verbal thinking, allows traumatic experiences to come back unrepressed into the mind's eye, and induces a state of relaxed concentration that can facilitate creativity.

There is no doubt that words, since they have profound suggestive powers, can influence our moods. Swiss psychiatrist Paul Dubois speaks of the "therapy of words" and suggests that when we are anxious or tense we should try the sedative effect of repeating words like *tranquility, serenity,* or *peace.* A similar suggestion was made by the poet Ella Wheeler Wilcox in her book *New Thought Common Sense.* She recommends the use of a rosary, which to her is "one of the oldest and sweetest customs among the religious denominations," used alike by Catholics, Buddhists, and Muslims. She suggests we sit quietly telling our beads, whispering gentle suggestions to our subconscious mind. If we are sick or depressed, we should recite such words as "I am health, energy and vitality. . . . Everything I do will succeed. . . . I am filled with happiness, optimism, and strength." If our problems are tension and anxiety, the litany could run, "I am serenity. . . . Nothing troubles me. . . . I am at peace with the world."

A similar effect can be obtained by slowly reading the Twenty-third Psalm, with its promise of comfort, support, and peace. Poetry used in this way can act with all the potency of a modern psychotrophic drug. John Stuart Mill, the nineteenth-century English reformer, suffered a severe depression at the age of twenty-two but found comfort and relief by reading poetry. "Wordsworth's poems," he wrote, were "a medicine for my state of mind . . . they expressed not merely outward beauty, but states of feeling, under the excitement of beauty . . . and I felt myself at once better and happier as I came under their influence."

The meetings of a local council in Devon, England, were constantly being interrupted by angry rows: The public gallery frequently had to be cleared of spectators, and during one particularly heated exchange a councilor collapsed with a heart attack. To remedy this distressing state of affairs, the town clerk introduced the novel idea of reading a poem before each session of the council. This worked like a charm in subsequent meetings and helped create the right atmosphere of reasonableness and calm.

Poetry therapy is now a recognized treatment in many American psychiatric hospitals. As Yale psychiatrist Albert Rothenberg, a leading member of the Association for Poetry Therapy, has explained, when patients suddenly decipher the meaning of an evocative poem, they experience a flash of understanding similar to the dramatic insights of conventional psychotherapy. Moreover, many inhibited patients find it much easier to express their innermost feelings through writing poetry.

Poetry is a much neglected antidote for psychic distress. Charles Darwin, who suffered a lifetime of mental ill health, said when he reflected sadly on his life during his seventieth year, "If I had my life to live over again, I would make it a rule to read some poetry and listen to some music at least once every week." Had he done so, he might have been a happier, healthier man.

We need to choose our words with care, for words, like dynamite, are powerful stuff, for either good or ill. They need to be labeled "Handle with Care."

Mastication

Fletcherism, though little-known today, was a popular health movement at the turn of the century. The cult was started by an overweight American businessman, Horace Fletcher, who was turned down for a life insurance policy at the age of forty as a bad health risk. He was so stunned by this experience that he gave up his business interests and immediately went in search of health. The panacea he formulated was based on the science of head digestion. He discovered that William Gladstone—the Grand Old Man of British politics, four times prime minister and noted for his exceptional vigor—made a strict point of masticating his food with great care before swallowing it. He taught his eight children to give every mouthful of their food a minimum of thirty-two chews—a chew for every tooth. This, Horace Fletcher decided, was the secret of Gladstone's health and the reason for his own malaise. Adequate nutrition depends on proper mastication. Food must be chewed until it practically "swallows itself." That was the message Fletcher preached throughout the world for the remainder of his life. But just how valid were his claims?

The object of mastication is to break foods down within the mouth into particles of manageable size and then to mix them thoroughly with the secretions of the three pairs of salivary glands. As there are no teeth in the stomach, the process of digestion is impaired if food is not properly prepared in the mouth. After two hours in the stomach, only the outer portion of a piece of meat is digested if the meat is swallowed whole. If it is thoroughly broken up in the mouth before it is swallowed, however, the digestive enzymes reach every fiber, with the result that after two hours in the stomach practically all the meat is digested.

A dental surgeon carried out hundreds of experiments that further emphasize the importance of proper mastication. He took samples of twenty-nine commonly eaten foods, sealed them in cotton mesh bags, and gave them to volunteers to swallow. In some cases the foods were chewed before they were placed in the bags. In others they were left in their natural state. On subsequent analysis it was found that there were far fewer residues left in the bags containing the samples of chewed food, which suggests that to get full benefit from our diet we need to chew food thoroughly before swallowing it. This is why some cows in Spain are now being fitted with sets of stainless steel false teeth: The veterinary faculty of Madrid University has found that this helps a cow to chew better and so improves its milk yield.

Chewing, as well as aiding the digestion, also helps protect the teeth. For one thing, it stimulates the flow of saliva, which helps flush away particles of food lodged around the teeth. In addition, the small particles of fiber released when we chew foods like apples and carrots act like wisps of dental floss to cleanse the crevices between the teeth. No doubt one reason why Eskimos and aborigines have such good teeth is their eating of large quantities of tough whale and kangaroo meat, which requires a lot of heavy chewing. And studies have shown that the native practice of chewing a portion of fibrous stick is a more efficient way of cleansing the teeth than brushing with a conventional toothbrush (see *Teeth Cleaning*).

Regular chewing also improves the circulation to the gums and helps to lessen the risk of periodontal disease which affects approximately 90 percent of adults in the western world and can give rise to bad breath, bleeding gums, and loose, decaying teeth (see *Gums*).

In young people the jaws are capable of exerting a pressure of up to three-hundred pounds per square inch. Elderly people with weaker jaw muscles may manage a bite of no more than fifty pounds, while the wearing of dentures may further reduce the strength of bite to ten to thirty pounds because of the uncomfortable pressure imposed on the sensitive tissues covering the jaws. For this reason elderly people and denture-wearers may need to avoid foods that require heavy chewing.

Meditation

The practice of meditation is not the perquisite of any one philosophy or religious doctrine. It is a technique that has been used over the ages by eastern mystics and Christian contemplatives alike to still the mind and expand consciousness (see *Mantras*). As Aldous Huxley wrote, "Meditation has been used in every part of the world and from the remotest periods as a method for acquiring knowledge about the essential nature of things." While it is not a panacea, it does help introduce an air of tranquility into our increasingly frenetic lives, and even a few minutes' daily practice will foster a feeling of well-being and produce an increased ability to cope with stress and strain.

Scientific studies indicate that meditation produces a state of calm alertness. Tests show that during meditation the output of the heart is reduced and oxygen consumption decreased, both signs of bodily relaxation. At the same time there is an increase in alpha brain-wave activity, which is an indication of heightened psychic awareness. These changes, according to Dr. David Orme-Johnson, head of the psychology department at the Maharishi International University at Fairfield, Iowa, signify "a unique physiological state in which the body is deeply rested, but the mind remains alert."

Most people claim to feel happier and more relaxed after meditating, and many find they are able to wean themselves of their dependence on tranquilizers, cigarettes, alcohol, marijuana, and even hard drugs. Dr. Peter Fenwick, research worker at the Institute of Psychiatry, London, believes it to be a useful tool in the treatment of drug addiction. He adds, "If the present substantial evidence is confirmed, meditation should also be able to make a major contribution in the treatment of stress disease."

To get the benefit of meditation, it is not necessary to make a pilgrimage to an ashram high in the Himalayan mountains, enter a Trappist monastery, rise at 4:00 A.M., dine exclusively on rice, or take a vow of absolute abstinence, piety, and chastity. The technique can be learned in three minutes and needs to be practiced only twenty minutes a day. The method is this:

Set aside a regular time and place for practice. To derive full benefit from meditation, it is essential to set aside a regular fifteen to thirty minutes every day, selecting a place conducive to contemplation where you are unlikely to be disturbed. (A quiet church or the corner of a bedroom is ideal.)

Be still. It is not necessary to adopt any particular posture when practicing meditation, providing the body is at ease. Some find it helpful to adopt traditional contemplative postures—sitting cross-legged in the lotus position or kneeling with hands clasped. Others prefer to sit in an upright chair. The important thing is to relax physically, for stilling the body helps to calm the mind (see *Relaxation*).

Most of us fill our days with a round of petty chores that leaves little time for quiet reflection. If we are to confront the major issues of life, we need to provide occasional pauses for reflection when we can stop to pick out the tree of knowledge from the dense forest of daily trivia. When psychoanalyst Erich Fromm was asked to give some practical advice on how to cope with the routine problems of modern living, he said, "Quietness. The experience of stillness." If we are too busily engaged in pursuing Course A, we cannot see the value of following Courses B and C. As Fromm says, "You have to stop in order to change direction." Periods of contemplation can also provide a breathing space that stops our rushing heedlessly into an unwise course of action.

The British Navy has a tradition that whenever danger threatens, the piper "sounds the still," a signal for all personnel on board ship to stand still for a brief period. This provides a pause for calm reflection and helps to prevent panic among the crew. Landlubbers too need to stand back occasionally from the battle of life and "sound the still," and this can often best be done during the daily "quiet time."

Stop striving. During meditation, all attempts at end-gaining should be avoided. We are so used to striving to *make* things happen, that we rarely stand back and *allow* them to happen. During meditation, we need to capture the spirit of the Zenrin poem of "sitting quietly, doing nothing," when "spring comes and the grass grows by itself." This can be the most valuable use we can make of our leisure time.

Moments of ecstasy and great leaps of creative thought are rarely achieved as a result of conscious effort. The subconscious mind, as well as being the storehouse of numerous repressions, smoldering fears, and guilty secrets, is also the wellspring of inspiration, creativity, and mystical delight. To tap this source of well-being, we need only still our bodies, quiet our minds, and let the subconscious mind speak. "Don't push the river, let it flow," is the Zen instruction. If we are content to do this, we will discover that, as Plotinus said, "There is always a radiance in the soul of man, untroubled, like the light of a lantern in a wild turmoil of wind and tempest." We will find that the kingdom of heaven and the gateways of peace and joy are truly within us.

Enjoy the timeless moment. We are normally so obsessed with the passage of time that we rarely have time to stand still and savor the passing moment. If we are forever living with past miseries and anticipating future anxieties, we must inevitably fail to extract the full delight of the here-and-now.

A Zen parable tells of a man who, running to escape a tiger, comes to a steep precipice. He escapes by lowering himself over the edge of the cliff on a slender vine with the tiger towering above him. Trembling, the man looks down and sees a second tiger waiting to devour him if he should fall. He also notices that two mice are gnawing through the vine. A short distance away, he sees a luscious strawberry. Gripping the vine with one hand, he reaches out and plucks the strawberry. How sweet it tastes!

When debts pile up or business anxieties mount, we need to stop and taste the fruits of the moment, to pause and smell the roses. "What is the point of making time to save time if we never have time to savour time?" asks Buryl Payne in *Getting There without Drugs.*

Our awareness of the passage of time is relative to the amount we attempt to cram into each waking hour. If during moments of meditation we stop to experience the here-and-now—to see, to smell, to feel, to hear—we will create our own brief moment of timelessness. As Thomas Aquinas said, "The apprehension of time in us is caused by the fact that we apprehend the flow of the now; so the apprehension of eternity is caused by our apprehending the now standing still."

Experience a sense of oneness with the universe. One of the limitations of conventional psychotherapy is that while it helps to integrate the discordant factions of an individual's psyche, it does little to integrate him with his environment. The goal of eastern philosophies, on the other hand, is cosmic union rather than any form of personal salvation. (The word *yoga* means a "yoke" or "union.") To the Zen Buddhist, the death of the self marks the beginning of liberation that does not mean the annihilation of the individual ego, but rather a merging of the self with the universe, just as a dewdrop shimmers on a lotus leaf and then slips down and merges, ultimately, with the mighty sea.

This experience of cosmic union is commonly encountered during periods of meditation. We are all inextricably linked with our environment. It is impossible to think of a breather without air, a walker without ground, a teacher without pupils, or a parent without a child. As John Donne said, "No man is an island, entire of itself." Contemporary society may have tended to encapsulate us from our fellows but, like fingers on the hand, we can never function in isolation. If we seek either happiness or business success, we should cooperate rather than compete; unite rather than withdraw. During our working hours we may sometimes feel aliens in a hostile world, but during moments of meditation, we can experience the peace and glorious assurance of being at one with the world.

Middle Age

Middle age has been described in a leading medical journal as the time "when youth fades, hopes, ambitions, and delight wane, and the shadows of decay and death are first perceived." It is recognized clinically by "thinning or greying of hair, increasing girth, lessening acuity of sight, and slackening of neuromuscular spring and agility."

Napoleon became emperor of France at the age of thirty-six and underwent a remarkable physical change. Within a few years the lithe, alert soldier with his finely chiseled features became a pudgy ruler with receding hair, thickened neck, and a decided paunch. As one historian put it, "His magnificent vitality slackened and he lost the capacity for prolonged constructive work. By the age of forty Napoleon had changed into a lethargic and hesitant man." But physical changes such as these are not inevitable. Most arise because we ignore the simple rules of health.

Healthy twenty-year-olds who eat ten calories a day more than they require—the equivalent of a lump of sugar or cube of chocolate—will put on a pound of weight a year. This means spare tires of twenty pounds by the time they reach the age of forty, more than enough to account for the average middle-age spread. Rheumatic pains, breathlessness, and tension headaches arise in a similar way. We exercise too little and so become weak and stiff; we damage our lungs by breathing polluted air and irritating tobacco smoke; and we succumb to tension ailments because we drive ourselves to unattainable goals, worry too much about nonessentials, and get too little rest, sleep, and relaxation. In this way we get the physical health in middle age that we deserve.

The same is true of the psychological problems that so often arise. Jung, in his book *Modern Man in Search of a Soul*, points to "a rise in the frequency of cases of mental depression in men about 40." Alfred Kinsey, in *Sexual Behavior in the Human Female*, notes that "the peak of extra-marital activities, both petting and coitus, occurs in the mid-thirties and early forties." Why is this so? Kenn Rogers, professor of Psychiatry at the New Jersey College of Medicine and Dentistry, made a detailed study of a group of predominantly middle-class British and American males in their fourth decade and found that many had reached a crisis point in their lives that bore no relation to their wealth, success, status, or degree of marital happiness. Many felt "their careers and their entire lives had reached some sort of plateau . . . that life did not hold out any excitement or opportunities for major satisfaction."

It is probably inevitable that many people will consider themselves over the hill when they reach the age of forty, for we live in a society that glorifies youth and denigrates age. But there is no physiological basis for this belief. Historically, middle age is the time when many make their major contributions in life. Dostoevski wrote the final words of *Crime and Punishment* at forty-eight, Edward Jenner successfully demonstrated vaccination at forty-seven, and William Harvey was forty-eight when he published his revolutionary work on the circulation of the blood. Yet commerce and industry tend to discount the contribution of the older person. In 1972 the American Labor Department investigated six thousand firms and found that at least one third were violating the laws against age discrimination, an injustice just as great as the more widely recognized racial or sexist discrimination. As the "Forty Plus Club" in America points out, youthful enthusiasm is no substitute for experience.

Boredom is a frequent problem for people in middle age. The psychiatrist Erik Erikson recognizes "eight ages of man," each with its own characteristic psychological problems. The seventh age he places in the fourth decade, a time noted for the conflict between "generativity" and "stagnation." The sickness of the period is boredom, the remedy the stimulus of change casting off the shackles of comforting routine and substituting adventure, expansion, and growth (see *Change*).

Muesli

Muesli—a mixture of grain, fruit, milk, and nuts—is a traditional Swiss dish. It was particularly popular among peasants living in the fruit-growing cantons of Switzerland, who valued it as a refreshing, energy-giving snack. It was adopted as a health food at the turn of the century by Dr. M. Bircher-Benner, the famous Swiss nutritionist. For generations it was the dream of physiologists "that a diet might be found for children and adults the composition of which would be identical with mother's milk." In muesli Dr. Bircher-Benner thought he had found the ideal dish: a mixture of "sunshine" foods with a balance of proteins, fats, and carbohydrates closely approximating that of human milk. He gave orders that muesli was to be served twice a day to patients staying at his Zurich sanatorium, and in numerous writings he extolled the virtues of the dish, which he judged to be "a wholesome breakfast and supper for children from the age of two, for sick people with digestive disorders and for healthy people who wish to remain healthy."

At the Bircher-Benner clinic in Zurich, a helping of muesli sufficient for one person was made from one large apple (or two small), a tablespoon of nuts, a level tablespoon of rolled oats, the juice of half a lemon, and one tablespoon of either condensed milk or cream mixed with honey. The dish was prepared by mixing the milk and lemon juice with the rolled oats (previously soaked for twelve hours in a little water) and adding to this mixture chopped nuts and grated apple. Dr. Bircher-Benner insisted that the entire apple was to be used, including skin, pips, and core, since the whole fruit contained more iron and phosphates than the pulp, and the core, twenty-four times more iodine than the rest of the apple.

Dr. Bircher-Benner called his concoction "raw fruit porridge" but noted that the dish was "becoming widely known in England as 'Muesli,'" meaning "mixture."

Today it is common to add bran, wheat meal, and dried fruit (currants, raisins, and chopped apricots) to the basic muesli mix. It is a versatile dish that provides a well-balanced nutritional meal, not just for breakfast but for any time of the day. Dieters should note that a helping of muesli prepared on the Bircher-Benner lines provides approximately 230 calories.

Music

Music is an integral part of our everyday existence. The rhythm of the rain pattering on a roof, the whistling of the wind through the trees, the pianissimo murmuring of a stream, and the thunderous crescendo of the waves beating against the shore, all form part of the symphony of life. The melody today is often shattered by the cacophony of pneumatic drills, sirens, typewriters, telephones, and the ubiquitous internal combustion engine. There is ample evidence that prolonged exposure to discordant sounds like these is damaging and that people have far too little appreciation of the healing properties of harmonious sound.

Music is one of the earliest therapies used by man. Musical shamans appear in cave drawings of paleolithic times, and in the Old Testament we find the account of David's curing Saul's fit of actue depression by playing the harp, whereupon "the evil spirit departed from him."

Everything in life vibrates. The smallest blob of protoplasm throbs and pulsates with ceaseless energy, and even a seemingly inert lump of wood, if examined under an electron microscope, would be seen to consist of a mass of constantly vibrating particles. This constant motion helps explain the powerful effect of musical vibrations. The resonance set up by a gentle note sounded from a church organ can make the hefty timbers in the belltower ring. In the same way a tenor reaching for a high C may shatter a glass standing on a nearby table. Two Indian research workers claim to have made mimosa grow faster by playing the violin to it, and it is said that the rate of growth of geraniums can be speeded by exposing them to the playing of a Bach Brandenburg Concerto. The same would appear to apply to human growth, for babies sleep longer and grow faster when they have played to them the amplified sound of their mother's heartbeat.

There are three main elements to music–rhythm, melody, and harmony–and the most fundamental of these is rhythm. Plato said, "Man's life stands in need of a good rhythm." To work easily and efficiently, we need to set a pace that can be easily maintained. This explains the value of work songs and sea chanteys, which help establish an easy flowing rhythm. Depending on the beat, rhythm can be made to exert a stimulating or a depressing effect. The basic beat, or *tempo moderato*, is set at the rate of the heartbeat. Quickening the beat, as with a Scottish reel or Irish jig, stimulates activity. A slower beat, like a funeral dirge, encourages a quieter, more reflective mood.

Harmony also follows certain basic physiological laws. Some combinations of notes we find soothing, others jar. Most people find it pleasing to combine two notes when the frequency of one is double that of the other (the octave above). Similarly, notes with frequencies in the ratio 4:5:6 provide for most people a harmonious combination.

The art of the composer lies in utilizing variations in rhythm, harmony, and melody to communicate with the listener, for music is, above all else, a means of communication. It is a universal language that can be understood by infants, autistic children, schizophrenic adults, and primitive tribesmen. Often it is possible to express with music feelings that words cannot possibly convey. As Mary Priestly, a leading British music therapist, writes in *Music Therapy in Action*, "mere talking seems to lack something as a completely satisfactory means of expression; it leaves an uncomfortable physical and emotional residue of the verbally inexpressible." This can often be conveyed through the richer, more colorful medium of music.

Music is also a form of socialization. A gathering of expatriates singing their national anthem is united in a unique way. So too is the crowd singing "Abide with Me," the group of instrumentalists gathered together to play an evening of chamber music, the family singing Christmas carols around the piano, and the football team singing bawdy ballads over a hogshead of beer. All are united by the experience of shared music-making, which is so much more potent than the more passive pleasure derived from listening to recorded sound. Many Japanese firms gather their employees together at the start of every working day to sing the firm's song, finding that this helps to boost morale and foster a feeling of group unity and joint commitment.

The making of music also provides a valuable outlet for personal creativity. Professor John Cohen, head of the Department of Psychology at Manchester University, England, recommends the teaching of musical instruments as a cure for delinquency and vandalism. "If a boy plays an instrument that gives him self-satisfaction, this can lead him away from mischief," he claims.

Another great therapeutic benefit of music is that it provides an outlet for emotional expression. The Greeks recognized the place of music as a vehicle for emotional release and credited Athena with its invention when, on hearing the heart-rending cries of Medusa's sisters after Gorgon had been slain, she created the art of aulos-playing. Few of us escape the emotional pull of music. Like the children of Hamelin, we dance to the tune the Pied Piper plays; like helpless sailors, we are drawn irresistibly to the Siren's song. We rally to the emotional call of the bugle; shed tears in response to the incidental music of a "weepy" film; grow amorous when seduced by the LP record "Songs for Swinging Lovers." Music can manipulate our mood, making us sad, gay, violent, or tranquil. Music therapists will often establish rapport with disturbed patients by playing music that matches their mood, choosing slow, haunting refrains in a minor key for depressed patients and vigorous, loud music for agitated patients. Then having established contact, they will endeavor to alter the mood by gradually changing the music. Even the most depressed patients will find their feet tapping when a cheerful tune is played.

A science writer suffered an uncharacteristic attack of the blues when he gave up smoking, but he found he could overcome his moments of despair by playing suitable music. "Mozart proved the most effective drug," he wrote, "and even the blackest despair couldn't survive twenty minutes' vigorous application of *The Marriage of Figaro*." Questioning his friends, he quickly discovered twenty-one who also found that music helped cure depression, several finding it more effective than antidepressant drugs. The favorite composer was Mozart, closely followed by Bach and Verdi.

Music can also be used to calm the agitated. As William Congreve said, "Music has charms to soothe a savage breast." Officials of Stoke City Football Club, England, found they had fewer outbreaks of violence among their crowds when they relayed soothing classical music to them before a match rather than beat music, which proved to be too stimulating. Hospitals have also found that by playing suitable music to patients before an operation, they can help sedate them. A safe method of letting off steam is to beat a violent rhythm on a drum or tabletop. Alternatively, conduct a violent piece of music like Bartok's Fifth String Quartet with all the vigor at your command or, while listening to the music, visualize yourself as an all-powerful being striding around crushing every inanimate object which comes in your way. Or follow the advice of a song introduced in the late 1960s by the rock group Sly and the Family Stone: "Dance to the Music." After some moments of this furious abreaction, all pent-up aggression will be assuaged and a delightful state of dynamic relaxation achieved.

At the University of Jena, East Germany, psychiatric patients are encouraged to relax by listening to such music as Handel's Largo or Bach's Air from the Suite in D Major. This exercise can be made more effective by accompanying it with the controlled use of the imagination. As you listen to the music, imagine yourself wandering barefoot through a country meadow. Savor the fresh smell of the blossom, listen to the call of the birds. There in front of you, picture a meandering brook. You sit down and dangle your feet in its cool water, run your fingers through the soft grass, and feel the warmth of the sun on your shoulders. Before long, fantasy becomes reality, and you will be at peace with the world.

Music used in this way can provide spiritual uplift and help us transcend the barriers and limitations of time and space. Music in ancient China was intended not only to entertain, but also to help people achieve their highest spiritual aspirations. They sought through their music to unite heaven and earth, and chose their harmonics in the ratio of 3:2 because 3 was the symbol for heaven, 2 the symbol for earth. Listen to any inspiring piece of music. Concentrate on the reverberating sound. Feel it throbbing through your body. Experience it echoing round the world, blending with the rise and fall of the tides, the swaying of the trees, and the pulsation of the stars. This is the transcendental experience of cosmic union. "Rhythm and harmony," said Plato, "find their way into the inmost places of the soul, imparting grace and making the soul of him who is rightly musical, graceful."

Nightcaps

Does eating and drinking affect our sleep? If so, what are the best foods to take last thing in the evening to insure a good night's sleep?

At one time fairly heavy suppers were consumed in order to stave off hunger pangs and prevent the development of a condition known as "night starvation." It was thought that eating cheese led to bad dreams, but now it is appreciated that eating a heavy meal of any kind last thing at night leads to restless sleep. On the other hand, it is a mistake to go to bed hungry, for we become restless if the level of sugar in our blood falls too low during the night. When human volunteers were put to sleep on a bed wired to record their every movement, it was found that they slept most soundly after a light supper of cornflakes and milk. With a heavy meal they were far more restless.

Taking a little alcohol as a nightcap can be relaxing, but too much will almost certainly spoil the quality of our night's rest. To begin with, we may sleep like logs, but as the effect of the alcohol wears off, we are likely to become abnormally restless and may wake with numb arms or stiff necks as a result of having lain for too long in a bad position.

A late-night cup of warm milk appears to make a more beneficial nightcap. Doctors at Guy's Hospital, London, have shown that drinking a cup of milk before retiring improves the quality of the night's sleep. After taking it, young people sleep more soundly and older people sleep longer, and if they happen to wake during the night, they find it easier to get to sleep again. Moreover, the more nights the drink was taken, the more effective it became as a sedative. In view of this, perhaps many people could rid themselves of their dependence on sleeping pills and establish instead the habit of taking a comforting bedtime drink of warm malted milk.

Nosebleeds

Bleeding from the nose was once considered a grave sign. An old text warned, "One drop of blood from the nose commonly foretells death or a very severe fit of fever; three drops are still more ominous." But the flux could be cured by magic. The pious found relief by writing on their foreheads in letters of blood the final words of Christ on the cross: "It is finished." The remedy for the irreligious was to stand on tiptoe and spit through a circle made with the thumb and forefinger, a folk cure which is still used in certain country districts of Europe.

Repeated nosebleeding can occasionally be a symptom of serious internal disease such as hypertension or cirrhosis of the liver, but more often than not it is a trivial incident which can easily be relieved by simple first-aid measures. The mucous membrane lining the nose is a highly vascular tissue which can easily be damaged by pollutants in the air like tobacco smoke, particularly if its protective layer of mucous is removed by constantly inhaling the dry air found in centrally heated rooms. The tissue is also sensitive to emotional stress and can become swollen and engorged with blood when we are anxious, resentful, or frustrated. This is the reason for the blocked, stuffed nose women experience on their honeymoons, sometimes referred to as a "honeymoon cold," and this explains why emotional stress can precipitate nosebleeding. Boulster's *Lectures*, published in the seventeenth century, tells the sad tale of the girl who protested her love to her sweetheart by saying, " 'Did my nose ever bleed when I was in your company?' and, poor wretch, just as she spake this, to show her true heart, her nose fell a-bleeding."

The increase in anxiety, emotional stress, smoking, atmospheric pollution, and central heating may explain why many hospitals report a sharp rise in the number of people admitted to emergency rooms in the throes of a severe nosebleed. Yet most of these cases could be safely treated at home if the right procedure were followed.

One popular remedy for nosebleeding is to apply a cold key to the back of the neck. In Russia, people suffering frequent nosebleeds were advised to wear an iron key as a pendant around their necks, and one book of Russian folklore tells of a man who from his youth onward suffered several nosebleeds a day which no orthodox medical treatment could relieve but who was eventually "radically cured by wearing an iron key between his shoulderblades, and has never been bothered by this condition again." Physiological research shows that cooling the skin of any part of the body produces a reflex contraction of the blood vessels of the nose and so helps to stop nosebleeding. Two hundred years ago, a Scottish physician reported that he could always stop a nosebleed by immersing his patients' genitals in ice-cold water, a first-aid measure that may be practical in countries given to wearing the kilt, but has little point elsewhere, when the same therapeutic effect can be obtained more easily by putting the feet in a bucket of cold water or applying a cold compress to the forehead.

While cold compresses help, they are not always available, and most nosebleeds respond to simple compression of the soft part of the nose with the thumb and forefinger. This should be maintained for ten minutes and should be carried out with the head tipped forward over a basin to prevent mess and reduce the drama of blood-soaked pillows and towels. Inhaling alum, flour, or starch is not an effective way of stopping a nosebleed. Packing the nose with cotton wool is a technique best left to medical workers, because fibers of the wool tend to get caught up in the clot. Remove the plug and bleeding often recurs.

Victims should not be given brandy to calm their nerves, because alcohol dilates the blood vessels and may increase the bleeding (an action that explains the warm glow that follows gentle drinking, and the red, engorged nose sometimes seen in heavy drinkers). Simple compression of the base of the nose while breathing gently through the mouth is all that is necessary to stop most nosebleeds. Cases that fail to respond to this simple approach and to the application of cold compresses, or cases that recur frequently need a physician's attention.

Once bleeding has stopped, care should be taken not to dislodge the clot by vigorously blowing the nose.

Obesity

While malnutrition is the besetting dietary disorder of large sections of the world, overnutrition and obesity are the curse of the West. It is estimated that 70 million Americans are overweight and spend among them a total of $400 million a year on reducing drugs and special dieting treatments. Many people regard obesity as a purely esthetic problem, but as Professor John Yudkin of London University points out, if you are 10 percent overweight, "You are twice as likely to have symptoms of chronic illness. You will be more prone to overtiredness and shortness of breath, more likely to have pains and swellings in your joints, to have indigestion and headaches and constipation." You are also likely to shorten your life, one British doctor having estimated that a person carrying ten pounds of excess fat has less chance of living a long, healthy life than one smoking twenty-five cigarettes a day.

The problem arises because we eat more than we need. The introduction of labor-saving machinery has meant that most of us need to eat considerably fewer calories than our greatgrandparents. But have housewives reduced their calorie intake since installing a washing machine instead of washing their clothes by hand (which uses up 250 calories an hour)? In the same way, how many farmers have trimmed their diets since they switched from walking behind a horse-drawn plow (which uses 400 calories an hour) and taken to driving a tractor (which uses only 130 calories an hour)? With this diminution of physical work and the introduction of a calorie-rich Coke, catsup, cookies, and candy diet, we have grown accustomed to eating more than we need.

This habit frequently starts in early childhood when mothers are coerced into overfeeding their babies by weaning them too quickly onto sweet cereal foods so that they make rapid weight gains. "You cannot overfeed a young baby" was the advice contained in many infant-care manuals. At baby shows the garlands went to "bonny," bouncing babies, and at mealtimes the credit went to the child who ate up his food "like a good boy" whether he wanted it or not. Winston Churchill tells in his memoirs that he was delighted when his only son Randolph tucked into his food like a good trencherman. "At his age," he explained, "greediness and even swinishness at table are virtues." So the habit of overeating begins. It is fostered further in adolescence when good behavior is rewarded with sweets, and any sign of obesity dismissed as "puppy fat" that will disappear as soon as the glandular imbalance of puberty is corrected. But the truth is that fat is fat whenever it occurs, whether as flabby thighs in teenagers, chubby cheeks in babies, or a middle-aged spread in the over-forties. The concept of "puppy fat" is a myth that must be dispelled, for the accumulation of fat early in life is neither normal nor ephemeral. The only glands involved in teenager obesity are the salivary glands. As 80 percent of obese youngsters go on to become obese adults, the condition can hardly be dismissed as a purely temporary, self-correcting aberration.

The habit of overeating, then, is the product of a lifetime and as such is not easy to correct, particularly as it is so widespread within our society. We seem discourteous if we decline the offer of a second helping of pudding at a dinner party or refuse to join in a third round of drinks at the bar. But if we are to avoid becoming obese, we must eat what we *need* to eat, not what others think we *ought* to eat.

Dieting is difficult, particularly for people in their middle years. As the decades go by we generally become less active and so require less food. At forty a man is probably burning up 15 percent-20 percent fewer calories than he did at eighteen, but still eating as he did in his athletic youth. In fact, with increasing affluence he may well be drinking Scotch instead of water, and eating crêpes suzettes instead of peanuts and potato chips, thus consuming more calories than ever before. So he puts on weight.

The mechanics of weight control are really quite simple. If we take in just enough calories to balance our energy output, our weight remains steady. If we take in too few our weight goes down; too many, and our weight goes up. It is rather like a bank balance, with the calories consumed corresponding to bank deposits and the calories burnt up in exercise equivalent to bank withdrawals. So our weight (as our bank balance) depends on the running total of inputs and outputs and can from week to week either go up, go down, or remain steady. The incredible thing about our body weight is that it remains as nearly constant as it does. The average woman eats about twenty tons of food between the ages of twenty-five and sixty-five and during this time gains on average only twenty-four pounds in weight, which is equivalent to an average daily error of only a hundredth of an ounce in excess of what is required. If she cut out the odd piece of chocolate or made a marginal increase in her level of daily activity, she would hold her weight steady throughout this entire period.

Losing weight is similarly straightforward. You can forget about exercise gimmicks, crash diets, drugs, slimming garments, and vibrating machines. The gimmicks don't work, and the crash diets and drugs are of only temporary benefit. The way to get slim and stay slim is to establish a healthy pattern of eating and exercising. According to Dr. Jean Mayer, a leading nutritionist, "Underexercising rather than overeating may well be the more important cause of the prevalence of overweight today." He studied a group of overweight schoolgirls and found that many of them actually ate less than average and put on weight simply because they were less active than their slim classmates, watching, for example, nearly four times as much television. A similar study of a group of women showed that those who were slim on the average walked twice as much as those who were fat.

To maintain trim figures, we need to introduce more exercise into our everyday lives: running up stairs instead of taking the elevator, cycling to the shops, walking to work, making love, playing games with children, and taking up active hobbies and sports (see *Exercise*). Brisk walking is one of the finest ways of controlling weight, since it uses up twice as much energy as scrubbing the floors (the most energetic of household chores) and burns up twelve times as many calories as watching television. Another excellent way of burning up excess calories is to leave off a layer of clothing and turn down the central heating in offices and homes as far as is comfortably possible so that the body is forced to step up its rate of metabolism in order to keep warm. Experiments have shown that when the body is subjected to a temperature of 4° C., (39° F.) metabolism increases on average of 35 percent. (Unfortunately the rise is less in obese people—4 percent-11 percent—because their extra layer of subcutaneous fat helps to insulate them from heat loss.)

At the same time as you adopt a more active way of life, start to modify your eating habits. Eat only when you're hungry, eat slowly, and make a point of enjoying every delicious mouthful of your food. Remember that it takes twenty minutes from the start of a meal before the brain begins to receive any signals of satiety, so don't rush the process of eating. Al Marston, professor of psychology at the University of California, recommends that people get into the habit of putting their knives and forks down after every bite. "If you eat slowly enough," he says, "you give the body time to decide when it's had enough." This practice also aids digestion and enables you to savor your food to the full (see *Mastication*).

You don't have to suffer to keep slim. Throughout his life American journalist Martin Lederman loved his food—not wisely, but far too well. As a result he was grossly overweight at somewhere in the region of 238 pounds. Over the years he had tried seventeen different diets, visited several spas, and taken countless Turkish baths. He calculated that in twenty-five years he had lost a total of over 400 pounds—but it had always come back. Then he made the simple discovery that his basic problem was that he *liked* food. The diets he'd tried in the past had failed because they were too dull and hadn't satisfied his delight in good food. So he set about creating a diet that would tickle his taste buds and do credit to the great Escoffier himself, and he found that the more he teased his salivary glands with succulent portions of ham laced with delicate slices of pineapple, and the longer he lingered over his Stilton cheese and burgundy, the slimmer he became. In his best-selling book *The Slim Gourmet*, he tells how in this way he trimmed his weight by nearly 84 pounds without having to sacrifice his gourmet's delight in fine food. The old dietary slogan was "If it tastes good, spit it out." Lederman showed that this negative approach is not necessary. The secret of getting slim, and the much more difficult art of *staying* slim, is to get into the habit of eating wisely but well.

Try to make as few changes as possible in your normal diet. Cut foods *down* rather than *out*. Eat smaller portions of everything, substituting, if you like, a few ounces of filet steak for a larger helping of rump. Step up your intake of fresh fruit and vegetables and cut down your intake of sugar and fried food (French fried potatoes, for example, contain three times as many calories as boiled potatoes because of their fat content). It also helps to spread your calorie intake as evenly as possible over the day to avoid the hunger pangs and lowered blood sugar levels that stimulate appetite and encourage excessive eating. Some people derive 80 percent of their daily calorie allowance from their evening meal, when they are just about to spend an idle evening in front of the television and then retire to bed. Others go without breakfast and a proper lunch, but stave off fatigue during the day by nibbling and may take up to 25 percent of their energy intake in calorie-rich between-meal snacks that are often of extremely low nutritional value. Both groups would benefit by having a substantial breakfast and a well-balanced lunch and avoiding eating between meals (see

Breakfast). Queen Elizabeth II is an extremely good example of what can be achieved by establishing a balanced, nutritionally sound diet that can be enjoyed without suffering undue privations. At one time she was considerably overweight and had to consult a Harley Street dietician. Now she keeps her slim figure despite the temptation of countless royal banquets by sensible eating habits. As a Buckingham Palace spokesman says, "She is a modest eater."

If you are overweight and will modify your diet and activity levels along these lines, you will undoubtedly lose weight. Once your body weight has settled down to its new resting level on this regime, weigh yourself and consider honestly whether this is now your optimum weight. If you have any doubt, strip and examine yourself in front of a full-length mirror. As an alternative, try the pinch test. Grasp a fold of skin from the center of your body midway between your navel and groin. If the fold is thicker than the little finger in men or the thumb in women, this is a sign that you are carrying excess weight. If you consult height and weight tables, ignore the allowance made for age and see what weight you should have been at twenty-five. And remember that most tables are based on statistics provided by the Metropolitan Life Insurance Company, which refer to the weights of people wearing indoor clothes. So if you weigh yourself in the nude, subtract approximately six pounds from the quoted figures to allow for the weight of indoor clothing and shoes. Better still, if you know the weight you were at age twenty-five, and were in good health at the time, this should be your ceiling weight for the rest of your life. In this way you should be able to get a fairly accurate idea of your optimum weight. Knowing this, deduct it from your present weight and see how many pounds you need to lose.

Let us say, for example, that you find that after making a permanent alteration in your habits of eating and exercising you are still ten pounds overweight. Set out to lose this at a rate of no more than one pound a week. This means reducing your calorie balance by 3,500 calories a week (the equivalent of one pound of fat). This reduction should be achieved by eating less and exercising more, for studies at Brigham Young University, Utah, have shown that a combined exercise and diet program is a more effective way of losing weight than dieting alone, and it produces a feeling of physical and mental well-being as an additional bonus. As a guide, an hour's brisk walking uses up 300 calories, and hour's dancing 250, tennis 350, golf 225, riding 250, bicycling 400, house-cleaning 150, rowing 400, swimming 400, jogging 600, ten-pin bowling, 250. Tables showing the calorie values of various foods are contained in most diet books but, as a rough guide, 100 calories are contained in a medium-sized roll or in one and one fourth slices of bread; one medium boiled potato or a cup of mashed potatoes; four lumps of sugar; one-half can of beer; one small slice of fruit cake; one glass of cola; one-half doughnut; or one-half scoop of ice cream. By making temporary alterations in your habits of eating and exercising, you should be able to lose a pound of fat a week without difficulty and so get down to your optimum weight. Don't be tempted to restrict your calorie intake below 1,200 calories for more than two days with-out seeking medical advice, and don't attempt to lose more than fifteen pounds without first consulting a doctor.

Once you have dieted down to your optimum weight, revert to your new exercise and activity program and adhere to this faithfully. Make a point of checking your weight at least once a week, and if it should increase by as much as a pound, immediately set aside the next week for cutting out the necessary 3,500 calories to get back to your base weight. In this way you will keep habitually slim and perpetually fit.

Orgasm

The Victorians had an unhealthy attitude to sex, but so, often, have we. They showed a morbid denial of their sexual feelings and needs; we tend to show an obsessive preoccupation with ours. Sexual performance, love-play techniques and coital positions have become a subject for constant analysis and debate. In our highly mechanized society sex has been dehumanized, and with the aid of sex manuals many go through the motions without the emotions. As a result the complaint commonly heard by psychiatrists today is not that people do not enjoy a full sex life, but that they have a full sex life that they don't enjoy. This is a frequent cause of marital stress and an utter tragedy, for sexual satisfaction and enjoyment is the birthright of everyone. Impotence, premature ejaculation and frigidity are functional disorders that can be cured and should never be accepted with resignation like club feet or spinal curvature.

According to a survey conducted by the London *Sunday Times*, 20 percent of Britons believe that women are incapable of experiencing orgasm, the satisfying climax of lovemaking described by author Vladimir Nabokov as "that routine rhythm that shakes the world." Modern research, however, suggests that the orgasmic potential of the female is as great as, if not greater than, that of the male. According to Dr. Alfred Kinsey, all females are capable of responding to the point of orgasm. Their frequent failure to achieve this innate potential most often stems, as it does in the male, from cultural repressions and deep-seated sexual taboos.

Human beings are the only animals that deliberately

inhibit their sexual drive, even to the point at times of making a virtue of total sexual abstinence. With our highly developed cerebral cortex we can exercise control over our sexual response as surely as we can hold our breath. By controlling our thoughts we can either facilitate sexual fulfillment or totally inhibit it. Sexual dysfunction is in nearly every instance a psychosomatic problem, stemming from disorders of the head and heart rather than the genitalia. Because of this, it is mental attitudes that generally need changing, not coital positions, and warmth and love that need stimulating rather than breasts and penises. Sexual maladjustment is the result of faulty conditioning in childhood and is relieved by unlearning rather than by learning. It is rarely characterized by a total absence of sexual desire, but rather by a blocking of sexual expression. The treatment is to remove the emotional blocks that inhibit the natural enjoyment of sex. This can be done mainly in seven ways.

1. **Banish Sexual Hang-ups.** With so many cultural restrictions and psychosocial taboos it is not surprising that many people today find sex less than fully satisfying; hedged around by these daunting prohibitions, we shouldn't be surprised if even porcupines find it easier to make love. If we wish to enable the positive emotions of affection and desire to flow freely, we must break down the barriers of guilt and fear, and accept sex for what it is, the perfectly natural, healthy expression of a close emotional relationship, a source of recreation as well as procreation. It is neither sacred nor profane. (If it is sacred, as some suggest, why is it not performed in church?)

To break down long-standing inhibitions and taboos, gradually accept and assert your sexuality. Take delight in the sight and touch of your naked body. Dance in the nude. Revel in your sensuality. Masturbate to your heart's content if, to begin with, you find it difficult to derive satisfaction from conjugal lovemaking. For most women coitus proves a less effective way of achieving orgasm than masturbation, which Alfred Kinsey and his co-researchers found led to orgasm in 95 percent of attempts. This explains one of the major differences in the sex histories of males and females, for while most males experience orgasm during their first coital act, this occurs in only 8 percent of females. Surveys, however, show that as the years go by and sexual inhibitions recede, the orgasmic satisfaction of the female during coitus grows.

No function of the human body is indecent unless you make it so, so never allow false modesty to inhibit your enjoyment of sex. Between consenting adults anything goes, provided it is acceptable and pleasurable to both partners and no bones are broken.

2. **Enjoy Erotic Stimulation.** Erotic thoughts help prepare the body for the sex act and can occasionally lead to orgasm without any additional physical stimulation. Thus one woman out of three has orgasms as the result of erotic dreams and a very small percentage can produce orgasms through fantasy alone. This faculty should be harnessed and used to enhance the sex act by allowing the mind to dwell on whatever proves sexually arousing. For some this may mean thinking of a particular piece of mood music, a scent, a book, a film, a voice or the fantasy of being carried off to a sheik's harem. For others the same effect can be obtained through erotic pictures.

A team of psychologists and psychiatrists at the University of New South Wales in Sydney, Australia, took a group of women who because of their upbringing had developed "a degree of aversion to the sight of the naked male body" that made it difficult for them to enjoy lovemaking. To begin with the therapists showed them straightforward pictures of naked males. Then, when they could view these without disgust, they showed them "more sophisticated hard-core pornography of women sexually aroused by men," and finally "couples engaged in the sexual act in various states of ecstasy." As a result of this gradual deconditioning, 70 percent of the women lost their inhibitions.

3. **Be more Sensual.** Sexual arousal is produced not only by thoughts, but also by the sight, smell and touch of

the one we love. It requires soft words and tender caresses as well as specific genital stimulation.

Every part of the surface of the body is richly supplied with nerve endings, but some more so than others. These particularly sensitive areas—the lobe of the ears, the neck, the nipples, breasts, the palms of the hands, the inner thighs, the abdomen and the instep and toes—are often referred to as the erogenous zones, since their stimulation is especially prone to produce erotic arousal. This arousal is a necessary prelude to orgasm, for just as laughter is the sudden release of emotional energy, so an orgasm is the explosive release of accumulated sexual tension.

Too many people try to make sex a hurried act of purely genital union, but if they bypass the soft words, the loving looks and the tender caresses they miss the mounting tension that alone insures a fully satisfying climactic release.

Couples who experience difficulty in their sexual relationships can derive benefit from a technique sometimes referred to as "sensate focusing." Retiring to the privacy of their bedroom, they should strip and then gently and lovingly explore the marvels and mysteries of each other's body without initially making any direct attempt at sexual intercourse. They should forget their anxiety, guilt and shame, forget their puritanical upbringing and their sexual failures in the past, and simply concentrate on maximizing their sensual enjoyment in the here-and-now. Backs should be massaged, necks rubbed and thighs stroked. Later, when this degree of intimacy can be enjoyed without anxiety, they can safely proceed to make more obvious sexual overtures.

Most people are aware of the special sensitivity of the penis, but many overlook the equal importance of the clitoris, the female homologue of the penis, which is more richly supplied with nerve endings than the penis and, when properly stimulated, is the most nearly certain way of ensuring female orgasm. According to Alfred Kinsey, failure to recognize the importance of this vestigial organ is the commonest cause of sexual dysharmony. He found, contrary to popular belief, that women were just as quick to reach orgasm as men providing they were adequately stimulated, and this means selecting coital positions or manipulative techniques that ensure maximum stimulation of the clitoris. The conventional, "missionary," position, with the man lying on top of the woman, produces a considerable degree of friction along the clitoral shaft, but greater clitoral stimulation can often be achieved in the "female superior" position, in which the female lies or sits on top of the man. This gives her the freedom to alter her position in a way that ensures maximum clitoral stimulation and allows her to set the pace which suits her best.

Since the tip of the clitoris is generally too sensitive for direct manual manipulation it is best stimulated indirectly, by gentle traction on the surrounding tissues. Dr. Helena Wright, one of the earliest sex researchers in England, introduced a technique whereby the man placed his hand lightly on his partner's pubic and vulval region, allowing her to move it in a way that gave her maximum stimulation. Since the woman knows what pleases her most, this ensures maximum clitoral stimulation, and since she retains command over the operation, it also helps women who are at first afraid to lose control during the sex act.

4. **Let Yourself Go.** It is impossible to derive deep satisfaction from sex if the mind utterly dominates the body. Fulfillment demands total surrender. Once a certain stage of stimulation has been reached, sex becomes an automatic act. From this point the body takes on a life of its own, moving rhythmically and energetically as nature dictates until a satisfying orgasm is reached. Only the conscious control of the brain can prevent this joyous, climactic release.

Many people find it difficult to permit themselves this degree of utter abandonment. Their superegos constantly watch over them. Undressing reminds them of childhood taboos against nudity. Genital caresses reawaken masturbatory guilt feelings. Grunting is unladylike; heavy breathing might waken the children. They find it impossible to relax while an overdeveloped conscience stands beside them as an ever-watchful, reproachful chaperone.

Others, outwardly more liberated, are inhibited not by guilt but by an excessively technical approach. Having read a variety of sex manuals, they try too hard to prolong the period of sexual foreplay, to adopt a certain copulatory position, to achieve maximum stimulation of the clitoris or stage-manage a synchronous orgasm. But lovemaking, unlike car repairs, cannot be performed by numbers according to an operating manual. Sex should be a spontaneous outpouring of physical affection, as infinitely variable in its modes of expression as are the people taking part. It cannot be choreographed and needs no guidebook, tutor or chorus master.

A Greek myth tells how Aphrodite was concerned that her youngest son Eros, the god of love, did not grow as other children but perpetually remained a tiny, chubby child. Wanting to know the reason, she consulted the oracle Themis, who said that the child's development was being held back by lack of feeling. "Love cannot grow without passion," the oracle declared. It is impossible to enjoy lovemaking with one eye on the clock, with a moralist's concern for decency or a technician's facination for performance data. Like the detonation of a bomb, love is an all-or-nothing response.

5. **Re-awaken your body.** Years of puritanical discipline have encouraged us to deny the pleasures of the flesh. We have accepted the Cartesian dichotomy of body and soul and learned to glorify the higher, cultural activities of the mind while rejecting everything related to the carnal, animal activities of the body. We have been trained to keep a tight rein on our emotions and limit the body's spontaneity. Once we leave childhood we no longer jump for joy or shout from sheer delight. Instead we envelop our bodies in a straightjacket of muscular tension, which inhibits our feeling or expressing either pleasure or pain. We tense our abdominal muscles to hold back the tears, freeze our muscles of facial expression to hide both anguish and ecstasy

and tighten our pelvic muscles to check the first quickenings of sexual delight.

If we are to reach the heights of sexual experience we must bring our bodies back to life. As Mary Calderone says in *Release from Sexual Tensions*: "You, yourself, must reawaken your body, rediscover it, re-educate it . . . find out for yourself how it feels to be touched in certain places. Find out which places arouse most pleasure in you when touched."

We must learn once more to enjoy the beauty of the human body, thrill to its sensuality, revel in its compulsive, rhythmic movement. We must laugh, shout, dance and cry, for these activities help relax the tensions in the abdomen and pelvis. Break down the protective muscular armoring and the body will come alive to a whole range of pleasurable sensations.

6. **Avoid Performance Anxiety.** Dr. William Masters and Virginia Johnson at their sexual dysfunction clinic in St. Louis, Missouri, have developed a technique that has helped many couples overcome the introspective anxiety that turns so many sexual encounters into a dreaded test of competence, supervised by two ever-watchful entities who award performance marks on the basis of the answers given to such searching questions as: Did you reach an orgasm? Did I maintain my erection long enough? Was it as good as last time/first time/on your own/with a vibrator/with the vicar? Are we having it often enough, or at least enough to satisfy the "norm"? Post-mortem questioning like this is best avoided since it increases anxiety, augments any latent feelings of inadequacy and debases sex by treating it as little more than a mechanical act.

Sex is not a time-and-motion study, and you can never savor its pleasures to the full while constantly analyzing what is taking place. Besides, there is far more to sexual happiness than the mere ability to have an orgasm. Physical intimacy, closeness and warmth are at least equally important and provide their own rewards. As Virginia Johnson says: "Just going from A to B may be enough; it is not necessary always to go from A to Z." At the St.

Louis clinic, couples experiencing sexual difficulties begin by studiously avoiding sexual intercourse. At the start they are advised to simply fondle each other's bodies in a nonsexual way. Later, when this degree of contact can be enjoyed without tension or strain, they are encouraged to become more intimate and overtly sexual be stroking breasts, buttocks, penis and genitalia. Only when this can be done without anxiety are they "permitted" to indulge in actual intercourse. In this way they are enabled to retrace the gently progressive stages of normal courtship and overcome the fears that previously limited their enjoyment of sex.

7. **Strive to achieve an equal partnership.** To enjoy sex in a natural, uninhibited fashion it is necessary for both partners to feel secure and to show a reasonable degree of self-assertion. Together they should discuss the factors that "turn them on" and see how best they can be satisfied.

As Dr. Alexander Lowen writes in *The Betrayal of the Body,* self-assertion in sex involves "the conscious reaching out for what one wants and the conscious rejection of what one doesn't want." It is time to reject the old stereotyped roles of man the active, aggressive hunter and woman his passive, meekly accepting prey. Sexual equality is as important in the bedroom as in the boardroom.

True sexual happiness can never be achieved while one partner feels denigrated or used, for just as a fulfilling relationship fosters love, so a loving relationship enhances sex.

Pets

The domestication of animals occurred several thousand years ago, originally to meet certain specific work requirements. Cats were reared in Egypt to protect stores of grain as early as 3000 B.C. and were soon raised to the status of gods. About the same time dogs were bred and employed throughout the world to herd sheep, hunt game, and pull sledges.

These domestic animals soon established themselves not only as trusted workmates but also as loyal, close companions. So they were reared as pets. The dog soon became man's best friend. "Lion dogs," practically identical in appearance to the modern Pekingese, became popular in China around 2000 B.C., and "lap dogs" were the pampered favorites of the Caesars in ancient Rome.

It is not difficult to appreciate the emotional appeal of pets. They provide a degree of friendship that is particularly valuable for the elderly, the childless, the lonely, and the bereaved. They can also help boost a deflated ego. The possession of a prize-winning collie or well-groomed Afghan hound is a recognized status symbol, and the accompaniment of an Alsatian straining at the leash can help to raise our confidence when we walk at night through a narrow alleyway. A man cowed by an overbearing boss at work and a nagging wife at home can raise himself at least one rank in the pecking order by dominating a submissive pet; and the woman who teaches her dog to come when she calls, to sit or fetch her slippers on command, proves without a shadow of a doubt that in this relationship she is the "top dog." Pets are also good "facilitators" of human contact: A dog taken for a walk in the park is a useful introduction to passing animal-lovers, and the unexpected entry of a cat into a roomful of strangers often helps to break the conversational ice.

Most important of all, pets are a focal point of human affection. In his book *Pets Can Keep You Sane*, psychologist Richard Ryder says, "Pets allow us to love and be loved–the experience of feeling loved and needed is the greatest psychotherapeutic service that they can give us." And they offer this love without attaching any emotional strings or counterdemands.

Often we endow pets with human characteristics. Sir Winston Churchill had a long succession of cats, all referred to as Mr. Cat and treated as people, all allowed the usual human failings and sensibilities. One had his tail amputated as a result of an accident. Churchill, feeling that this was a source of great embarrassment to him, gave orders that everyone coming into contact with Mr. Cat should make a point of behaving as normally as possible without mentioning or drawing attention to his deficiency. Such is our anthropomorphic approach to our pets.

These human substitutes can also help children develop a sense of responsibility and an ability to enter into a close, caring relationship with other living creatures. They also provide useful lessons in sex education. For these reasons they have been introduced into schools and sometimes employed in children's hospitals as "silent therapists." Pet therapy has proved itself to be of value in the treatment of delinquent children, alienated narcotic addicts, and sociopathic criminals. "Pets can be of real benefit to the emotionally disordered," concludes Ryder. He points out that they provide valuable opportunities for play (see *Play*). "The only chance that most adults have of playing silly uninhibited games is either with the children or with pets." Sadly, as we get older we indulge in fewer games, and those we play tend to be exessively formal and competitive. Our play with animals, however, is more childlike in its expression–freer, gayer, and altogether more spontaneous. Because of this, it provides greater opportunities for personal expression and emotional release.

Sometimes the emotional bonds we develop with our pets are closer than those we have with our friends. Often pets become our substitute babies or surrogate lovers. As Desmond Morris points out in *Intimate Behavior*, we all feel the need for close bodily contact: "If those humans closest to us cannot supply us with what we want, and it is too dangerous to seek intimacies with strangers, then we can make tracks to the nearest pet shop and for a small sum, buy ourselves a piece of animal intimacy." We find a pet that will curl up in our lap, nuzzle against our leg, or lick our face and hands. In return, if we feel like it, we stroke it, nurse it, pat its back, rub its belly, or run our fingers slowly through its hair. As Morris says, "Blocked in our human contacts by our cultural restrictions, we direct our intimacies towards our adoring pets, our substitutes for love." Unfortunately, this close contact is not without risk.

Dogs can provide comfort for the lonely, protection for the insecure, and guidance for the blind, but they also annoy, pollute, damage, and kill. These problems are particularly acute in the world's major cities. There are 280,000 dogs in Tokyo, 300,000 in Los Angeles, 500,000 in London, 700,000 in New York, and over a million in Mexico City. In each of these cities the dog presents a health hazard.

The Englishman treats a dog with the reverence a devout Hindu shows to a sacred cow. In fact, it is suggested that many Britons in their worship and devotion spell *god* backward. "He cannot be a gentleman who loveth not a dog," says an old English proverb. And yet the dog in Britain is responsible for nine road deaths or serious injuries every week, kills more than ten thousand sheep and poultry every year, can pass on to its master at least twenty different diseases, and brings a medieval filth to twentieth-century streets. It is estimated, for example, that the streets and parks in London now receive about one million pints of urine and seventy tons of feces a day from the city's dogs. Yet Britons still adore their dogs and will cheerfully send their children to boarding school for several years while refraining from sending their dogs to a kennel for even a few days, in case they should pine. Britain's cats and dogs also consume as much meat as 700,000 humans and in a world faced with mass starvation, it seems only proper that, in the words of one conservation group, "the dire physical needs of the hungry should come before the emotional needs of pet owners."

But Britain does not head the dog-ownership league. The ratio of dogs to humans is higher in France (1 to 6.8) and America (1 to 6.2) than it is in Britain (1 to 9.4). In all these countries many injuries arise each year from dog bites, particularly with the current vogue for owning large protector dogs. In America 1.5% of emergency hospital admissions are for dog bites and, in a quarter of these cases, the wounds become seriously infected. Newsboys, door-to-door salesmen, and rent-collectors are constantly at risk. The toll of bites in New York now runs at 75,000 a year, affording a much more serious health hazard than fouling of the streets and parks. Public concern is being focused on the wrong end of the dog.

In addition to its population of 40 million dogs, the United States also finds room for 40 million cats, 15 million birds, and 10 million miscellaneous warm-blooded animals ranging from hamsters to orang-utans. All these can contribute to the spread of human disease.

At one time rabies was thought to be the only disease transmitted from animals to man. Now it is realized that there is a whole range of these shared diseases, known collectively as the zoonoses. Fleas, lice, mites, and ticks can carry disease from pets to their owners. Veterinarians working at the Royal Veterinary College at Hatfield, Hertfordshire, have shown that a number of skin rashes commonly treated by tranquilizers, antihistamines, or prolonged psychotherapy are in fact due to mite infestations transmitted through contact with domestic cats and dogs. Another study has shown that 5 percent of the diseases referred to skin clinics in the West of England stem from this source.

A short while ago the pet dog of the governor of New

Mexico was found to be carrying fleas infected with bubonic plague, the disease that ravaged Europe in the Middle Ages. Concurrently there was an outbreak of the plague among several people in New Mexico.

In Britain about one in eight of the country's cats and dogs is infected with toxocariasis, a worm disease that can affect humans. Infected animals house worms in their intestinal tract and shed eggs in their excreta. Normally these eggs find another animal host, but if they should enter a human mouth, they can hatch into larvae lower down the gut. These may invade the bloodstream and settle in the liver, chest, heart, brain, and eyes, causing chest troubles, blindness, and brain damage. Crawling babies, toddlers, and adults not too careful of their hygiene, who lead literally a hand-to-mouth existence, are particularly at risk. A related infection is toxoplasmosis, a disease caused by a minute protozoan parasite which, while rare and generally mild, can if it affects pregnant women lead to abortion or brain damage of the unborn child. Blood tests show that 30 percent of adults in Britain have been infected by toxoplasmosis. Far fewer suffer actual disease symptoms. Generally this desease is spread by cats, which pick up the infection by eating infected rodents and birds. In view of this, Dr. W. M. Hutchinson, of Strathclyde University, Scotland, recommends that cats should be "belled" to minimize their hunting efficiency and adequately fed so that they have less need to hunt.

Considerably more common are the cases of food poisoning transmitted by pets. A recent study in Florida showed that 15 percent of the dogs in the state excreted salmonellae, the bacteria that are the commonest cause of food poisoning. Yet how many doctors faced with a case of enteritis in a child bother to check whether they have picked up the infection from the family dog or cat? In Britain it has been found that 80 percent of the 250,000 tortoises imported into the country every year carry salmonella infection.

Leptospirosis is another of the zoonoses. It is reckoned to affect a quarter of the dogs in America at some time in their lives and can give rise to fever, muscular pains, jaundice, and serious liver pathology in their owners. Birds can transmit pneumonia-like diseases called ornithosis and psittacosis, which do not necessarily produce symptoms in the bird. Parrots and parakeets are common carriers, which may explain why cases of ornithosis have doubled in Britain since the lifting of the ban on the import of these exotic birds.

But the zoonoses are not common causes of human disease, and to ban dogs and cats because they spread disease and foul the streets, as some suggest, is akin to eliminating the entire human race because some pollute the environment and are carriers of tuberculosis. The world would be a poorer place without pet animals. Moreover, many of the troubles they cause can be reduced by responsible pet-ownership. No one should own a pet unless he or she needs it and is prepared to care for it. Puppies and kittens are born in America at the rate of ten thousand every hour. Many of these are unwanted and are eventually put to sleep, but others go on to become strays, the doggy drop-outs of our affluent society. This pet explosion, which continues at a rate far greater than the growth of the human population, can and should be curbed by higher license fees for pet-ownership, the control of strays, and the wider use of neutering as a means of birth control "Don't let them stray; neuter or spay," says one animal welfare society.

Tattooing a registration number on the inside of the hind legs of dogs would help by making it easier to trace the ownership of strays. The provision of subsidized clinics offering low-cost animal sterilization, as introduced in Los Angeles in 1970, would also help to reduce the number of unwanted pets. In Britain many authorities are also reviving the old post of dog-catcher to reduce the number of strays. Other authorities wisely insist that dogs in town be held on leash. This by-law, when introduced in Slough, Buckinhamshire, caused an immediate 75 percent reduction in the number of road accidents caused by dogs. Local authorities should also take steps to reduce the fouling of pavements. Holland has introduced street signs with a picture of a dog "performing" on the pavement with the caption "Don't let your dog foul the pavement." Several town councils in Britain have built special doggy lavatories along the lines of the ones first provided in Hove, Sussex, in 1968. These consisted of special silver-painted lampposts surrounded by clinkered compounds containing attractively perfumed disinfectants. Many towns levy fines on the owners of dogs who foul the pavements, and in 1972 the New York authorities toyed with the idea of insisting that pet owners should be required by law to carry special "pooper-scoopers" to clear up any mess their animals make.

At home, pets should be trained not to dirty lawns, paths, and children's play areas. As an additional precaution, nets should be placed over children's sandboxes.

More care should also be taken to keep pets away from food intended for human consumption. They should never be allowed to enter food shops or restaurants, "share" meals, or lick food from the family plates. And pets should not be kissed.

Regular washing and grooming helps reduce the mite and flea content of animal pelts, but with even the most careful grooming, it is still advisable to wash the hands after handling pets. Flea collars impregnated with pesticides are best avoided, for while they successfully kill fleas, they can also be hazardous for owners and pets. Veterinarians at Washington State University put flea collars on fifty cats and found that twenty-one of them developed symptoms of nervous disease—listlessness, loss of appetite, lack of coordination, and—in four cases—death. The Environmental Protection Agency also warns that these collars can produce dizziness, nausea, and skin rashes in humans.

Pillows

The earliest pillows were just bundles of straw or logs of wood, but gradually they became elaborate. The ancient Egyptians slept on semicylindrical bolsters made of metal, wood, or stone; the early Anglo-Saxons in Europe on two or three firm pillows stuffed with loose or plaited straw; and wealthy Romans on luxurious cushions filled with the finest down. Cultures favoring intricate hairstyles developed head rests that would protect coiffures during sleep. In Japan this led to the "butterfly" pillow, and in Africa to the stool, which was often heavily carved and decorated with vegetable dyes and intricate poker work.

Ideally, during sleep the head, neck, and spine should be kept in a straight line so that no strain is thrown on the spinal joints and no undue compression exerted on the nerves as they emerge from the spine. Many stiff necks result from sleeping on too high a pillow. It is said that Enrico Caruso, the famous Italian tenor, slept in a bed with eighteen pillows and three mattresses, which is enough to support an entire operatic cast. One firm pillow should be enough to insure comfortable sleep. Those who find it difficult to lie flat because of heart failure, hiatus hernia, or chronic bronchitis need to sleep with the entire mattress or bed tilted; and none of us should attempt to raise our bodies by simply lifting the head. This places far too much strain on the neck.

It is possible to dispense with a pillow altogether, but most people find it adds to the comfort of their sleep. Desmond Morris, the celebrated ethologist, points out in his book *Intimate Behaviour* that an infant receives comfort by placing its cheek against its mother's breast. This explains the subtle appeal of the advertisements that show a woman snuggling up against a fleecy blanket or a soft mink coat. It also explains the basic attraction of the pillow, which acts as a substitute for the mother's breast. "The caress of this tender pillow breast," says Morris, "provides a major soothing element at the end of the day, helping to calm us into a condition where we are prepared to sink at last into a deep slumber and give up the adult battle of the day."

To provide adequate support, a pillow needs to be reasonably firm; but to provide comfort it needs to have some of the softness of a mother's touch. Dr. Marie Stopes, the pioneer authority on birth control, was a great advocate of soft pillows. She tried sleeping with a flat stone for a pillow while touring but found "they numb one's nerves and are not to be recommended." She was also firmly opposed to rubber mattresses and pillows on the grounds that "rubber is an insulator and cuts you off from the electric currents of the earth." The selection of a pillow for an adult is largely a matter of individual preference. For infants the choice is more critical. Soft, impermeable pillows may be the cause of some crib deaths, those inexplicable cases of sudden, silent death which occur in sleeping infants. A child can easily suffocate by burying its face in a soft pillow. Or, if the pillow is nonporous, it can regurgitate a litte milk from its previous meal and drown in the vomit trapped in the hollow formed by its head. For this reason a baby's pillow should be firm and porous so that any vomited milk is quickly absorbed. Dispensing with a pillow and lying flat on a mattress covered with a waterproof sheet is no alternative, for that too can retain a pool of milk. Researchers at a children's hospital in Sheffield, England, suggest that one of the safest sleeping surfaces for a child is a manger filled with hay or a mattress stuffed with straw.

Play

Play is an essential part of our lives. It is an activity that normally comes to the fore during periods of relaxation when all our basic instinctual needs are met and we are warm, fed, secure, and happy.

In 1960 the Central Council of Physical Recreation in Britain published the Wolfenden Committee Report on *Sport and the Community.* One of its major conclusions was: "Man needs play. In the form of a game, a sport or an outdoor activity of some kind, it is desirable in itself, for its own sake as a valuable element in a full and rounded life."

Considerable research has been done on the physiology of work; far more needs to be done on the biology of play. All work and no play, we know, makes Jack a dull boy—staid, timid, and uncreative.

When we play we temporarily suspend the rigid framework of our normal, routine lives. This gives us a chance to explore and test out new patterns of behavior. As Dr. Hans Hass, the noted German ethologist, concludes after studying the play activities of both primates and man, "our play and curiosity impulse is responsible not only for discovery, exploration and innovation, but also, in large measure, for promoting our artistic development."

This learning content of play is particularly noticeable in children. Little girls train to become mothers by playing with dolls. Little boys equip themselves for their generally more combative futures by learning to climb, fight, and wrestle. Playing games in the dark, or games involving sudden frights, helps infants of both sexes to overcome some of their basic fears. Skills are acquired in much the same way. Plato recommended that miniature tools should be given to three-year-olds who were to become builders in later life. Experiments with chimpanzees have shown that it is easier to solve a problem if the objects involved have formed the subject of previous play. Children don't need expensive toys; often all they require is a bundle of old newspapers, a pot of paint, and a ball of string. Playthings are not objects to keep infants quiet: They are the tools with which they learn new skills, the tickets to carry them to unexplored lands, the props to act out their fantasies, and the weapons to conquer their fears. Play serves many functions. As one educator has put it, "Understanding the atom is child's play compared with understanding child's play."

Even adults learn from play. An indoor adventure playground has been built at the Farleigh Mental Hospital, near Bristol, Somerset, "to stimulate patients to explore their potential." At Ulm, in Germany, psychiatrist Tobias Brocher has set up a "play school for parents." Here grown-ups are encouraged to use the play activities of childhood–finger-painting and clay-modeling–to explore and overcome some of their adult hangups. With these techniques they are often able to relive and resolve early childhood conflicts. Many have become better parents as a result.

Brocher gives as an example the stern, unbending judge who when first asked to finger-paint could only dip his little finger into a pot of white paint and make rows of orderly dots. Three weeks later he had overcome his inhibitions to the extent that he was now up to his elbows in paint, happily daubing the walls with splashes of vivid reds, yellows, and browns. "Isn't it fun?" Brocher asked. With a shy grin the judge replied, "I must tell you something. I was never permitted as a child to play with mud; my mother punished me when I came home dirty. My wife and I got into lots of fights about our son because I couldn't stand seeing him playing with mud. Now I know how it feels and I am happy we can give our son a different experience from the one I had."

As well as providing a learning experience for adults, play also contains an element of fun that can be described but not easily analyzed. "The play mood is one of rapture and enthusiasm," says historian Johan Huizinga in his fascinating study *Homo Ludens.* "A feeling of exaltation and tension accompanies the action, mirth and relaxation follow." It was of course this element of fun that was so roundly condemned by the Puritans. John Bunyan considered that to dance, or to play hockey on the village green, was "an ungodly practice." These Puritanical strictures still haunt us in our play today. We do not find it easy to frolic and let off steam. We indulge in organized games, with their strict boundaries and formal rules, but find it difficult to enjoy the uninhibited freedom of spontaneous play. But the very nature of their regulations makes organized games a poor substitute for unfettered play, for within their rigid framework we cannot expect to express our total personality or develop our full potential.

Play, then, is a thing of many parts. It can be creative or cathartic. It can help us express our feelings, develop our talents, and conquer our fears. It is part of the primary business of childhood and in an ideal world would be one of the major activities of adults.

Psychiatrist Erik Erikson made a special study of a group of children, which he followed up thirty years later when the children had matured. He found that the adults leading the most interesting, fulfilling lives were the ones who had managed to keep a sense of playfulness at the center of their lives. "What then, is the right way of living?" asks Plato. "Life must be lived as play," he replies.

Potatoes

Potatoes are an ancient crop. They were first grown by the Incas on the slopes of the Andes well over three thousand years ago. From there they were introduced into Europe by the Spanish conquistadors, who little realized that this curious plant would come to produce an annual world crop far more valuable than all the gold they plundered from the New World. The European aristocracy took quickly to the new dish. They regarded the South American papas herb as a rare delicacy, an elixir of love. One seventeenth-century writer described it as "of great value to comfort and strengthen the body."

As the food became in more abundant supply, it lost some of its exotic appeal. In Burgundy, its cultivation was banned by law following an outbreak of leprosy for which it was held responsible. Elsewhere it was condemned as the cause of madness, tuberculosis, and rickets. But some continued to see a future for the crop.

Frederick the Great thought it would make an excellent substitute for grain and sent a wagonload of seed potatoes to a famined town with orders that they were to be grown and used to supplement the meager diet. But the townsfolk complained. "These things have neither smell nor taste," they said, "not even the dogs will eat them, so of what use are they to us?" Unable to get his own people to eat them, Frederick used the crop to feed some of his French prisoners, who included among their number Antoine Parmentier, chef to King Louis XVI of France. He was one of the few prisoners to appreciate the new food. On his release he took a sample to show the French king. King Louis was obviously impressed and showed his approval by making public acceptance of a bunch of potato blooms. Marie Antoinette, his wife, even used the blooms to decorate her hair. Later Parmentier organized a series of royal banquets at which every dish was created from potatoes. This helped popularize the food among the French nobility, but it was still not accepted by the poor who considered it "not for the likes of them." So Parmentier resorted to a subterfuge. He obtained from the king a hundred acres of land on the outskirts of Paris and raised there a crop of potatoes in conditions of feigned secrecy, and under a twenty-four-hour military guard. When the crop was mature, and he had obtained maximum publicity for his clandestine activities, Parmentier gave orders for the guard to be stood down. As he hoped, the crop was quickly pilfered. Next season potatoes flowered throughout the back gardens of Paris.

From this checkered start, the potato has become one of the world's major staple foods, valued particularly in times of famine and world food shortage because it yields four times as much food per acre as wheat. Adam Smith, the "Father of Economics," points out in *The Wealth of Nations* that at that time the strongest men and the most beautiful women in the British Empire were fed on potatoes. "No food can afford a more decisive proof of its nourishing quality, or of its being peculiarly suitable to the health of the human constitution," he said.

Today many people shun potatoes because of their calorie content. They fear that eating them will make them fat. However, the potato is 80 percent water and contains only a third as many calories as an equivalent weight of bread. (One medium-sized potato contains about 120 calories.) In 1969 a nutritional survey was carried out in Britain to see how well people understood the basic principles of human nutrition. When asked what foods we could do without, the majority of people said, "Potatoes." But as the report pointed out, "The potato is probably the one food that as a nation we could *not* do without." Few people questioned realized that potatoes are an important source of Vitamin C and yet the average Briton gets a third of his or her Vitamin C intake from potatoes, with the proportion rising to as much as a half during the winter months when fruits and vegetables are in short supply. The potato is not particularly rich in protein, but in Britain, because of the large quantities of potatoes consumed, it supplies more protein than traditional sources such as fish. (Potatoes supply 5 percent of daily protein intake, fish 4 percent.) It is also an important source of iron, supplying 10 percent of the recommended daily intake, according to the United States National Research Council.

In order that potatoes yield the maximum Vitamin C, they should be subjected to a minimum amount of preparation. Storing, cutting, mashing, boiling, and reheating all destroy some of the Vitamin C content. (French fries contain more Vitamin C than boiled potatoes because of the speed with which they are cooked, but as they also contain 70 percent more calories because of the fat they absorb during the cooking process, they are best avoided by dieters.) The ideal way to prepare potatoes is to bake them in their skins. This retains the largest amount of Vitamin C and also insures the maximum intake of iron, which is found mainly in the skin. Potatoes roasted in their jackets make a nutritious and tasty dish. They were popular in Victorian England when they were sold by hot-potato vendors, familiar figures who wandered through the streets selling their wares from charcoal-heated containers strapped around their necks. For added variety, baked potatoes can be opened up and the contents mixed with grated cheese, chopped herbs, cooked onions, or fried chopped kidneys.

Relaxation

Our lives are growing increasingly anxious and tense. With our noses to the grindstone and our shoulders to the wheel, we are constantly striving to climb the ladder of success, grasping to take hold of a bigger share of the world's material wealth, or sometimes merely fighting to keep our heads above water. Each image conveys a state of tense, earnest struggle.

Children are told to pull themselves together. From an early age classmates compete for scholastic and athletic honors, while teachers in their end-of-term reports urge further effort with the time-honored comment "Must try harder." In business the competition becomes keener still. Instead of being surrounded by friendly members of a tightly knit supportive pack, the executive animal finds himself or herself alone in an alien jungle, prey to attack at any time from any quarter.

As we pick our way through life, we are constantly on guard. Like tortoises or hedgehogs, we show the primitive animal response of retracting our heads and curling up our bodies when we are under attack to try to shield our necks and soft underbellies. When we are anxious we contract our bodies and become "uptight." When we relax, our bodies expand and "swell with pride" or "burst with enthusiasm."

Like other animals, we also freeze into immobility when we are alarmed or frightened, in the hope that in this way we may escape the attention of our enemies. This happens even when the "threat" comes from the sudden ringing of a telephone bell.

In order to avoid giving vital clues to our enemies, we

try to hide any show of our true emotional feelings. The German ethologist Hans Hass has noted that some races are much more "open" than others. The Samoans, for example, are content to live in huts that are open on all sides. "They do not hesitate to expose their private lives to the gaze of others," says Hass. "The play of emotion in their faces is no less undisguised." We, on the other hand, make a point of keeping poker faces and stiff upper lips to prevent exposing our inner selves or true feelings. Wilhelm Reich has shown that this suppression of feeling involves the muscles of the entire body. We hold ourselves in muscular straitjackets, which prevent our experiencing or expressing strong emotions. We tense our abdominal muscles to choke back tears, freeze the muscles of our thighs to stop our legs from breaking into panic-stricken flight, and clench our jaws to keep our teeth from chattering. In this way we develop a characteristic pattern of "body-armoring" that sets out to defend us, but ends up confining our movements and deadening our ability to experience even pleasurable feelings.

Further tension stems from our constant battle with time. We seem obsessed with deadlines and struggle to do yesterday what we start and couldn't possibly finish today and don't in any case need until tomorrow.

Increased speed is the constant goal, even though at times it leads to decreased efficiency. As the old adage puts it: "More haste, less speed." We employ machines to do our work, but instead of sitting back and letting the wheels spin round, we insist on pushing. Automation, instead of providing more time for rest and recreation, is making us more restless. The faster the industrial machine travels, the quicker the pace of our lives.

Once introduced, a state of tension tends to be self-perpetuating. The feedback of stimuli from tense muscles arouses the brain and keeps it in a state of constant alarm. This high degree of arousal maintains a condition aptly named by psychiatrists as "free-floating anxiety," in which the brain is constantly informed that trouble is just around the corner but cannot identify what it is. So the cerebral finger is kept permanently pressed on the

Red Alert button. Muscles remain ready to spring into action, the heart beats rapidly, blood pressure soars, and stress hormones are poured out into the circulation as the metabolic engines race, ready to burst into sudden action. This leads to breathlessness, palpitation, and a variety of other alarming psychosomatic signs that are themselves further causes of anxiety. Sleep is disturbed; we tire more readily and suffer a variety of muscular aches and pains. The common response to this dilemma is to struggle harder. We have been taught to combat every obstacle we meet in life by making an increased effort. Yet, like persons thrown into the sea without life jackets, we are often more likely to survive if we lie quietly on our backs than if we thrash our arms and scream.

Tension and effort are often self-defeating. The tighter a golfer grips his club, the worse his swing becomes. The harder a stammerer tries to control his speech, the worse his stutter. Relaxation is the secret of efficient movement. Every set of muscles has an antagonist group that must be relaxed as the prime movers contract. Even the burliest weight-lifter would find his efforts ineffectual if he contracted both triceps and biceps when he set out to hoist a barbell overhead. In the same way, a sprinter would be hamstrung if he contracted the flexor muscles of his thigh at the same time as he straightened his knee. Smooth, powerful movements can be made only when the body is otherwise completely relaxed. Sustained tension leads to anxiety, fatigue, stiff necks, headaches, and unsightly facial wrinkles, frowns, and worry lines. We can take tranquilizers to suppress anxiety, vitamins for fatigue, aspirins to deaden headaches, hot baths and massage to relieve fibrositis, and cosmetics to hide wrinkles, but these measures provide only temporary symptomatic relief. Tension is cured not by taking drugs, but by learning to relax.

We are all subject to changes of mood, to times of great joy and moments of despair, to frustration and elation, spells of bright euphoria and periods of dark depression. These swings of mood give color and purpose to our lives. If we suppress them with drugs, we become little better than cabbages. We need to live life fully and passionately, even if it involves at times a little suffering, for suffering may be the scourge that goads us into making much-needed changes in our environments or lifestyles. It is a mistake to try to banish anxiety from our lives. We need to be aware of both the dangers and the opportunities that we'll face and function best at a certain optimum level of arousal that varies with the occasion. An athlete needs to be keyed up before an event if he is to perform well. Similarly, the conductor of an orchestra should aim to be calm and composed in his dressing room, but needs to be tense and alert the moment he walks on stage if he is to be at concert pitch. The same applies to business executives, who need to act and react quickly if they are to work effectively. Tranquilizers may filter off the stress of business life, but they also reduce a person's confidence and drive. Like ear plugs that assist sleep by quieting the noise of passing traffic but also deaden the sounds of alarm bells and cat burglars, tranquilizers are insufficiently selective. Business executives need to learn to relax without the aid of drugs, for then they can lessen strain without suffering any reduction of their creativity and drive. This also supports their qualities of leadership, for when psychological tests were administered to a group of over four hundred men and women, it was found that the dominant individuals signaled their presence in the pecking order by the easy, relaxed manner in which they held and used their bodies. Less dominant subjects were more tense and inhibited in their movements; they spoke quicker and in higher pitched voices.

These forms of nonverbal communication are often cultivated by politicians and used to great effect by cowboys, who signal their dominance by their easy, loping gait and slow drawl. Similar dominance signals are shown by rhesus monkeys, and scientists at the Yale School of Medicine have demonstrated that leader monkeys lose some of their power and authority when they receive injections of Librium, a tranquilizer commonly given to harassed executives. Monkeys lower in the hierarchy, spotting this diminished dominance, often seize the opportunity to take over leadership of the group, a usurpation of authority that could equally well happen in the boardroom if sedated executives show a lessening of their authority and drive.

Tension is a bad neuromuscular habit. Too many people drive themselves through life with the handbrake on, allowing themselves no time for rest, recovery, or repair. They need to learn the art of relaxation so they can switch off as well as on. This saves unnecessary fatigue, prevents the development of tension, aches and pains, improves performance, reduces accidents caused by clumsiness, and cures a large number of psychosomatic ailments.

In Croydon, Surrey, an Indian G.P., Dr. Chandra Patel, taught hypertensive patients to relax and secured a significant reduction of blood pressure in 76 percent of the cases, with 24 percent able to dispense with their antihypertensive drugs altogether. At the Menninger Foundation, in Kansas, relaxation therapy has been used to get a "significant degree of improvement" in 81 percent of migraine patients.

Learning to relax, as well as relieving stress disorders, will also enrich our emotional life, for as Wilhelm Reich showed, bodily tensions produce blocks that prevent us from feeling emotions as deeply and fully as we should. When we are tense, we tend to overreact to irritating stimuli. We jump when the telephone rings, shout at the children when they knock over a cup of water, and throw a temper tantrum when we can't undo a jammed zipper. Learning to relax checks these overreactions, gives us greater control over our emotions, and enables us to switch on to health-giving, positive emotional states. We experience the emotion of depression as a heaviness and tightness of the body; we feel bowed down with problems, knotted up with worry, with a weight on our shoulders and a load on our minds. Conversely, when we are elated, our bodies seem light and free, as if we were up in the clouds walking on air. Since the power and quality of the emotions we feel depend to a very large extent on the strength of the sensations recorded throughout the body, we can often evoke elation and overcome despair by controlling the level of tension within our bodies.

All this can be achieved by learning to relax, an art that can be acquired by systematic practice and that can then become part of our everyday lives. The steps are quite simple. Choose any time of the day when you can be sure of being on your own for at least fifteen minutes. (Last thing at night is often an ideal time.)

Step One: Stretch the body as fully as you can, for just as stretching breaks down cramp, so it relieves lesser degrees of tension in the muscles. This is why a yawn accompanied by a delicious overall stretching of the body makes such an excellent prelude to sleep. In Japan a transistor manufacturer has instigated thirty-second breaks for yawning during the day when he encourages employees to stand back from the production line, stretch their arms and yawn in unison. This has reduced tension and led to significant increases in production.

Step Two: After stretching the body thoroughly, lie on your back on the floor with your legs and arms comfortably separated from your body. (This, in yoga terms, is the *Shavasana*, or Corpse Posture.") If any discomfort is felt in the small of the back in this position, place a large cushion under the knees. Now go from top to toe, tensing every muscle group within the body, then letting them relax. Tense the left foot, calf, and thigh, then let them relax. Do the same with the right leg. Contract the buttocks and pelvic muscles, then let these muscles go. Do the same with the left hand and arm; the right arm; the chest and shoulders; the face, neck, and forehead—each time letting the degree of relaxation grow deeper and deeper.

The employment of tension before relaxation may seem self-defeating, but in practice this has proved to be the easiest way to gain control over tight muscle groups and enter a state of deep relaxation. Dr. Knight Dunlap of John Hopkins University, Baltimore, Maryland, has found that exaggeration is a useful technique for breaking other bad neuromuscular habits. He urges stutterers to deliberately increase their stammer until they tire, stop trying too hard, and so speak better. (This is similar to the method used by Demosthenes, the great Greek orator, who cured his stammer by putting pebbles in his mouth. This made speech yet more difficult, but correspondingly easier when he removed the pebbles and spoke in an unimpeded fashion.)

When employing this alternate cycle of tension and relaxation, pay particular attention to the key spots where tension is most frequently encountered: the jaw, the tongue, the brow, the eyes, and the hands. Don't employ any special effort to make these muscles relax, just tense them firmly, then *let* them relax. Relaxation cannot be forced–it can only be allowed to happen. The sensation should be like stepping out of a tight girdle or ill-fitting pair of shoes.

Step Three: When the body is relaxing well, concentrate on breathing slowly, deeply, and rhythmically. With each expiration, feel the tension easing from your body (see *Breathing*)

Step Four: After several cycles of relaxed breathing, use your imagination to conjure up pictures of heaviness and warmth. J. H. Schultz developed an effective system of relaxation known as *autogenic training*, which is based almost entirely on the controlled use of the imagination. He hypnotized a number of people and asked them to report the sensations they experienced as they slipped into a state of deep relaxation. Most reported experiencing sensations of heaviness and warmth permeating their bodies. Schultz then gave these suggestions without any attempt at inducing a hypnotic trance and found his subjects relaxed equally well. In a low voice he intoned, "Your arms and hands feel heavy and warm." "Your whole body is peaceful and relaxed." "Warmth is flowing into your feet; your legs feel heavy and warm." Giving ourselves similar suggestions of heaviness and warmth is a definite aid to relaxation.

It also helps to go on fantasy trips. Imagine you are lying on a beach in the South of France bathed in sunshine, the hot sand beneath you, a gentle breeze fanning your body, the cry of the gulls in the distance, the smell of hibiscus flowers wafting past your nostrils. Or in your mind's eye take a country stroll, wander through a meadow and lie down beside a rippling stream, run the soft grasses through your fingers, feel the touch of the sun on your cheeks, and enjoy the sound of the birds and the delicate scent of the wild flowers.

Just as an undisciplined imagination can make us afraid, so a controlled imagination can induce feelings of quiet repose and deep relaxation.

Step Five: End each session of relaxation by implanting into the subconscious mind the suggestion that the calmness and peace you have secured will remain with you throughout the remainder of the day. Then stretch, like a cat emerging from a deep sleep, blink the eyes, yawn, and slowly resume your normal activities.

To be effective, these exercises must be repeated every day, for acquiring the habit of relaxation is rather like climbing a rope. If you let go for even a moment, you fall to the bottom and have to start to climb again. But the habit, once acquired, will last a lifetime.

Rest Pauses

The body protects itself from damage in an often-remarkable way. We can move from the tropics to the Arctic Circle with no variation in our body temperature; we can go on a fluid-free diet or a prolonged beer-swigging binge and suffer neither desiccation nor overhydration, and we can leap from bed after a night's rest and chase after a bus with no alarming leap in our blood pressure. In each of these instances we bring into play complex automatic-control mechanisms that protect the body from self-inflicted abuse. If the body cares for itself so well in these fields, why is it that we suffer so much mental breakdown and nervous fatigue? Is there no thermostat to protect our nervous systems from overheating–no similar protection for us against excessive psychic stress and strain?

The answer is that there is a device to prevent nervous fatigue, but we have an ability to override its operating cut-out mechanism that we all too often abuse. Most systems of the body show alternate cycles of work and rest. The heart beats 100,000 times a day and manages to maintain this incredible work output without fatigue by interspersing periods of contraction (systole) with longer periods of rest (diastole). The strong postural muscles of the back also enjoy regular intervals of rest, operating a shift system among their muscle fibers so that, like a gang of laborers, while one group of fibers contracts, the others take a needed break.

The same work/rest cycle can be seen in the activity of animals and children. A dog will chase a ball vigorously for several minutes and will then lie panting on the ground to rest and recover. A few seconds later he will return refreshed to the chase. The same occurs with children. One minute they are chasing the cat over and under the dining room table, the next they are curled up on the sofa asleep. These cycles of alternate work and rest characterize the activity pattern of most animals. They form the natural biological rhythm of work, but they are not immutable like the work/rest cycle of the heart. We can, if we choose, deny the desire to rest and keep on working for long periods without relief. Society in fact encourages us to do this, and by the time we have reached adulthood, most of us have substituted for this natural work/rest cycle a completely artificial division of the day into a prolonged period of work, followed by a period of recreation and sleep. We have made such a vice of sloth, moreover, that many people consider it positively sinful to succumb to the natural urge to rest during the working day. Yet the introduction of regular intervals of rest during periods of work enables us to achieve the maximum output of work with the minimum expenditure of energy and the least risk of fatigue.

Scouts have found that the most economical way to cover long distances is by alternately running a mile and then walking a mile. Athletes have adopted "interval training," which involves alternate spells of all-out running and short recovery spells of relaxed jogging, since they find that in practice this is the most effective way of extending the limits of athletic performance.

Laboratory experiments confirm the results of this practical experience. In Sweden a group of fit men were given an hour in which to perform thirty minutes set work on a cycle trainer. Some worked flat out for thirty minutes, then rested for the remainder of the hour; others worked for shorter intervals and took more frequent breaks. When the results were analyzed, it was found that the most economical way of performing the task was to divide the hour into thirty-second intervals, working for half a minute and then resting for half a minute. This produced the smallest consumption of oxygen, the lowest elevation of pulse rate, and the least accumulation of the fatigue-producing waste products of muscle metabolism.

Manual workers have always appreciated the value of regular rest pauses. As Henry Thoreau observed, "A really efficient labourer will be found not to crowd his day with work." If he allows himself to work to the point of fatigue, the efficiency of his work suffers. This was the experience of Henry Ford, who once admitted, "We would have had our Model A car in production six months sooner if I had forbidden my engineers to work on Sunday. It took us all week to straighten out the mistakes they made on the day they should have rested."

Most manual workers instinctively take these much-needed periods of rest. A team of German physiologists, who carried out a detailed study of the work pattern and energy expenditure of a large group of factory workers in Dortmund, discovered that the men took rest pauses whenever they were physiologically required but concealed them from their foremen by indulging in activities such as idly polishing their machines. In one factory it was found that 11 percent of the working day was spent in these unauthorized breaks. In view of this it was decided to introduce official pauses of five minutes at the end of every hour. When this was done, the hidden breaks disappeared, fatigue was lessened, and production rose 13 percent.

Analysis of the lives of people noted for their prodigious output of work invariably shows that they have made a habit of taking regular periods of rest whenever nature required. It doesn't pay to whip the body on with doses of caffeine, nicotine, or other chemical stimulants. This only staves off fatigue for a while. Maximum efficiency can be achieved only by alternating periods of work with periods of rest.

Resuscitation

Countless lives would be saved each year if more people knew how to resuscitate the unconscious victims of accidents involving head injuries, drowning, poisoning, and electric shocks. Casualty experts in Britain estimate that 20 percent of people killed in car crashes and other accidents could be saved if they were placed in the correct position. Generally, the worst thing to do with unconscious victims is to lay them on their backs, for then they tend to inhale their own blood and vomit, and to face the added risk of suffocation should their tongues fall back and close their throats. The correct procedure is to place injured persons face downward, their heads turned to one side and one arm raised to prevent rolling over. This is the "recovery position" which, although not widely known, is recommended in all modern textbooks of first aid.

It is absolutely essential for the brain to be constantly supplied with oxygenated blood. If this supply fails for more than four minutes, permanent damage to the brain is likely to occur. Speed, therefore, is absolutely vital when coming to the relief of an unconscious person, so much so that skilled life-savers are now taught to apply the "kiss of life" in the water as they bring casualties to the safety of the shore.

The three essential steps to take when administering emergency resuscitation are:

Ensure a clear airway. Remove tight clothing around the neck and any obstructions in the mouth such as débris, vomit, blood, and loose false teeth. Make sure the tongue is brought well forward so that it does not block the throat.

Restart the heart if it has stopped. This can be done by briskly striking the chest lightly to the left of the lower part of the breastbone. If this fails, apply external heart compression. (Place the heel of the hand over the lower part of the breastbone and press down towards the spine. Repeat this sixty times a minute, each time moving the breastbone a distance of about 4 centimeters (1½ inches). *Neither of these techniques should be used if the heart is beating, however weakly.*

Apply artificial respiration. Over eighty different methods of artificial respiration have been described. In the wine-making districts of Europe, unconscious victims were rolled over a barrel; comatose sailors in the Mediterranean areas were tossed in a blanket; and Maoris in New Zealand were suspended over an open fire in the hope that the irritating smoke would help revive them. (In fact, it is more likely to do the reverse, and any one in danger of being burnt to death can obtain practically instant oblivion by taking a few deep drafts of smoke.)

> ***Silvester Method:*** In the nineteenth century a number of physicians endeavored to perfect a method of artificial respiration that could be used by one person without the need for any special apparatus. The most effective of these techniques was developed by Silvester and involved placing the victim on his back, preferably with a folded blanket or jacket under his shoulders. The rescuer knelt astride the casualty's head and bent forward to grasp his hands at the wrist. It was then possible to inflate the lungs by raising the arms upward and backward, and to deflate them by crossing the arms over the chest and pressing gently downward. This cycle was repeated twelve times every minute until normal breathing was resumed.
>
> ***Holger-Nielsen Method.*** The great disadvantage of the Silvester Method is that with the victim lying on his back, it is

difficult to keep the tongue from dropping back and closing the throat. To overcome this drawback, a Dane, Lieutenant Colonel Holger Nielsen, introduced an alternative method that had the victim lying face downwards with his hands placed one on top of the other underneath the head, which was turned to one side. The rescuer kneels at the head of the unconscious victim and forces expiration by pressing forward on the rib cage. Inspiration is achieved by grasping the elbows and elevating them so that the ribs are raised. Again the cycle is repeated twelve times a minute.

During the war it was thought advisable to test the efficiency of the various available techniques of artificial respiration. Accordingly, in 1950, the United States Department of Defense took a team of volunteers, anesthetized them, and paralyzed their muscles by injecting the drug curare. In this critical state they were entirely dependent on artificial respiration to maintain their lives. Several different techniques of artificial respiration were used and these were analyzed to compare their relative effectiveness. It was found that the Silvester and Holger-Nielsen methods were, in many cases, twice as effective as many of the other and had the added attraction of being easily taught to students during the course of a ten-minute lecture demonstration.

A still more effective method is provided by mouth-to-mouth resuscitation, popularly known as the "kiss of life." This, the earliest known form of artificial respiration, was recorded in the Old Testament as the technique used by the prophet Elisha to revive the child of the Shunamite woman. (In 1530 Paracelsus, the great Swiss physician, mechanized the technique by using a pair of fireside bellows, inserting one into each nostril to inflate the lungs.)

To perform the "kiss of life," tilt the victim's head backwards to elevate the tongue, with her or his nostrils closed between your fingers. Take a deep breath, seal your lips around the victim's mouth, and blow into her or his lungs until the chest rises. Then relax the mouth contact to allow the chest to fall under its own weight. This cycle is repeated in time with the rescuer's natural rate of respiration until normal breathing is resumed.

This is the technique of choice, unless there are severe injuries to the face or jaw, or the victim is pinned face downward or suffers from recurrent vomiting. In these instances, the Holger-Nielsen method should be used, or the Silvester technique, if it is necessary to combine artificial respiration with cardiac resuscitation.

In the days of Queen Anne, the Thames watermen used to say, "The only thing to do for a drowned man is to pick his pocket." That may then have been true, but now it is possible to save his life, providing effective techniques of resuscitation are commenced quickly and maintained until the spark of life returns.

Rocking Chairs

Gentle rocking of the body has a marked sedative effect. Mothers instinctively calm their fractious children by rocking them either in their arms or in a cradle. Disturbed children and the inmates of mental hospitals often console themselves by making some rocking movement, while Jewish tradition encourages mourners to comfort the bereaved by rocking them backward and forward in their arms. Others find tranquility and rest in the use of an old-fashioned rocking chair.

These made their appearance during the latter half of the eighteenth century, the first rockers being placed on ordinary chairs, possibly to enable nursing mothers to lull their babies to sleep without effort. Subsequent rocking chairs were built for the purpose and quickly became a vogue in America when Benjamin Franklin popularized the Boston rocker and Abraham Lincoln the Lincoln rocker. These chairs were later imported into England and marketed as "American Common Sense Chairs . . . specially adapted for rest and comfort." About this time one Dr. Calvert, a Londoner, developed a brass-framed rocker, described as a "digestive chair" since its regular use was thought to aid the digestion and prevent "livershness." Folding rockers were made for people on the move, miniature mahogany rockers with inset chamberpots for constipated children, and special "crinoline rockers" with low seats and half arms for women wearing fashionable hooped skirts.

In addition to its sedative effects, the rocking chair also provides a valuable stimulus for the circulation. Sitting motionless in front of a television set retards the circulation and can predispose to blood clots. Gentle rocking helps to minimize this risk, a fact known to the ancient Greeks, who made therapeutic use of swings and hammocks to provide "passive exercise." Many people who suffer leg cramps at night find that an hour's rocking before retiring assures them of a good night's sleep.

Rocking chairs also help reduce the spinal strain of prolonged sitting, which is why they were recommended to President Kennedy by Dr. Janet Travell, who claims, "The constantly changing position will relax your muscles and rest you."

A short while ago Thomas Saxe, president of a chain of restaurants, started a club for rocking-chair enthusiasts in Stamford, Connecticut, called the Sittin' Starin' 'n' Rockin' Club. This club now has a worldwide membership of housewives, statesmen, clergymen, footballers, and policemen, all devoted to the gentle art of contemplative rocking. Too many people today are "pools for ever blown upon by restless winds, that never grow calm enough to reflect anything beautiful." Thomas Saxe suggests that these restless souls should consider the advice carved into the headpiece of many old rocking chairs: "Sit ye, Rock and Think." This can bring needed peace of mind.

A Canadian doctor recently published an article in a leading British medical journal on "The Therapeutic Value of the Rocking Chair," in which he pointed out that this tranquilizer is "cheap and easily obtainable, has no side effects, is non-toxic and needs no prescription."

Roughage

Epidemiological studies have shown that noninfective diseases of the lower bowel such as appendicitis, diverticulitis, polyps and cancer are much more common in industrialized countries than in developing nations. One possible explanation is a difference in diet, in particular our much lower intake of nondigestible vegetable fiber or roughage. In the last ninety years the fiber content of our diet has fallen by over 3000 percent. When blacks first arrived in America, they suffered little bowel disease, but when they exchanged their native diet of maize, millet, and beans for white bread, sugar, and jam, the incidence of bowel disorders soared. The same is happening throughout the world where traditional diets of rice, corn, and yams are giving way to highly concentrated convenience foods. With less roughage in the diet, the bulk of the stools grows less, food passes more slowly through the intestines, and more of its fluid content is absorbed so that the stools become smaller and harder, increasing the tendency to constipation.

Mr. D. P. Burkitt, a leading member of Britain's government-sponsored Medical Research Council, has carried out considerable research on the effects of the reduced roughage content of our contemporary diet. He says, "I believe the removal of the indigestible fibre from our diet may be one of the most important single factors for the rise of bowel cancer and other conditions in the western world." He has compared the diet and bowel habits of English public school boys with those of African villagers and senior boys at an African boarding school living on a transitional diet containing quantities of white bread and sugar. The differences found were marked. The average weight of stools passed by the African villagers was 470 grams, for the African public school boys 185 grams, and for the English public school boys 108 grams of "solid formed rock." Parallel with this were changes in the rate of passage of food through the gut, which took thirty-five hours in the case of the African natives, forty-seven hours for the African public school boys, and for the English public school boys, living on a diet of doughnuts, chocolate cookies, and cakes, a sluggish eighty hours. As Burkitt says, "There is no change in our food in the last one hundred years which compares in magnitude with the way we have removed our cereal fibre from our diet." This creates mechanical problems that predispose to constipation, colicky pains, appendicitis, and diverticular disease, and also increases the risk of intestinal cancer by prolonging the length of time potential carcinogens are in contact with the gut wall. It is also possible that this dietary change may be partly responsible for the incidence of gallstones and coronary disease, which while becoming increasingly prevalent in the West remain relatively uncommon in less developed countries. Normally a careful balance is maintained between the production, excretion, and reabsorption of bile salts. If the transit time of food through the bowel is slowed down, there is more time for the reabsorption of bile salts and a corresponding increased chance of developing gallstones from the deposition and concentration of bile salts in the gall bladder. This increased reabsorption means there is less need to synthesize fresh bile salts by the breakdown of cholesterol, so the level of cholesterol in the bloodstream rises, and with it possibly the tendency to coronary disease. Experiments with human guinea pigs had confirmed that there is a definite link between blood cholesterol levels and the fiber content of the diet.

It would seem prudent in the light of this research to modify our contemporary western diet. If we value our health, we need to replace concentrated convenience foods, cakes, and cookies with vegetable foods, fruits, and cereals, which are rich in cellulose fibers, for cellulose, which forms the wall of plant cells, is resistant to the action of human digestive juices and so passes through the bowel unchanged and provides much-needed roughage and bulk. Whenever possible these fruits and vegetables should be eaten raw, since cooking, freezing, and canning all tend to soften the cellulose fiber and so make it less effective as roughage.

Vegetables with a high fiber content are cabbage, beetroot, carrots, broccoli, tomatoes, Brussels sprouts, eggplant and squash (or marrow, if you're British).

Cereal fibers probably provide more effective roughage and are found in whole wheat bread, cookies, oatmeal, bran, and brown rice. Cereals which have lost their outer coat in the refining process, like white flour, white rice and white sugar, have also lost their fiber content.

Dr. Burkitt believes that the addition to the daily diet of two tablespoonfuls of bran or five ounces of wholemeal bread would provide sufficient fiber to improve bowel function and help prevent disease. This additional roughage could also help to keep us slim, because, as research at Bristol University's Department of Medicine has revealed, people on high-fiber diets absorb fewer calories than those on low-fiber diets.

Salt

Salt is an essential ingredient of our diet and without it we would die sooner than if deprived of any other item of food. Its importance has been recognized for generations. In Africa, Abyssinia, and Tibet, cakes of salt were used as money. In the Roman army officers and men were given a regular ration of salt, and when this was stopped they were given instead a salt ration, called a *salarium* (the root of our word *salary*).

Although an adequate supply of salt is essential for the maintenance of health, an excess is equally deleterious. Drinking salt water can cause death and was a method of suicide in ancient China. In recent years there have been several cases of accidental death caused by taking an overconcentrated dose of salt water as an emetic. The recommended dosage of salt to induce vomiting is two tablespoons of salt to a glass of tepid water. Exceeding this concentration can prove fatal.

There is evidence too that an excess of salt in the diet predisposes to high blood pressure. Races with a low intake of salt, like the Eskimos, suffer little hypertension. Those who use copious quantities of salt to preserve or season their food, like the Japanese, frequently succumb to high blood pressure. Salt also appears to potentiate the harmful effects of stress, while for the figure-conscious, there is the added disadvantage that a high intake of salt can give rise to fluid-retention and a temporary increase in weight of a pound or more.

Our total daily requirement of salt is small. There are only three ounces of salt in the entire body. The majority of people get sufficient salt in the foods they eat without adding more either at the table or during the process of cooking. Cases of salt deficiency are rare, and even after sweating profusely on a hot summer's day or performing hard manual work in the tropics, there is rarely a call for taking additional salt. The only time it may be necessary to take salt supplements is after periods of prolonged vomiting or diarrhea, and these are conditions that require proper medical investigation and treatment, particularly in children, who are especially prone to suffer the effect of rapid changes in the body's salt and water balance.

Siestas

Most animals, when left to their own devices, take their sleep at irregular intervals throughout the day. When they are tired, they automatically take short catnaps and wake refreshed and reinvigorated. Taking regular periods of rest like this helps prevent the build-up of tension, postural strain, and nervous fatigue and is undoubtedly the most efficient way of performing the day's labors (see *Rest Pauses*).

Unfortunately the demands of modern society have made it necessary for many adults to dispense with this natural pattern of rest-taking. Youngsters and elderly people in retirement may take frequent naps during the day, but working men and women have to train themselves to sleep only at night and as a result often build up a backlog of fatigue that even a good night's sleep cannot assuage. But we are gradually rediscovering the value of the midday snooze, and many executive office suites now boast a relaxation couch or reclining catnap chair.

Many of the world's most prolific workers took physical refreshment in this way. The Duke of Wellington, during the clamor and frenzy of the Battle of Waterloo, could be found dozing behind a copy of the London *Sun.* Edison would work long irregular hours in his laboratory and, when he was tired, would snatch three or four hours' sleep on a couch, then return refreshed to the fray. President Kennedy, when conferences at the White House became deadlocked, would call a five-minute break; while others smoked or drank coffee, he would rest his head on his desk and snooze. Even more remarkable was the work schedule of the world-famous architect and inventor,

Buckminster Fuller. He trained himself to sleep for half an hour every three hours of the day and night and found he could work in this way at peak efficiency even though he had only four hours' sleep a day. (Fuller ultimately gave up this schedule because it made it difficult for him to meet his clients.) A similar pattern of work is adopted by Dr. Alton Ochsner, head of the Ochsner Clinic, New Orleans, Louisiana, who takes only four hours' sleep a night but reinforces this with occasional five-minute catnaps during the day. "The siesta habit is a good one," he claims, adding, "It is difficult for many to store up a day's energy needs with a single stretch of a night's sleep."

It is a practice we could all adopt with benefit, for there is evidence that a midday rest reduces fatigue, increases efficiency, and provides a brief respite from mental strain that helps protect us from the effects of what may be otherwise unrelieved stress (see *Stress*). It offers a balm for tired bodies and a restorative for burdened minds.

Sitting

This is the age of the sedentary man, a world dominated by *Homo sedentarius*, who reigns in godlike splendor over a slave world of labor-saving machinery from a cushioned throne, generally of the most appalling design.

Both during our working day and in our leisure hours, an increasing proportion of our lives is spent in the sitting position. This has a harmful effect on our health, leading to discomfort, fatigue, backache, sciatica, and varicose veins.

Many people suffer pain in the lower part of their back after a long car journey. This is because of the considerable postural strain thrown upon the spinal ligaments. Radiological studies have shown that in the slumped sitting position the lower lumbar vertebrae are flexed forward as far as they will go. This means that three hours' driving in a poor posture can produce as much ligament strain as a morning spent crouching over the garden.

The slumped sitting position can also produce cramps, numbness, and sciatic pain if weight is borne by the fleshy parts of the thigh instead of the strong bony haunches of the pelvis. Pressure on the soft parts of the thigh can also compress the main saphenous vein and so predispose to varicose veins, which are considerably more common among western peoples than among Africans and Orientals, who squat or sit cross-legged on the floor rather than on chairs.

Although we spend so much time sitting down, we are still poorly adapted to the use of chairs. It takes an animal species millions of years to undergo any substantial anatomical modifications as a result of evolutionary change. We are still poorly adapted to the erect position that we adopted 800,000 years ago. Chairs were introduced only 5,000 years ago, far too recently to produce any structural change other than a slight thickening of the skin overlying the buttocks. Probably to begin with, chairs were used as status symbols by kings and priests to raise them head and shoulders above the common herd. By the seventeenth century, workbenches and stools were in common use, but easy chairs were still rare and were possessed by only a few wealthy noblemen, such as King Charles II of England, who was the proud owner of a handsomely carved, well upholstered chair that traveled with him on his journeys. (Very few of the kings's subjects owned chairs at this time, which is why doubt must be placed on the authenticity of many of the "Carolean" chairs offered for sale in antique shops today.) Easy chairs became common pieces of household furniture only during the latter half of the nineteenth century. By this time mass production and the introduction of metal coil springs had led to a marked deterioration in design.

But then, what is the optimum shape of a chair? Is the ideal to be found in the functional simplicity of the slatted chairs constructed in the 1920s by Dutch architect Gerrit Rietveld? In the classical lines of the Barcelona chair of Ludwig Mies van der Rohe? in the plush upholstery of Le Corbusier's Grand Confort chair? Or in the ever-shifting contours of the modern amorphous sack filled with polystyrene granules? The market choice today is wide, but it includes very few chairs of sound anatomical design, and so particular care needs to be taken when buying a chair to see that it meets the basic requirements of good functional design.

In the first place, the seat needs to be firm. It is a big mistake to equate comfort with softness when purchasing either beds or chairs. No position–standing, sitting, or lying–is comfortable if maintained for too long. Slight shifts of posture are necessary to lessen fatigue and prevent the prolonged compression of delicate tissues, and these minor adjustive movements are best made from a firm base. Five hundred people were recently invited to test the prototype seats in a new experimental railway coach. Nearly all expressed a preference for the soft luxury of the first-class seats, but concealed cameras showed by their constant wriggling that they were in fact considerably more comfortable in the more austere second-class seats, which provided firmer support for their bodies.

Functional studies have also shown that comfort is at a maximum in the sitting position when the weight of the body is shared between the feet and the ischial tuberosities, the bony humps at the base of the pelvis. As no weight should be taken by the thighs or fleshy outer parts of the buttocks, the height of a chair seat should be slightly less than the length of the lower leg from foot to knee, so that the weight of the body can be shared between the feet and the bony haunches, with the feet firmly planted on the ground and the thighs running more or less parallel with the ground. There is then no risk of compressing the blood vessels and nerves running along the under surface of the thighs and so causing numbness, pain, and a tendency to varicose veins.

With an adjustable typist's chair, it is easy to adapt the chair to suit the individual, with a resultant lessening of tension and strain. As an American orthopedic surgeon has said, "Seat a stenographer properly and she will make fewer typographical errors and probably have less menstrual distress and less lame back." But what of the ordinary household chair, which cannot be lowered or raised? The only possible adjustment here is to throw away an unsuitable chair and start again, and this is well worth doing. Chairs need to be bought for individuals. Three-piece suites may be the delight of the furniture salesman, but they are the bêtes noires of the orthopedist. How can a chair designed for a six-foot male suit his five-foot-three wife? The ideal chair of the future will be custom-made, and this will prove to be a more valuable service than custom tailoring, for an ill-fitting, off-the-rack suit does not cripple, but an ill-chosen chair can.

Furniture manufacturers are trying to make their

products suit the requirements of the average person in the hope that in this way they will suit most of the people most of the time, but they are chasing a myth, for there is no such thing as an average American. If seats are constructed of a height to suit the "average" American male, they will leave the legs of 90 percent of American women dangling precariously in mid-air. Furniture designers discovered this somewhat belatedly when they took ten vital statistics of four thousand men and used them to derive the shape of the "standard" man, only to find that not a single member of the group measured up to the standard dimensions in every respect. Comfort will not be found by buying chairs built for "average" people. The chair of the future must be custom-built to suit the requirements of the individual. This will also enable adequate support to be given to the small of the back.

At quick glance at the backs exposed to view at a swimming pool will show that there is as much variation in the curvature of the human spine as there is in the shape of the nose. No one chair, therefore, can be expected to give proper support to all shapes and sizes of back. And support is needed, for electromyographic studies have shown that maintaining an upright sitting position without the support of a chair-back requires more muscular effort than standing erect. One alternative is to slump, which lessens the muscular fatigue but throws strain onto the spinal ligaments and so gives rise to chronic postural backache. The only real solution is to provide chairs with suitable lumbar supports that maintain a slight hollow in the small of the back without the need for the back muscles to remain in constant tension. A cushion can provide a measure of support, but ideally chairs should incorporate a built-in back rest of a size, shape, and position to suit individual needs.

To make full use of the support provided by a chair, the seat should not be too deep (not more than two-thirds the length of the thigh) and should slope back slightly so that the weight of the trunk is constantly coaxed into the chair's lumbar support.

For comfort, a reasonable width of seat must also be

allowed. Architects designing New York's Lincoln Center for the Performing Arts found that the seat of the American male is getting larger, with the result that they had to allow 22-24 inches to accommodate his bulk, compared to the 18–19 inches provided by the seats at La Scala, Milan. This meant one-third more room to accommodate the same number of people.

Custom-built chairs of proper ergonomic design would go a long way toward lessening the strain of prolonged sitting. Better still, we should attempt to reduce the amount of time we spend sitting down and try to lessen the strain by reverting occasionally to some of the earlier resting positions: reclining on a couch, squatting, or sitting cross-legged on the floor. All three of these postures involve less muscular effort and are less productive of spinal strain.

Skiing

Skiing is an ancient method of traveling over snow-covered ground. Primitive skis, fashioned from animal tusks, unearthed in Sweden, are believed to date back over four thousand years, although skiing became a fashionable pastime only with the development of ski lifts and cable cars, the first of which was opened at St. Moritz in 1935.

Unfortunately, this exhilarating and deservedly popular sport carries a high accident rate. The Swiss Accident Insurance Advisory Board reports that Switzerland's ski slopes are now as dangerous as its roads. People using the slopes at Sun Valley, Idaho, can on the average expect one injury for every 137 days' skiing. The risk is so high that some American firms now forbid their key employees to ski, while the United States Public Health Service, in an endeavor to reduce the absenteeism caused by skiing injuries, has found it advisable to support research into the cause of skiing accidents.

Experience shows that a large proportion of these injuries could be prevented if skiers observed the following simple safety-first rules.

Get fit first. Skiing is a strenuous exercise that demands a higher degree of strength, flexibility, and balance than the average sedentary worker possesses. Because of this, expert skier and novice alike should take a six-weeks conditioning course before their winter sporting seasons start. During this time they should carry out a program of pre-ski exercises for at least fifteen minutes every day. To this should be added jogging, hopping on alternate legs, running in place, and skipping. While getting fit, elevators and escalators should be shunned, and flights of stairs tackled at a steady trot, ascending two or three stairs at a time.

Members of the Westchester (New York) Ski Club averaged five thousand skiing days a year for eleven years. During this time they carried out pre-ski conditioning exercises and suffered only two minor strains. After inadvisably abandoning their pre-ski exercise program, they suffered three fractures within the next season. As a doctor commenting on this report said, "Strength and flexibility of the skier play the largest part in avoiding injuries by making fatigue less likely and by improving the ability of the skier to meet inevitable spills."

Increase your skill. Experienced skiers receive fewer injuries than beginners because they are fitter, have better judgment, and possess the skill to cope safely with difficult ski conditions. In the course of a thousand days, skiing novices can expect to suffer 16 accidents, intermediate skiers 4, and experts 3. A five-year study of skiing injuries at Sun Valley, Idaho, also showed the value of expert teaching; 676 injuries were recorded among independent skiers, but only 320 among a similar-sized group which had received instruction from a ski school.

Use properly adjusted safety bindings. The skier traveling fast develops considerable momentum. If his or her ski tip gets caught, the ski acts as a lever and applies a rotational strain to the ankle that is equivalent to the momentum multiplied by the length of the ski from boot to tip. Similarly, if a 150-pound man is skiing downhill at 30 miles per hour and enters deep snow, he may be brought to a stop within a distance of two feet. This means that a braking force of 2,250 pounds is applied to his body. In the past, these sudden strains easily led to injury, but the risk has been reduced by the introduction of safety bindings, which release the foot when the leg is subjected to strong forward or rotational strains. A study of over sixty thousand German skiers showed that safety bindings reduce the risk of fracture by as much as twenty times. To be effective, they must be properly adjusted, particularly to suit the weight of the individual skier. A binding that is too tight provides no protection; a binding that is too loose may free the ski prematurely and so cause the very accident it is designed to prevent.

Women in the past have derived little benefit from wearing safety bindings because their lighter frames often fail to activate the release mechanism. The Ski Club of Great Britain's Accident Prevention Group tested eighteen of the most popular safety bindings and found that only one (the unfashionable American Cubco) would release a woman safely at its lowest setting. (Of the remainder, fourteen had minimum settings which were too high even for men.) This may help explain why women skiers suffer nearly twice as many accidents as men.

Warm up before skiing. An athlete always "warms up" before an event, but skiers often travel up an exposed ski lift and then stand still in the cold for several minutes before making their descents. This invites muscle injury. Skiers should avoid the lifts for the first few runs of the day, which should be taken on the nursery slopes. Later on, when using the lifts, they should make a point of climbing an extra few yards of the slope on foot, just to make sure their muscles are properly tuned up for the downhill run.

Never ski when tired. Most accidents to skiers happen when they are tired, either at the end of the morning, or more particularly, at the end of the day. A check at ski resorts in the Berkshires in Massachusetts showed that 90 percent of all injuries occurred after 3:00 P.M. In Switzerland, it has been found that the dangerous times for skiing vacationers are on their third and final days–the last day because when they are taking too many risks and the third day because they tend to be overcome with fatigue. Skiers should always quit the slopes when they're feeling fit enough for another run. Accidents occur to skiers fitting in "just one more" descent when muscles are tired and the slopes growing increasingly icy.

Avoid overcrowded slopes. Because many serious injuries are caused by collisions, it pays to avoid overcrowded slopes. Accidents would also be reduced if every skier adopted the "Skiway Code" offered by the Ski Club of Great Britain, which suggests, "Never run out of control. Don't stand on the piste to rest; move to the side. If you fall, get out of the way quickly. Look behind you before restarting after a rest or fall."

As one doctor commented after reviewing the causes of injuries sustained at several popular American ski centers, "Judgment and courtesy are just as necessary in preventing skiing accidents as they are in preventing traffic accidents."

If these simple precautionary measures were taken, it is probable that skiing accidents would be reduced by 60-70 percent.

Sleeping

Asklepios was a highly successful physician in ancient Greece. When he died he was raised to the status of a god and worshiped in hundreds of temples throughout the Hellenic world.

An integral part of the cult of Asklepios was the practice of incubation, or temple sleep. Patients suffering from a wide variety of disorders visited the temples and, after taking a ritual bath to purify their bodies, lay down to sleep in long, open-air corridors. They were led to believe that the god would visit them during their sleep and advise them on their cure. The custom, suitably modified, persisted into the Christian era, the sleeping pilgrims now expecting to receive advice from one of the Christian saints rather than the pagan god. The preliminary ritual cleansing of the body was also reduced from total immersion to a mere sprinkling with holy water. Temple sleep is still practiced in certain Mediterranean areas, and each year many miracles are reported from the sacred island of Tenos, where the sick are permitted to sleep in the temple during the island's two special religious festivals.

Sleep cures of a different kind, without any suggestion of faith-healing, are practiced now in many medical centers throughout the world, generally in the treatment of nervous disorders.

At Montreal's Allan Memorial Hospital, mentally sick patients who have failed to respond to other forms of therapy have been put to sleep with sedatives for several days, being wakened only for food, drink, and essential toilet requirements. The hospital reports that 57 percent of these chronically sick patients have shown either marked or moderate improvement. At London's Charing Cross Hospital, doctors have used deep sleep treatment to help coronary patients over the critical days following their attack, believing that this lessens the inevitable fear and mental shock. They report only one death in their first fifty-nine cases, and that from a peptic ulcer rather than a second heart attack. In Russia prolonged sleep, induced by applying a low pulsating electric current to the skull, has been successfully used in the treatment of asthma, ulcerative colitis, and various chronic skin disorders. In Israel the same treatment has been used to cure cases of depression, insomnia, and anxiety states. One computer executive suffering from acute anxiety was given electrosleep treatment for one hour every afternoon for twenty days, and at the end of this time was able to dispense completely with his heavy dosage of sleeping pills and daytime sedatives.

The basis of all these cures lies in the restorative powers of sleep, described by Shakespeare as "the balm of hurt minds." People deprived of sleep soon show signs of mental malaise. One scientist, as an experiment, gradually reduced his sleep from seven hours a day to four and quickly became irritable, sarcastic and, according to his wife, "quite unlike his normal self." After two full nights' sleep he regained his normal cheerful disposition, so much so that colleagues commented on the remarkable personality change. More severe forms of sleep deprivation are used in the brainwashing of political prisoners. One prisoner relates how he was prevented from sleeping by day and awakened every fifteen minutes at night by flashing lights, shrill whistles, and heavy banging on his cell door. At the end of ten days he collapsed with shivering fits and severe hallucinations. But the loss of sleep need not be as severe as this to affect our health. At the University of Florida Sleep Laboratory, a team of psychologists and psychiatrists subjected sleeping volunteers to gentle electric shocks that were regulated so that the level of their sleep was lightened without actually waking them up. With this mild level of sleep disturbance, the subjects complained of depression, apathy, and general malaise within a few days. As an Ohio psychiatrist has suggested, "Lack of sleep–perhaps chronic or accumulated sleep loss–may be the villain of some functional psychiatric disorders." He blames the introduction of inexpensive electric lighting, which has turned night into day. Others would add to this the attraction of late-night television. Many people stay up late purely out of habit. Parents wanting a little time to themselves are forced to stay up after their children have gone to bed. Commuters find that if they retire early, their lives become a ceaseless round of working, traveling, and sleeping with no leisure time between.

More and more commonly, people induce sleep with pills; yet sleeping pills are a poor remedy for mere insomnia. Their use leads to dependence. And they are not without side effects, the chief of which is a drowsiness that may linger well into the following morning. Research has shown that they also decrease the amount of time spent dreaming, and dreaming serves a psychologically useful function.

We need to get enough sleep so that we wake spontaneously in the morning feeling refreshed and eager to start the day's activities. The only practical way to discover whether we are having adequate sleep is to get a little more and see what happens.

A study of a group of Canadians over the age of sixty showed that subjects who got less than seven hours' sleep a night were more prone to suffer from anxiety, tension, and fatigue than those who normally sleep longer. For a month these sleep cheats were encouraged to sleep an extra two hours a night. At the end of this time, they all felt better, their complaints of tension, fatigue, and anxiety lessened, and they discovered that with more sleep to sustain them, they were better able to cope with extra effort and stress.

Smoking

Smoking is an expensive way of ruining your health. Future historians, seeking to understand our age and its prevailing habits, will no doubt be at a loss to explain why the people of the twentieth century should knowingly contribute to their own destruction. In the past, many attempts have been made to curb the spread of this pernicious habit. At one time Russians caught in the act of smoking were flogged and castrated; Persians had their mouths filled with boiling oil and Turks were sentenced to death. Today, there are no legal sanctions against the consumption of tobacco, but the punishments continue, administered now by smokers themselves who masochistically flog their lungs and fill their mouths with burning tar while cheerfully ignoring the sentence of death constantly hovering over their heads.

Most smokers choose to ignore the medical risks. Few would enter a plane if they knew it had a one-in-eight chance of crashing, yet they blissfully smoke a pack or more of cigarettes a day even though they know that in doing this they run a similar chance of contracting cancer of the lung. Why? What reasons can there be for persisting in so dangerous a habit?

When quizzed, smokers generally excuse themselves on five main grounds: "It's too late to stop"; "I know people who've smoked heavily for years without suffering"; "You've got to have one vice"; "I'm afraid I'll put on weight"; "I haven't the will power to stop." None of these arguments bears close examination. In the first place, it is never too late to stop smoking. The risk of contracting lung cancer falls the moment you stop smoking;

it is halved at the end of the first year and thereafter is progressively reduced until it becomes practically as low as it is for lifelong nonsmokers. Second, it is true that some heavy smokers do not contract lung cancer, but it is equally true some people fall out of fifth-floor apartment windows and live to tell the tale, and this is hardly justification for taking a similar risk. If "you've got to have one vice," why choose one that ruins your health and shortens your life? Smoking is not the harmless peccadillo these apologists suggest.

Nor is it a purely personal vice. People who smoke in public places endanger the health of those around them. Dr. Donald A. Dukelow, of the American Medical Association's department of education, estimates that a nonsmoker in a smoke-filled room inhales as many harmful tobacco by-products as a smoker consuming four or five cigarettes. So smokers cannot shelter behind the plea "I'm only harming myself."

It is true that giving up cigarettes may present a weight problem, but this should be purely temporary; it affects only certain people and is normally limited to a gain of a few pounds, which will be rapidly burnt up with the surge of energy that should follow giving up smoking. The people who claim they haven't the will power to stop smoking should gain encouragement from the many who have. The British Medical Association estimated recently that since the appearance of the first reports linking smoking with lung cancer, 30 million people in the world have stopped smoking. If they can do it, so can you. It's not easy, but then the things that are really worth achieving rarely are. The first thing to do is determine, without any equivocation, whether you really want to quit. Success depends on the strength of your motivation. If you sincerely want to break the habit, you can. If you have any lingering doubts, you'll almost certainly be one of the backsliders who try half-heartedly to give up but time and time again slip back into the old familiar routine.

How to stop smoking. There are two basic methods of giving up smoking: by making an abrupt halt or by gradual withdrawal. Of these the sudden break is the quicker, surer, and more certain of producing permanent results. The smokers who gradually wean themselves of cigarettes are liable to think, "One more won't make any difference," so they take just one more cigarette and then another until all the bad old habits are resumed. The only sensible way to give up smoking is to make a sharp, clean break. Choose a day in the future when you're not likely to be under stress and fix this clearly in your mind as D-day, your day of liberation from enslavement to the tyrant nicotine. (The first day of a week's holiday makes an admirable starting point.) From this fixed point, count back four weeks. This marks the month of intensive preparation that you may need to equip you for the battle ahead. Devote the first of these weeks to learning all you can about smoking. Read about it. Study the section in this book on *Will Power.* Talk to friends and colleagues who've stopped smoking. Learn from their experience. Don't try to frighten yourself with the thought of what *might* happen if you carry on smoking. Take a more positive line and list the things which undoubtedly *will* happen when you give up smoking. This, in brief, is what you stand to gain:

Your breathing will improve. Every week you're free of cigarettes you will cough less and breathe more freely. It is estimated that 90 percent of lost lung function is regained nine months after quitting smoking.

Your senses of taste and smell will return. Journalist Stewart Alsop found this one of the greatest rewards for giving up cigarettes. "I took a walk in the country about two weeks after I'd stopped smoking," he wrote, "and found myself smelling the countryside again as I hadn't done for years . . . All sorts of subtle flavors, long forgotten, became apparent in the most familiar dishes."

You'll feel fitter. Experience at special antismoking clinics in Sweden shows that habitual smokers can expect a

20 percent improvement in their general physical condition after a month's abstention from cigarettes.

Your resistance to infection will increase. Smoking reduces the vitality of the blood's phagocyte cells (the scavenger cells that help combat infection) and impairs the efficiency of the body's antibody system (the mechanism responsible for maintaining immunity to specific disorders). This makes the heavy smoker more prone to infectious disease. Experiments with animals show that this lowered resistance is 80 percent back to normal within four months of giving up smoking.

You'll look younger. Smoking makes the skin increasingly dry, dull, yellow, and blotchy. One survey in America showed that middle-aged smokers have facial lines and wrinkles similar to those of nonsmokers twenty years older. Stopping smoking helps to prevent this premature aging of the skin.

Your sex life will improve. The tobacco companies in their advertising campaigns suggest that smoking increases vigor, potency, and sex appeal. In fact, it does the reverse. Catarrh, bad breath, stained fingers, and a hacking cough are hardly attractive, and far from improving potency, smoking tends to lower a man's fertility by reducing the mobility of his sperm. Dr. Carl Schirren, a professor at the University of Hamburg, recommends that "in every case of reduced male fertility, smoking should cease completely if children are desired." Many people attending antismoking clinics have reported that their enjoyment of sex has increased since they gave up smoking. This is probably due to an increase in the output of the male hormone testosterone. As Dr. Alton Ochsner, one of the pioneer researchers in the field, remarks, "The ironic thing is that many men don't recognize that they have a libido problem until after they stop smoking and then they realize what they've been missing."

You'll feel less tense. Many people believe that smoking helps them relax. If this were so, heavy smokers would be as limp as rag dolls, whereas more often they are tense and jittery, with an often perceptible tremor of the hands. This is because the chemical effect of nicotine mimics in some ways the the action of the stress hormone adrenaline, making the pulse race and increasing the body's neuromuscular excitability. Without regular shots of nicotine to excite him, a smoker becomes calm and often enjoys a sounder night's sleep.

You'll gain in self-esteem. It is degrading to live with a habit you can't control. As Stewart Alsop put it, "There is something deeply humiliating in being wholly dependent on cigarettes. It is humiliating to have to drop all work and venture out into a snowstorm to get cigarettes . . . humiliating to have to beg a cigarette from a passing stranger like a whining mendicant . . . humiliating to feel the fear which a compulsive smoker feels, at the mere idea of living without tobacco." Quitting the habit will enable you to become master of your life once more.

You'll help your children live a longer, healthier life. Smoking in Britain is twice as common among children whose parents smoke as it is among those whose parents abstain. So by setting a good example you are more likely to produce nonsmoking children and to live long enough to see them marry and to enjoy the company of their healthy offspring. Dr. Harvey Flack, editor of *Family Doctor,* feels that setting a good example to children is the most important reason for giving up smoking. "If we could stop our children smoking until they are 21," he says, "we would save one million lives by the end of the century."

You'll save money. In addition to the immediate economy of not having to buy packets of cigarettes, nonsmokers can enjoy other cash savings. Some auto insurance companies offer reductions of up to 20 percent in the premiums of nonsmokers, since they find that drivers who smoke have twice as many accidents as those who abstain. Some life insurance companies offer a discount for nonsmokers, knowing that they are better life insurance risks, and several companies have introduced bonuses for employees who sign a no-smoking pledge on the grounds that they have less absenteeism from sickness and put in an extra half hour's work a day through not having to buy, borrow, and smoke cigarettes.

Make a list of the benefits you personally will gain from giving up smoking, keep it prominently displayed, and read it through whenever you feel the temptation to smoke.

Then try and analyze why you smoke. At the start of your four-week preparation for D-day, make a point of jotting down on a slip of paper details of every cigarette you smoke. Do you smoke mainly in company? Do you like to have a cigarette with meals and cups of coffee? Is the early-morning cigarette particularly important? Do you smoke most when you're under tension or when you're feeling socially ill at ease? Keep detailed notes for at least a week, and you will gain a better understanding of your own particular habit pattern and as a result will find it easier to break the habit when D-day arrives. (The inconvenience and embarrassment of having to keep this detailed inventory may well have the effect of making you reduce, before D-day, the number of cigarettes you smoke, which is all to the good.)

There are five main motivations for smoking:

1. *Stimulation:* Cigarettes are employed by some people to give them a boost when their energies flag. To curb this particular craving, try taking some form of brisk exercise whenever you feel the urge to smoke. Go for a brisk walk, do twenty half-knee bends, or run in place for thirty seconds. This provides the same stimulus as smoking with none of the attendant risks.
2. *Handling:* Many smokers derive great pleasure from the actual manual manipulation of a cigarette. They may find doodling with a pencil, or playing with worry beads, coins, or pieces of jewelry, useful substitutes. Toying with cigarettes is playing with fire.
3. *Pleasure:* Smoking is for many primarily a source of

self-indulgence. They may derive substitute satisfaction from chewing gum, eating nuts and raisins, or massaging their forehead and neck.

4. *Crutch:* A large number of smokers use a cigarette as a crutch to tide them over periods of stress or social discomfort. They may find the cultivation and use of techniques of relaxation a valuable substitute (see *Relaxation*).
5. *Habit:* Smoking is to a very large extent a self-perpetuating habit, and many smokers light up a cigarette automatically without realizing they are doing so. They should take steps to break the habit cycle by making themselves acutely aware of every cigarette they smoke (see below).

To get some idea how strong these various motivations are for you, complete the questionnaire below (a modified version of the questionnaire devised by Daniel Horn while working for the U.S. Department of Health, Education, and Welfare).

Answer the following questionnaire, giving yourself points according to your replies to each of the sixteen questions. Score five points if your answer is Always; four points for Frequently; three points for Occasionally; two points for Seldom; one point for Never.

A. I smoke cigarettes in order to keep myself from slowing down.
B. Handling a cigarette is part of the enjoyment of smoking.
C. Smoking cigarettes is pleasant and relaxing.
D. I light up a cigarette when I feel angry about something.
E. I smoke cigarettes automatically without even being aware of it.
F. I smoke cigarettes to stimulate myself, to perk myself up.
G. Part of the enjoyment of smoking comes from the steps I take to light up.
H. I find cigarettes pleasurable.

I. When I feel uncomfortable or upset about something, I light up a cigarette.
J. I light up a cigarette without realizing I still have one burning in the ashtray.
K. I smoke cigarettes to give myself a "lift."
L. When I smoke a cigarette, part of the enjoyment is watching the smoke as I exhale it.
M. I want a cigarette most when I am comfortable and relaxed.
N. When I feel "blue" or want to take my mind off cares and worries, I smoke a cigarette.
O. I've found a cigarette in my mouth and didn't remember putting it there.

The strength of the various factors motivating you to smoke is assessed as follows (scores of 7 or less are low; scores over 11 show strong motivation):

Stimulation:	Total the scores of A + F + K
Handling:	Total the scores of B + G + L
Pleasure:	Total the scores of C + H + M
Crutch:	Total the scores of D + I + N
Habit:	Total the scores of E + J + O

Smoking is a habit and not an addiction. There is a chemical craving that drives an addict to drink or to take heroin, but there is no similar addiction to nicotine. A person chain-smokes purely to repeat a long-established habit. There is something reassuring in the series of movements that is reenacted every time a cigarette is smoked: the removal of the cigarette from its packet, the gentle tamping of one end, the lighting of the match, the soft glow as the paper ignites, the aroma of the first puff, the casual flicking of the ash, and the final grinding of the butt in the ash tray. The sequence has an obsessional appeal that encourages its constant repetition. Once caught in its grip, the smoker becomes an automaton, programmed to repeat the same act over and over again. To break the habit, it is necessary to disturb this natural sequence of events. Dr. Henry Link realized this when he set out to stop smoking his ration of over sixty cigarettes a day. His plan was simple. "I shall contrive frequent interruptions, frictions, delays in the smooth-flowing chain of habitual action," he resolved. "I shall do this gradually to break down the mechanism I have spent years in perfecting." With this simple technique he managed to overcome a habit that he knew was ruining his health.

This is the plan to be followed during the remaining three weeks before D-day. Get a large calendar and clearly mark D-day, in large block letters. On each of the twenty-one preceding days, add an instruction that will help you break your established habit pattern. Suitable instructions are:

Today don't smoke before breakfast.
Today keep an elastic band round cigarette case or packet.
Today hold all cigarettes in the left hand (right for left-handed smokers).
Today no cigarettes after 9:00 P.M.
Today carry no lighters or matches.
Today smoke with the back of the hand facing the mouth.
Today change brand of cigarettes for one with a totally different flavor.
Today no cigarettes before lunch.
Today no cigarettes with drinks or meals.
Today hold all cigarettes between the third and fourth fingers.

Keep a careful record of the number of cigarettes you smoke each day, and you will probably find that during these three weeks you have succeeded in reducing your consumption of cigarettes as well as breaking (or at least bending) the smoking habit cycle. Both achievements will make it easier for you to stop completely when the time comes. During the three weeks, save the stub of every cigarette you've smoked and hoard them in a large ashtray. From time to time look at the revolting sight and sample the nauseating odor. The disgust you feel will help strengthen your determination to conquer the habit that has been mastering you.

As D-day draws nearer, step up the intensity of the campaign. Try to get a friend to give up smoking with you. Offer him or her the price of a packet of cigarettes for every day he gives up smoking, providing he or she does the same for you. Arrange to spend your winnings on a joint celebration at the end of the first month's abstention. Plan other rewards to spur you on. If you like a glass of wine, make a diary entry on the third day after D-day: "Reward: Bottle of Claret." Work out what you will save at the end of a fortnight and plan to spend that on a trip to the theater or other entertainment on Day 14. Try to arrange a series of simple rewards like these every two or three days after D-day. Mark them clearly in your diary and use them to lure you on.

With the advent of D-day, the battle proper begins. With most of the ground work done earlier, success should be assured. Don't acknowledge the possibility of failure. Every day you refrain from smoking, the burden becomes lighter. The following ploys may help you in your campaign.

1. *Use the De Gaulle opening.* Make a bold start to your campaign. Charles de Gaulle gave up smoking while President of France by walking into his office and announcing to his staff that he had given up cigarettes and they would never again see him smoking. Since he was a proud man, he could not turn back, having made this pronouncement.
2. *Permit no exceptions.* Smoking is a habit. If a habit is not repeatedly fed it quickly dies. Each time you say No makes it easier to say No next time. Just as one drink is too much for a onetime alcoholic, so is one cigarette for a reformed smoker.
3. *Don't rely on smoking "cures."* The desire for a cure shows that a smoker is not prepared to take full responsibility for quitting smoking through her or his own efforts. If the going gets tough, it is easy to shift the responsibility for failure onto the cure rather than on one's own weakness. Moreover, there is no evidence that smoking cures offer any more than purely

psychological aid. As the American Medical Association's committee on drugs has stated, "No substance intended to deter smoking has proved to be more effective than a placebo."

4. *Pamper yourself.* Smoking is largely a form of self-indulgence, so during the withdrawal stage provide substitute oral satisfaction by chewing gum, sucking licorice drops, or sampling small pieces of ginger root, cinnamon, or cloves whenever you feel the urge to smoke.
5. *Keep your mouth fresh.* Freshen your mouth at frequent intervals during the day by drinking fruit juice, brushing the teeth, or gargling with any suitable mouthwash.
6. *Avoid provocative situations.* If you normally smoke in the train on the way to work, choose nonsmoking compartments. If your first action on waking up in the morning is to light a cigarette, get out of bed the moment the alarm rings. If you usually have a cigarette after meals with your coffee, cut out the cup of coffee. Don't invite temptation.
7. *Try deep breathing.* The people who smoke primarily to relieve tension derive help from the sedative effect of the steady deep inhalations they make. This benefit can be obtained without cigarettes (see *Breathing*). Dr. Donald Fredrickson, director of the New York City Health Department Smoking Withdrawal Clinics, advises tension smokers to imitate the action of smoking whenever they feel the urge to smoke—to take a series of deep breaths, each followed by a slow emptying of the lungs. This helps to steady the nerves and suppress the desire to smoke.
8. *Take brisk exercise.* If you smoke to obtain stimulation, make a point of taking some form of brisk exercise whenever you feel the need to smoke.
9. *Hold a nightly review of the battle.* Each night carry out a survey of the day's battle. Compliment yourself on your success so far. Analyze your weaknesses. When did temptation nearly get the better of you? How could your defenses be improved? As you relax, em-

ploy the techniques of autosuggestion (see *Will Power*). Remind yourself of the rewards to be gained from stopping smoking. Try to feel the benefits you're already experiencing. Say to yourself as you fall asleep, "Day by day I'm losing the urge to smoke. My health is being renewed. The battle is being won." Don't make the mistake of looking too far ahead. Set yourself the target of not smoking for just the day ahead. That is a resonable goal. As each day without smoking makes it easier to refrain the following day, the days will flow gradually into weeks and months until eventually the insidious habit is broken.

Sneezing

Sneezing is a reflex action initiated when the lining membranes of the nose are irritated. A sneeze clears the nasal passages of all irritating particles by blasting them through with a stream of air. The velocity of the air stream is high during sneezing, and particles are propelled a distance of several feet from the nose. The same applies to a cough, which is a reflex action designed to clear the throat and bronchial tubes. Dr. George Trimble, writing in the *Journal of the American Medical Association,* reports that the airstream velocity of a full-blooded American cough is 760 miles per hour, whereas the more genteel British cough generates speeds of only 200 miles per hour.

Coughing and sneezing serve the vital function of keeping the airways clear, but unfortunately they also spread disease. Even the gentle act of quiet talking distributes a spray of germs two or more feet from the mouth. This contributes to a spread of disease known as droplet infection which is the most important method of disseminating diseases such as measles, whooping cough, mumps, influenza, and the common cold. Bacteria and viruses, although they are heavier than air, may be kept afloat for hours by gentle currents of air. If a passenger in a subway train sneezes openly while suffering from a heavy cold, a spray of germ-laden droplets will travel throughout the entire compartment, spreading the infection to every fellow passenger. This can be avoided by covering the nose and mouth with the palm of the hand or, preferably, a handkerchief. Children from an early age should be taught the slogan "Coughs and sneezes spread diseases, cover your face with a handkerchief."

Despite the risk of droplet infection, it is a mistake to try to block a sneeze, for this, according to Dr. David Mezz of New York, can lead to nose-bleeding, ringing in the ears, and sinus trouble. He recommends an open mouth and a natural sneeze—plus a handkerchief.

Similar principles should apply to the act of nose-blowing. This should never be performed with both nostrils closed, since such action entails a build-up of pressure within the nose that may drive infected material into the sinuses. When blowing the nose, the nostrils should always be cleared one at a time.

Soap

Regular washing of the body is accepted now as an essential part of personal hygiene, but this was not always so. At one time, there were religious objections to any form of personal grooming or ablution. Some of the early Christian saints abstained from washing throughout their entire lives, in the belief that dirtiness was one of the insignia of holiness.

Throughout the Middle Ages and well into the nineteenth century, Europe was divided into two social groups: the great unwashed working class, which was expected to reek of the sweat of its daily labors, and the nobility, who washed no more than the proletariat but took pains to conceal the fact by drenching their skins with perfume and draping their bodies with highly scented sachets, fragrant nosegays, and sweet-smelling boutonnières. Whereas the Roman nobleman had taken at least one bath a day, Queen Elizabeth I of England set an example to her subjects by taking one bath a month "whether she need it or no." Now the daily bath is a commonplace.

The hygienic function of bathing is to cleanse the skin of its accumulation of dead skin cells, sebum, and sweat. If allowed to remain, this débris blocks the pores and provides an ideal breeding ground for germs. Since this dirt is bound together on the skin by grease, it is not removed by washing with water alone. Hence the need for soap, which lifts away the dirt by emulsifying the fats and dissolving the surface grease.

Soaps are made by treating fats with caustic soda. Pliny records that the Romans made soap by boiling goat's tallow with causticized wood ash. Today soaps are made from tallow, whale oil, coconut oil, palm oil, corn oil, olive oil, and cottonseed oil. Generally a blend of oils is used to derive a soap with the required properties of lathering and hardness, and to this basic product is added a wide range of coloring agents and perfumes. The choice of a brand of soap is largely a matter of personal preference. Even the cheapest soap cleanses the skin adequately, but some can prove too harsh.

The skin is normally mildly acid in its reaction, which helps suppress the growth of surface bacteria. Soaps, which are strongly alkaline, tend to remove this natural protective "acid mantle." Fortunately this effect is too short-lived to harm the majority of individuals. People with particularly sensitive skins, however, or those prone to spots and pimples, may benefit by using one or other of the "neutral" soaps, which are formulated so that they are only very mildly alkaline in their reaction.

Another disadvantage of soap is that, as a detergent, it removes not only grease and grime but also some of the natural fats, secreted by the sebaceous glands that prevent the skin from drying out. Samia Gamal, the late King Farouk's favorite belly dancer, traveled to America after marrying a Texas playboy and quickly found fault with the dry skin of the average American woman. "They wash too much and use too much soap," she said. "I take a bath twice a week and other days I sponge myself with olive oil." Dermatologists believe that the skin is unlikely to be harmed by daily bathing with soap and water, but people with excessively dry skin may find it helpful to use one of the "superfatty" soaps, which include free fats such as lanolin and cold cream to replace the lost skin oils and so seal the skin from excessive moisture loss. In addition, they could do worse than to follow the example of Samia Gamal and occasionally massage the body from top to toe with a body oil. (A lotion made up of one part of glycerine to five parts rosewater serves excellently for this purpose.)

A further problem arises when soap is used together with hard water. It is common knowledge that soap lathers best in soft water. This is because hard water contains lime and will not form a lather until all the lime is converted into an insoluble lime soap. This explains the curdlike suspension that arises when soap is mixed with hard water. It is also the reason for the greasy sludge left around the rim of the bath. To avoid leaving a similar irritating scum on the body, it is necessary to rinse the skin thoroughly with plain warm water after bathing. This practice is frequently neglected and leads to much needless irritation of the skin. It is a particularly important habit for people suffering from blocked pores, pimples, and acne, who may benefit, if they live in hard-water areas, by using a water-softener or washing in rainwater.

All soaps have a mild germicidal action. In some the germ-killing action is strengthened by the inclusion of such substances as phenol and hexachlorophene. These specially medicated soaps should be used only on medical recommendation. Recent tests have shown that hexachlorophene can cause skin irritation and brain damage, with greatest risk for infants and young children. (When baby monkeys were bathed daily for ninety days with a soap containing 3 percent hexachlorophene, all developed brain lesions.) To replace these medicated cleansers, the American Academy of Pediatrics has recommended a substitute that keeps a baby just as clean as hexachlorophene: plain soap and water.

Spring Fever

Dictionaries describe spring fever as the listlessness that overtakes some people at the onset of the first warm days of spring. The subject receives no mention in medical textbooks, but it is thought that the sudden increase in environmental temperature at this time of the year causes a dilation of the vast network of blood vessels in the skin, which requires a corresponding increase in the volume of circulating blood. To begin with, this increase in volume can be achieved only be drawing fluid from elsewhere in the body, which means that until fresh blood corpuscles can be found, there is a temporary decrease in the concentration of red blood cells. Since these cells are responsible for carrying oxygen through the body, there may be some substance in the old belief that springtime fatigue is due to a "thinning" of the blood.

Springtime also signals other changes. It appears to stimulate the nesting urge in many housewives, who take it as a sign to embark on a round of spring cleaning and general house improvements. Market reports show that the sales of paints and household cleaners rise 20 percent in the Spring.

The increased exposure to light that occurs with gradually lengthening days also appears to increase the sexual activity of many animals. Most birds normally breed only in the spring, although a number can be made to produce a second batch of eggs in the winter if they are exposed to repeated doses of artificial light. In the same way, sheep that have lambed in the Northern Hemisphere can be made to breed again if they are taken to latitudes south of the equator. Human sexual activity, on the other hand, appears to be stronger in the autumn than in the spring. When public health authorities in New York made a seven-year survey of over 1.25 million births, they discovered that most babies are conceived in the autumn. Contrary to popular belief, they found spring the slackest time of the year for conceptions; this discovery suggests that it is in the autumn rather than the spring that a young man's fancy is most likely to turn to thoughts of love.

In recent times spring has proved a popular time of the year for weddings; yet there is evidence that spring romances may tend to be less successful than those that blossom at other times of the year. A German psychologist recently conducted a survey of one thousand married couples and found that the majority of them (53 percent) met and fell in love in the autumn. "Thoughts of a cold grey winter ahead make people feel the need for warmth, affection and love," he claimed. Similar evidence came from a short survey of divorced couples, which showed that the majority (62 percent) of divorces stem from "spring romances."

Stings

People's reactions to bee and wasp stings vary enormously. Some beekeepers become increasingly immune and show little or no reaction to repeated stings. Others, thought to number 2 percent of the population, show an allergic reaction and after being stung feel faint, sick, and dizzy, and may even collapse and die if left untreated. Hypersensitive reactions like these require immediate medical attention, as do stings at the back of the mouth, which can cause choking. The remainder respond to simple first-aid measures.

The first step is to remove the stinger if it has been left behind, which is frequently the case with bee stings. This is best done by placing the blade of a knife flat against the skin and drawing it slowly toward the wound, applying pressure without cutting into the skin, so that the sting is lifted out complete with barbs and poison sacs. It is a mistake to try to pull the sting out with the fingers or a pair of tweezers, as many contemporary first-aid manuals suggest, for this carries the risk of squeezing more poison into the wound.

Then comes the hoary question of "neutralizing" the sting. It used to be thought that bee stings were acid and wasps stings alkali. The recommended treatment was to neutralize a bee sting with mild alkali like bicarbonate of soda or ammonia and a wasp sting with a mild acid like vinegar. It is now known that both bee and wasp stings are a complex mixture of acids and alkalis, so there is little point in trying to "neutralize" their stings. As the Reverend Charles Butler wrote in 1609 in one of the earliest books about bees, *The Feminine Monarchie*, "No antidote can follow after a sting." All we can do is to provide a degree of palliation, to lessen the swelling and allay some of the irritation. The best way of reducing swelling is to apply cold water to the sting, and the most effective way of lessening the irritation is to smoothe in a little antihistamine cream.

In the case of wasp stings, it can be helpful to apply a mild antiseptic, for while bee stings are generally sterile, wasp stings are not. The wasp is a carnivorous creature and gets her feet into all kinds of putrefying rubbish while feeding; and it is a case of "her" feet because the male wasp does not carry a sting. It is the old story—and a true one, in this case—of the female of the species being deadlier than the male.

Stress

The stress of modern life comes in for more blame than it rightly deserves. It is frequently cited as a cause of nervous breakdown, strokes, heart attacks, and peptic ulcers. But how many appreciate its positive aspects?

To begin with, a life without stress would be unbearably dull. We need the stimulus of occasional anxiety and fear to keep us alert. Psychiatrists in Northern Ireland have noted that there is a decrease in the rate of admission to psychiatric hospitals in areas affected by violent civil disturbance. In times of communal stress there are fewer suicides and less depressive illness, probably because exposure to danger stimulates the adrenal glands to secrete stress hormones like adrenaline, noradrenaline, and cortisone, which act as powerful pep-pills. Boredom is the root cause of much mental illness, and many people leading drab, uneventful lives seek out the stimulus of risk-taking activities like gambling, skiing, and motor racing to avoid suffering ennui.

Laboratory experiments have shown that rats subjected to repeated stress live longer than those protected from stress. This is probably because repeated exposure to intermittent stress stimulates the adrenal glands and keeps the body's hormonal defense mechanisms working at peak efficiency, in the same way that exposure to infection stimulates the body's immunity responses.

It is interesting in this light to note that Presidents of the United States, unless they meet unnatural deaths, live longer on the average than Vice Presidents and longer still than unsuccessful candidates for the Presidency. Similarly, in industry it is found that people who get to the top live longer on average than those who face the daily frustration encountered lower down the promotion ladder. A survey taken at the Bell Telephone Company showed that workers on the shop floor had twice as many heart attacks as the company's top executives. This is because the harmful effects of stress lie more in its quality than in its overall intensity.

An animal's normal response to stress is to prepare the body for "fight or flight." The muscles are tensed, the pulse is quickened, the blood pressure is raised, and the bloodstream is flooded with sugar and fatty acids, which are the basic fuels for muscular activity. In our primeval past, when the most likely source of stress was the approach of a saber-toothed tiger, these changes had some point. We needed then to take some immediate action, to stand our ground and fight, or take to our heels and run. But these responses are largely inappropriate today. We get annoyed with a pettifogging boss and show a general alarm reaction, but we don't punch him or her in the nose or run screaming in terror from the office. So our muscle tension remains, and we get a stiff neck and visit a health club for a sauna bath and massage. The boss has literally become a pain in the neck. In time our blood pressure may become permanently elevated, so we start taking hypotensive drugs, and we become candidates for the Coronary Club if excess fats coursing round the body become deposited in the blood-vessel walls, causing a dangerous narrowing of the coronary arteries.

This is the harmful aspect of stress, which comes when stress is unrelieved and unaccompanied by appropriate physical activity. Some of the danger would be averted if after exposure to stress we took some form of vigorous physical activity to work off the unwanted muscle tensions and burn up the superfluous sugars and fats circulating in the bloodstream. The ideal antistress activities are swimming, jogging, brisk walking, and cycling. Lifting the lid off the emotional pressure-cooker and letting off steam by swearing, shouting, or stamping the feet is an alternative way of coping with unrelieved tension.

Another important precautionary measure is to intersperse periods of stress with regular periods of relaxation (see *Holidays*). Even an hour or two's repose a day is sufficient to counteract the harmful effects of otherwise unrelieved stress (see *Meditation*).

As an experiment, two psychologists at Cornell University subjected sheep to repeated stress. They made them apprehensive by ringing a bell and then subjecting them to a mild electric shock. In time this produced signs of mental malaise. The sheep lost interest in their food, stopped following the rest of the flock, and eventually lay down listlessly on the grass. But it was found that these symptoms of functional disturbance failed to develop if the sheep were given relief from stress for a minimum of two hours every day. Exercise, then, is the perfect antidote for stress, regular relaxation the ideal prophylactic.

Sunbathing

As an old English proverb affirms, "The sun is the best physician, but the most difficult to make an appointment with." It plays a part in the production of Vitamin D, sometimes called the "sunshine" vitamin because it can be formed by the action of ultraviolet light on the skin. This vitamin is intimately involved in the formation of bone and the utilization of calcium within the body. Deficiencies in children can give rise to rickets, a disease characterized by deformities of the growing bones that was once extremely common in the almost sunless, polluted cities of northern Europe. Deficiencies in adults can lead to a painful softening of the bones called osteomalacia. In Britain, the Medical Research Council studied a group of over a hundred pensioners admitted to a hospital in Harrow, Middlesex, and found that while many elderly patients entering hospital were existing on diets deficient in Vitamin D, only those who rarely went out in the sun developed a weakening of the bone structure. The Council concluded, "Too little attention has been given to the role of sunlight in osteomalacia." Regular exposure to sunlight in childhood aids the development of the bones; in adulthood it helps maintain their health and strength.

Sunlight also helps protect the skin. Niels Finsen, the Danish doctor who developed the first ultraviolet lamp, showed as early as 1893 that natural sunlight helped eradicate certain chronic skin complaints. Even today, exposure of the body to liberal doses of sun and air is accepted as one of the finest treatments for psoriasis. Doctors working at the Copenhagen Kommune Hospital report that 93 percent of Danes suffering from psoriasis lose their unsightly psoriatic patches after spending a sunshine holiday by the Dead Sea.

Sunlight also helps to kill some of the numerous germs that linger on the skin and that can cause pimples, spots, boils, and that plague of teenagers, acne. It is, in the words of one doctor, "incomparably the best, cheapest, most natural and universal antiseptic of all." It must also rank as one of the finest skin care products, for sunbathing, in addition to cleansing the surface of the body, also stimulates the circulation to the skin and speeds up the sloughing off of dead skin cells, which might otherwise accumulate and block the pores.

The bactericidal action of ultraviolet light has also been employed clinically to kill bacteria suspended in the air in aerosol dispersions. Experiments in schools show that children have fewer coughs and colds, and less need to visit a doctor, when the air in their classrooms is treated by artificial sunlight. This confirms the old Italian proverb, "Where the sun enters, the doctor never comes."

Experiments suggest that exposure to sunlight stimulates metabolism and increases the number of white blood cells circulating in the blood, but its beneficial effects probably extend much further than this. It is an all-around tonic which, in the words of one doctor, induces an "I-don't-know-what's-the-matter-with-me-I-feel-so-grand" feeling that defies close analysis.

Sunbathing became a health cult in Europe soon after the end of the 1914–1918 war. Niels Finsen had shown the value of heliotherapy in the treatment of chronic skin complaints. In 1910 Dr. A. Rollier opened his famous "School in the Sun" in the Vaudois Alps, where ailing children received their schooling stripped to the waist in the open air. Sunlight helped dramatically to restore their health and foster their rate of growth. Later he built a sanatorium where he demonstrated that sunlight aids the recovery of children suffering from tuberculosis of the bones and joints in a way that was often little short of miraculous. Then in 1915 Sir Edward Mellanby discovered that rickets is a deficiency disease that can be prevented by exposure to natural or artificial sunlight. These exciting medical discoveries, combined with a general naturist revival, started the great crusade. Everywhere bodies were bared to the sun. Actinotherapy clinics were opened in all major industrial centers so that sick city children could receive the healing rays. Solariums were built at pit heads so that sun-starved miners could get their daily share of ultraviolet light. Schoolchildren took their classes in the open air. Nudist clubs were opened. Shipping lines cashed in on the craze by offering special sunshine cruises. The Riviera coast of France, which had previously been purely a winter resort, now became a summer playground, a Mecca for sun-seekers. Open-neck shirts and shorts were the order of the day. Everywhere people basked in the sun.

Then the reaction set in. Reports hinted that excessive exposure to sunlight was harmful. Too much sun could lead to premature aging of the skin. Excessive irradiation could cause skin cancer, which was shown to be four times as common around the sunny Black Sea coast as along the Baltic Sea.

These risks undoubtedly exist, but they should not be exaggerated. The sun is far too valuable a medicine to waste but, like all other remedies, it needs to be taken with care. Skin cancers are rare even where conditions are favorable for their development, and the best prophylaxis against them is not total abstinence from sunbathing but moderation of exposure.

The body should always be exposed to the sun in carefully graduated stages, with extra care taken when sunbathing at high altitudes or close to water, sand, or snow, which will reflect the sun's rays. Before going into the sun, people with sensitive skins should take the precaution of acquiring a measure of tolerance by using an ultraviolet lamp, and they should always cover their bodies with a special protective cream, the best of which will filter off up to 90 percent of the burning rays.

If sunburn occurs despite these precautions, the finest treatment is to bathe the skin immediately in cold water for at least ten minutes. Applying a simple baby cream the following day helps allay irritation and protects the skin from excessive drying-out.

Sunbathing today is carried out less in the search for health than in the pursuance of vanity. At one time a dark skin was the sign of a peasant; a pale "peaches and cream" complexion, the mark of a lady of leisure. Now it is the urban worker who develops a pallor by spending most of the hours of daylight working in a factory or office. So people of leisure, to emphasize their difference, cultivate a tan. A bronzed skin is now a status symbol worn proudly by the well-to-do, who rest secure in the knowledge that only they can afford the time and money to winter in St. Moritz and summer in the Seychelles.

This bronzing of the skin is now so highly prized that the pharmaceutical industry offers a wide range of cosmetics guaranteed to give an instant, overnight tan. They offer tablets containing psoralens which, when taken by mouth, sensitize the skin to ultraviolet light and so hasten the natural tanning effect. But these drugs are unpredictable in their effect and can produce unfortunate side effects that render their use hazardous. An alternative range of products is provided by creams containing dihydroxyacetone, a drug that darkens the outer, horny layer of the skin almost literally overnight. Tests on animals and human volunteers have failed to reveal any adverse effect of using these creams. The British Consumers' Association, after testing the drug, concludes, "While it may be wise to wait for some evidence of the effects of long-term applications to human beings before using it for long periods, we believe that most people need to have no fear of occasional use for limited periods." But the value of these creams is purely psychological. They confer no health benefits, and as they do not reach or affect the pigment layer of the skin, do not convey any protection against sunburn.

The acquisition of a tan is purely a matter of vanity. The benefits of sunbathing can be obtained by gentle exposure of the body without the need for deep tanning, which merely indicates that the body has strengthened its defense against the harmful effects of excessive sunlight by increasing the density of its dark, pigment layer. This exposure must of course be done out of doors, for ultraviolet light cannot pass through ordinary window glass. Specially manufactured "Vita" glass is available in America (not in Britain for the last forty years) that permits the passage of a certain proportion of ultraviolet light, but even if buildings were completely glazed in "Vita" glass, the amount of ultraviolet light penetrating them would rarely equal the amount that can be obtained by spending a few minutes outdoors in the middle of the day. City-dwellers need to make a habit of doing this.

All living matter responds to the stimulus of the sun, but as the French historian Jules Michelet observed, "Of all the flowers it is the human flower that needs sunshine most."

Sunglasses

Before the development of optically satisfactory transparent glass, spectacle lenses were made from sections of quartz, beryl, and other semiprecious stones. Nero is said to have watched the persecution of Christian slaves through an emerald lens. Wearers of these early spectacles believed that their eyes benefited from being bathed in colored light. Today, tinted spectacles are again in vogue, being worn as fashion accessories and partly as veils to shield the oversensitive psyche and to conceal the telltale signs of late nights, old age, tears, bruises, and drug addiction. Only rarely are they medically required.

The normal eye is well adapted to stand bright light, being protected by a pigment layer, a pupil that automatically contracts in strong light, and a pair of eyelids that when closed prevent the passage of ultraviolet light. There is no need to wear sunglasses when basking in the sun if the eyes are closed, for this provides complete protection without producing those ugly, panda-like patches around the eyes.

The only nonmedical indication for wearing sunglasses is a situation in which the sun's rays are reflected strongly from water or snow, particularly at high altitudes. Under these conditions it is possible for the cornea to sustain a sunburn, a condition known as photophthalmia or snow blindness, which, while exceedingly painful, is easily cured and leaves no permanent disability. The damage that arises from looking directly at the sun can be more serious, for this can lead to a degree of permanent blindness ("eclipse blindness") by causing a retinal burn. If there is ever a need to look directly at the sun, as when watching an eclipse, it is essential to look through a glass heavily coated with soot or through several layers of overexposed photographic or X-ray film.

Apart from these exceptions, and a handful of medical conditions, there is no necessity to wear sunglasses. For children, the habit is potentially dangerous. "They do not need them," says the British Medical Association in one of its publications, "and they may interfere with the normal development of the eyes." In adults the constant wearing of colored lenses may lead to habituation. "The somewhat neurotic patient can easily become addicted to such lenses," writes one eye specialist, "and then finds great difficulty in being without them." People who show a true sensitivity to bright light should not resort to sunglasses without first consulting a doctor, for photophobia like this can be a sign of underlying pathology that requires proper medical diagnosis and treatment.

On the rare occasions when sunglasses are indicated, there is a choice of four basic lenses: absorptive, polarizing, coated, and photochromatic. Absorptive lenses are made by adding certain chemicals to the molten glass that selectively filter off infrared and ultraviolet rays while letting through most of the remainder of the visual spectrum. Polarizing lenses contain an "optical screen" that cuts out light reflected from horizontal surfaces. Coated lenses are covered with a thin metallic film that can be graduated so that it is denser at the top than at the bottom to cut out overhead glare. Photochromatic lenses contain silver crystals that have the property of growing progressively darker when exposed to bright ultraviolet light. But simple glasses of tinted plastic or glass can provide as much protection as these expensive lenses and, contrary to popular opinion, there is no evidence that the cheaper sunglasses damage the eyes. If they are of poor optical quality, they may give rise to a degree of eye strain during use, but this does not result in any permanent harm.

Sunglasses should not be worn by motorists except on medical recommendation. If they are dense enough to cut out 30 percent of incident light, they may reduce glare and increase the comfort of night driving, but they also reduce visibility and increase the time taken to adjust to fluctuations in light intensity by as much as 92 percent. Tinted glasses also alter color values and may make traffic signals less readily seen, while Polaroid lenses introduce the additional hazard of bringing out the stress patterns in toughened windshield glass, which can prove extremely irritating for many motorists.

The wearing of sunglasses by motorists is dangerous. Their use at other times is an unnecessary habit which is regrettable, not because it harms the eyes, but because it drains the world of color and deprives the wearer of the simple sensuous delight of observing nature in all its richness and variegated hues.

Swearing

Swearing, as the anthropologist Ashley Montagu pointed out in his book *The Anatomy of Swearing*, is "as old as man and coeval with language." The actual words we choose depends to a large extent on the cultural repressions we are subjected to. The English poet and scholar Robert Graves noted in his book *Lars Porsena: The Future of Swearing and Improper Language* that with the decline in the number and potency of our gods, there has been a corresponding decrease in the incidence of blasphemy and profanity. Dr. Vladimir Piskacek, a New York psychiatrist, found on the basis of a linguistic study of various European countries that the choice of swear words depends largely on prevailing cultural taboos. In religious countries like Poland and Austria, a blasphemy appears to be the common expression of rebellion. In countries like Germany that place great emphasis on order and cleanliness, obscenities tend to relate to the excretory functions of the body, whereas in America, with its long tradition of Puritanism, the tendency is to use sexual obscenities.

At times swearing is a more effective way of letting off steam than laughing or crying. In some cultures this harmless form of abreaction is ritualized. The Eskimos, for example, hold "drumming contests" at which feuding rivals indulge in a slanging match, egged on by members of the tribe. Their vituperative battle of words is continued until honor is satisfied, anger dissipated, and friendship restored. Since 1973 people needing to blow their tops in Tokyo have been able to use a twenty-four-hour telephone service. After listening to a tape-recorded message of female sympathy, embittered employees and henpecked husbands are encouraged to scream, yell, grumble, or curse. This "grudge line" became so popular that the service was extended into a battery of 200 telephones in order to cope with the 1,500 calls each day.

In time, swear words tend to lose their cathartic powers and need to be replaced. When the Romans ceased to worship their planetary gods, they ceased to swear "By Jupiter" or "By Jove." Britons, once they stopped showing allegiance to their patron St. George, ceased to swear "By George." But replacement oaths, profanities, and curses have always arisen to take their place.

Sweating

We tend to think that the human animal is the King of the Jungle, the Lord of all Creation. Yet if the Olympic Games were opened to all comers, man would almost certainly lose every event. The sprint events would be taken by the cheetah, the mile by the gazelle, the marathon by the wolf, most of the swimming events by the dolphin, and the high jump quite easily by the kangaroo. But there is one thing we excel at: Because we carry little body hair, we sweat more effectively than other mammals, and this enables us to exist in temperatures hot enough to fry an egg.

We lose from one to two pints of sweat a day, but this amount can be increased to as much as three pints an hour if strenuous physical exercise is taken in hot climates, for the production and evaporation of sweat is one of the major mechanisms for keeping the body cool. Insensible perspiration occurs throughout the day and becomes noticeable during exercise only when the rate of evaporation fails to keep pace with the rate of sweat-secretion. In the same way sweat is particularly noticeable in the armpits, groin, and feet, not because sweat production is greater in these areas, but because it evaporates less easily. The answer to sweaty underarms and feet is to wear lighter, more porous clothing and shoes (See *Clothing*).

At one time it was thought that sweating facilitated the removal of toxins from the body. This followed the observance that children taking part in religious festivals became ill and sometimes even died when their bodies were covered with gilt paint. This was attributed to the retention of poisons within the body, but this is a myth, for the amount of waste products voided from the body in sweat is negligible. When sweating is restricted we suffer from an unchecked rise in body temperature, not from the accumulation of toxins within the body, because, despite its large surface area, the skin is of little importance as an organ of excretion compared with the kidneys and lungs.

It is pointless, therefore, to take a Turkish bath after a heavy drinking spree in the hope that this will rid the body of its toxic waste. (At this time it is better to rehydrate the body by drinking plenty of water; see *Hangover Cures*.) Similarly, when suffering from influenza, don't go to bed with hot-water bottles and extra blankets in the belief that this will "sweat out" the infection. (During fevers, attempts should be made to reduce the temperature of the body, by cold sponging, if necessary.)

Another corollary of this theory is the mistaken belief that taking strenuous exercise to work up a "healthy" sweat helps rid the body of its accumulated waste products, toxins, and miscellaneous impurities. The value of exercise is in no way related to the sweating that accompanies it. It is pointless and in fact potentially harmful to encourage the formation of sweat while exercising by wearing sweatsuits or heavy sweaters.

Similarly, although strenuous exercise is of help in reducing weight, there is little benefit to be derived from passively induced sweating. Sitting in the extreme heat of a Turkish bath for an hour may lose a pound or more of fluid weight, but this is quickly replaced when the resultant thirst is quenched.

As a result of persistent advertising, we have been persuaded that sweat and natural body odors are undesirable. In fact, there is nothing nicer than the skin fragrance of the person one loves. The Song of Songs is filled with references to the lover whose cheeks smell of herbs, whose breasts smell of spices, and whose breath bears the sweet scent of apples. At one time, sweat was thought to be an aphrodisiac, and love philters filled with sweat were worn around the neck.

According to Paracelsus, if a man "ate or drank anything given off by the skin of another, he would fall desperately in love with that other." Oriental potentates would get the ladies of the harem to exercise to make them perspire, and would then choose, as concubine of the day, the girl whose clothes bore the most attractive scent. Now a whole industry has grown up to help us suppress these natural odors, and another to enable us to replace them with synthetic scents. It seems paradoxical that people will spend money to obliterate the odor of the product of their own apocrine glands and still more to replace it with the odiferous secretions of the sex gland of a skunk.

Most animals have special scent-secreting glands. Elephants have theirs on their foreheads, rhinos on their feet, rabbits near their anuses, and marsupials generally on their necks. Mankind has only a scattering of modified sweat glands (apocrine glands) under the armpits and in the genital area. These produce a secretion containing certain aromatic substances of pheromones, which, like hormones, are active in extremely minute quantities. The tracking abilities of a dog seem incredible. A man loses only a pint or so of sweat a day; little of this leaves the soles of the feet, and 99.5 percent of this is water. Yet a dog will pick up odor traces left by the feet of a man who may have passed days before. This is because only a few molecules of aromatic substances like butyric acid and acetic acid are required to trigger off the sense of smell, and each footstep carries 250 billion molecules of butyric acid. These pheromones are also responsible for increasing the sexual attractiveness of female monkeys when they are in heat, and it is possible that a woman excites a man, and a man a woman, by the chemicals they emit with their sweat. If this is true, antiperspirants are likely to prove antierotic, reducing rather than enhancing a person's attractiveness. This would be particularly true of vaginal deodorants which are, in any case, to be condemned because they interfere with the natural defenses of the skin and can cause rashes, irritation, and occasionally severe burns.

In Britain, the Housewives Trust tested out a typical vaginal deodorant on one thousand of its members and concluded, "We do not believe these products do anything a twice daily wash would not do better."

The same is true of all body-odor problems. Sweat is sterile and sweet-smelling when it reaches the skin (unless it carries the odor of certain drugs or aromatic foodstuffs such as onions and garlic). It becomes offensive only if allowed to stand, if the fatty substances it contains become broken down by bacterial decomposition. The answer to the problem of B.O. for most people therefore, is not to douse the skin with antiperspirants, deodorants, and all-concealing perfumed talcs, but to remove sweat secretions from the body by regular washing with plain soap and water (See *Soap*).

Tea Drinking

Tea drinking originated in China early in the fourth century. It became a fashionable beverage in Europe in the sixteenth century and spread soon after to America. The Englishman started out as a coffee-drinker but rapidly converted to tea, while the American started out as a tea-drinker but converted to coffee largely as a result of the iniquitous tea tax imposed by the British government. As a result Britons now drink five times as much tea as coffee, while Americans drink twenty-five times as much coffee as tea.

Tea, soon after its introduction, was described as a pernicious drug that destroys lives and causes chambermaids to lose their bloom. Others hailed it as "the sovereign drink of pleasure and of health." Drunk in moderation, it acts as a mild and harmless stimulant. An ancient Chinese legend relates that a Buddhist saint fell asleep during the course of his devotions and as a penance, when he woke up, cut off his eyelids and threw them to the ground. Here the lids took root and blossomed into a tea bush, the leaves of which were provided so that man forevermore could have an herb that would banish sleep.

Tea contains three main constituents: caffeine, tannin, and various essential oils and aromatic substances that provide its flavor and bouquet. Most cultures possess an indigenous drink derived from coffee beans, tea leaves, cocoa beans, or kola nuts, which all contain the stimulant drug caffeine.

The tannin contained in tea gives the drink its body and astringency. If taken in excess on an empty stomach, it can impair digestion and may in time damage the mucous membrane lining the stomach. This is not altogether surprising when one considers that tannin is the substance used in the process of tanning to convert soft, supple rawhide into tough, dry leather. People prone to indigestion should drink China tea, which contains considerably less tannin than Indian tea, and should dilute their tea with milk, since the milk protein casein combines with tannic acid to form a harmless inorganic salt. They should also avoid tea that has brewed too long. The ideal period of infusion is from three to five minutes, which is long enough to extract the caffeine and aromatic oils from the leaves. Longer periods of infusion merely increase the tannin content, which doubles when tea is left to stand for half an hour. In view of this, experts recommend straining tea into a second heated pot if it is to be kept for periods of longer than five minutes.

In 1973 a research worker at Oxford University reported a statistically significant link between drinking tea during pregnancy and the incidence of a severe form of brain damage known as anencephalous. This disorder, a common cause of stillbirth and neonatal death, was found to be ten times as common in Britain as in countries drinking less tea. It was found that there was a significant excess of babies with brain damage born to women drinking three or more cups of tea a day, and the probability that this relationship was due to chance was estimated to be less than one in a thousand. These findings, however, await confirmation and further analysis.

On the credit side, Professor Leslie Hardwick of the Turner Dental School at Manchester University has pointed out that tea contains fluoride to the extent that a generous consumption of tea would provide adults with as much protection from dental decay as the fluoridation of water supplies at the recommended levels. Drinking tea also seems to be safer than drinking coffee, for a team of doctors working at the Boston University Medical Center have found that people who drink six or more cups of coffee a day appear to have twice as great a risk of coronary thrombosis as those who either drink none or drink only tea. (This may, of course, be because the highly competitive people who are known to be prone to coronary disease also have a predilection for drinking coffee.)

Teeth Cleaning

Dental decay is the commonest disease in the western world, affecting 97 percent of American children, according to the Public Health Service. In the developing nations it is far less common. (One African tribe accepts an attack of dental caries as an adequate cause for divorce, the disease being far less prevalent there than adultery in the West).

In their natural state, teeth are remarkably resistant to disease. They are shaped in such a way that they are as far as possible self-cleansing, with saliva to bathe them and the constant movement of tongue and cheeks to polish their exposed surfaces. They are covered with enamel, probably the hardest animal substance known, which is extremely resistant to wear and which, like flint, will make a spark if struck with steel. It may seem odd that this structure, which is most resistant to rot in death, is most likely to decay in life, but this paradox is easily explained. Dental caries occurs only when certain parasitic bacteria are present in the mouth, and these are found only during the lifetime of their host.

The human mouth is normally teeming with bacteria, of up to eighty different varieties. Some of these—notably the lactobacillus acidophilus, or milk-loving bacterium—break down the simple sugars found in certain foods to form acids. If allowed to remain in contact with the teeth, these acids eat into the protective enamel coating and so start the process that we recognize as dental caries. At present, there is no way of ridding the mouth of these bacteria, but it is possible to deprive them of the sugar on which they feed, and to wash away or neutralize the acids they form. This involves a planned dietary regimen and a proper routine of dental care.

Some teeth are more resistant to decay than others, and there is evidence that a good diet in childhood, rich in dairy foods to provide adequate calcium and vitamins A and D, helps to build sturdy teeth. More controversial is the value of dietary supplements in later life. Dr. Alfred Aaslander, a Swedish agronomist, advocates the taking of a teaspoonful of bone meal every day to provide the calcium and trace minerals necessary for the continued health of the living tooth. "To build up the teeth is like building a house," he says. "If you use good bricks and mortar, you get a good house. Without them it falls apart." Foods that are unusually hot or cold should be avoided, since dental enamel can suffer "thermal fatigue" when exposed to extreme changes of temperature, leading to the formation of fissures that can permit the entry of bacteria.

The most important dietary advice, however, is to cut out sweet, sticky foods and to avoid eating between meals. Some years ago the Swedish Dental Institute studied the effect of giving volunteers sugar to eat either in drinks, with meals, or as between-meal snacks of toffee, caramels, and chocolate. They found that eating sticky sweets between meals increased the rate of dental decay over ten times. Chocolate was less damaging than toffee, and sweet-eating with meals less harmful than sweet-eating between meals. As a result of these and other studies, some doctors suggest that packets of sweets and toffees should carry a government warning like that on a packet of cigarettes: "WARNING: Sweet-eating is dangerous to your health." This is particularly true of children, who are especially prone to dental decay. They should never be offered sweets as a reward for good behavior nor, as infants, given sweetened pacifiers. In England it has been found that the number of children completely free from dental decay is 28 percent higher in schools without tuck shops selling ice creams, sweets, biscuits, chocolates, and ice pops. If children are to eat between meals, they should be offered apples, nuts, raisins, carrots, and potato chips. Sweets should be reserved for eating after meals.

Sticky foods containing sugar remain in contact with the teeth for about an hour. This means that if twelve sweets are eaten at hourly intervals, the teeth are exposed to risk for twelve hours. If twelve sweets are eaten together after a meal, the teeth are exposed to risk for only an hour. This explains why sweets should not be taken between meals and why sucking peppermints, with their slow release of sugar, is so damaging for the teeth. Eating potatoes and bread is less harmful than eating sweets because carbohydrates are not broken down into simple sugars until they reach the intestine and so cannot be converted into acids by the bacteria in the mouth.

Dietary change alone, however, will not prevent dental caries, for this problem existed long before the refinement of cane sugar and the development of the confectioner's art. Even Stone Age man—living on a diet of fruit, nuts, berries, and raw meat—suffered dental decay. A survey of twelve thousand Stone Age teeth showed that 8 percent of these were affected by decay. With even the healthiest diet, teeth need to be cleaned, and this can be done in a variety of ways.

One of the earliest methods involved the use of chewing sticks, portions of fibrous wood that when chewed cleansed the crevices between the teeth. Muslims frequently employed this technique, using a piece of wood called a *miswak*, to follow the Prophet's instruction recorded in the Koran: "You shall clean your mouth for that is the way to praise God." In Roman days teeth were generally rubbed clean with a piece of cloth. This was also the method used by Queen Elizabeth I of England who, one New Year's Day, received presents which included gold toothpicks and Holland tooth-cloths edged with black and gold. She used these devices regularly, together with a mouthwash containing rosemary, myrrh, and cinnamon, to such good effect that when the emissaries of King Henry VII of Naples visited the queen to assess her potential as a spouse, carrying the instructions "to approach as near to her mouth as they honestly may, to the intent that they may feel the condition of her breath, whether it be sweet or not," they were able to report that "the said Queen is like to be of a sweet savour and well aired." (Cleaning the teeth, in addition to preventing dental decay, serves a cosmetic function, whitening the teeth and sweetening the breath.) Toothpicks of silver, gold, or porcupine quills are another time-honored way of removing lodged particles of food from around the teeth. In seventeenth-century France it was a common practice for diners to pick their teeth after a meal with the pointed end of their knives. This so offended Cardinal Richelieu that he ordered that table knives were to be fashioned with a rounded end so that they could not be used as picks, a shape that many still carry to this day.

Toothbrushes are a natural development of toothpicks. They were first used in China over five hundred years ago but were developed independently by William Addis while he was languishing in England's Newgate Prison after being convicted for inciting a riot. Addis, like most of his contemporaries, was in the habit of cleaning his teeth with a cloth, but the thought occurred to him that the job might equally well be done with a brush. So he shaped a piece of bone, drilled minute holes in it, and inserted tufts of hair provided by a sympathetic prison warden. On his release, he marketed his new invention, which quickly became a great success.

Despite its current popularity, the toothbrush is probably not the most effective way of cleaning the teeth. One study showed that while a toothbrush is 60 percent efficient in removing biscuit débris from around the teeth in the space of thirty seconds, eating just a quarter of an apple does the same job with 90 percent efficiency. This is because the fibrous portions of the apple scour the crevices between the teeth, while the juice of the apple stimulates the flow of saliva and so helps to wash away particles of food that might escape a brush. (Saliva, which is mildly alkaline, also helps to neutralize any acids that come into contact with the teeth.)

At a dental conference in London, Professor R. D. Emslie reported on an experiment carried out in the Sudan to test the effectiveness of various indigenous methods of cleaning the teeth. It was found that the most effective way was using a chewing stick, followed in turn by cleaning with a piece of towel, using a toothbrush, and eating fibrous fruits (oranges and sugar cane). The chewing stick proved to be 80 percent effective and the orange 40 percent effective.

Rinsing the mouth with water is another proven way of cleaning the teeth and schoolchildren in England are now taught a "bubble, swill, and swallow" technique for use after meals—a mouthful of water bubbled between the teeth, swilled round the mouth, and then swallowed. There is evidence that if this were done three times after every meal the incidence of dental decay would be reduced by as much as two-thirds.

Whatever cleaning technique is chosen, it must be employed as soon as possible after a meal, for it takes less than ninety seconds for bacteria to start acting on sugars adhering to the teeth to form caries-producing acids. Studies carried out for the Swedish Government show that rinsing the mouth with water greatly reduces the concentration of sugar in the mouth if it is performed immediately after a meal.

The most important time of the day to clean the teeth is last thing at night, for during sleep the normal mouth-cleaning mechanisms are in abeyance, with the result that any sugar molecules that are not removed before retiring are likely to remain in contact with the teeth throughout the night. Ideally, each meal should end with the eating of a portion of fibrous food (apple, orange, celery, or raw carrot), followed by thorough mouth-rinsing.

If a brush is used, it must be employed correctly, with both surfaces of the teeth cleaned, together with the upper biting surfaces of the rear teeth. Brush strokes should travel from the gums to the apices of the teeth, brushing the upper teeth downward and the lower teeth upward. Since brushes wear out, they need to be replaced at least every six to nine months. A survey in Holland showed that 67 percent of people were using toothbrushes that were too worn to be of any practical value. In America the position is thought to be even worse; the American Dental Association estimates that four out of every five brushes in use throughout the country are in urgent need of replacement. Dentists recommend that children under the age of five should have their teeth cleaned for them, partly to make sure the job is done correctly and partly to get them into the right habit at an early age.

The choice and use of toothpaste is largely a matter of personal taste. There is no evidence that toothpaste helps to prevent dental decay, it merely adds a little piquancy to what is otherwise a rather boring task. The British Consumer's Association studied fifty-one different brands of toothpaste and found that none was more effective in preventing decay than brushing with water alone. Moreover, most contain either precipitated chalk or finely ground pumice, which may prove too abrasive for some teeth, eroding the protective dental enamel and wearing away the neck of the tooth. In addition, there is a risk that lead from the tubes can contaminate the paste and prove toxic, particularly for children. In view of this, toothpastes are probably best avoided. (If the teeth should become stained, they can be cleaned periodically by brushing with ordinary bicarbonate of soda.)

Vegetables

Diets vary, but the basic principles of human nutrition remain the same the world over. We need to eat vegetables for the proteins, vitamins, and minerals they contain, and some races show great ingenuity in obtaining adequate supplies of these important foods. The Otomi Indians of Mexico live in semidesert conditions in the Mesquital Valley but keep themselves fit by eating thistles, pigweed, and cactus fruit. The Zulus eat berries and the Chinese peasants the young sprouts of germinating plants. In these ingenious ways they keep themselves healthy—healthier often than races with far more money to spend who, in their ignorance, often end up overfed but undernourished.

A number of myths surround the eating of vegetables. At one time it was thought that eating greens helped purify the blood. (In fact, it merely provides *some* of the iron required for the formation of the oxygen-carrying red blood cells.) At an earlier date it was held that vegetables acted as potent aphrodisiacs. Onions were said to "excite Venus," artichokes were believed to "heat the genitals," and carrots were described as the "great furtherers of love's delights." More recently carrots were recommended as a sure way of improving night vision, which is only true in the rare cases of people suffering night-blindness from deficiency of Vitamin A. The importance of vegetables as a source of iron has also been exaggerated.

If we wanted to obtain all our requirements of iron from vegetables, we would have to eat the equivalent of four and one half pounds of Brussels sprouts a day. Most of our iron comes from meat (29 percent), and bread and cereals (31 percent), rather than from vegetables (19 percent).

Vegetables, however, are an important source of Vitamin C, the antiscurvy vitamin. It is common to regard the citrus fruits oranges and lemons as the major sources of Vitamin C, but in fact red and green peppers contain five times as much Vitamin C as the equivalent weight of oranges, and vegetables such as broccoli, parsley, and kale twice the quantity.

To get the maximum nutritional benefit from vegetables, they should be subjected to the minimum of preparation and eaten when they are really fresh. Vitamin C is easily destroyed by cooking, shredding, dicing, frying, or boiling. Greens kept warm on a hot plate can lose up to three quarters of their Vitamin C content. Ideally they should be boiled in a minimum of water in a closed saucepan and cooked and served as soon as possible. Even then some of the vitamins and minerals escape into the cooking water, which is far too valuable to be thrown away and should be saved and used for gravies, stocks, and soups.

As no one vegetable contains the entire range of vitamins, minerals, and essential aminoacids, it is advisable to vary the vegetable diet as much as possible. Eat plenty of fresh, mixed salads of sliced carrots, chopped mushrooms, shredded white cabbage, grated raw beetroot, mustard and cress, fine-chopped onions, chives, and parsley, with a few raisins, chopped nuts, and apple and onion portions thrown in for good measure, mixed in a large bowl together with a few tablespoons of healthful French dressing or home-made mayonnaise.

Tossed salads like these are well worth making and merit taking as a separate course either after the main dish as the Continentals do, or at the start of the meal as the Romans did, their first course or "gustation" consisting generally of an hors d'oeuvre of vegetables, herbs, radishes, and purple asparagus.

Walking

Very few people walk well. Stand at the corner of the street and watch the world walk by: In the parade you'll see hobblers, waddlers, mincers, and strutters, but very few people who walk with elegance and ease. This is perhaps not altogether surprising, for it is not easy to walk well. Every step forward we take involves the starting, stopping, acceleration, and deceleration of thirty different muscles. Human gait is also basically unstable. It involves balancing an unwieldy structure of five feet or more on a base that is constantly shifting and that, at times, is no larger than an identity disc. This feat is every bit as difficult as the juggler's trick of balancing a six-foot pole on his chin. Both acts take time to learn. A child requires many months to learn to walk. Many people never learn to do the job properly and as a result suffer needless fatigue and pain throughout their lives.

Fortunately, in recent years considerable research has been carried out into the mechanics of walking, most as a by-product of the drive to develop a more nearly perfect artificial leg for amputees. This makes it possible to provide a simple guide to the art of walking with elegance and ease. There are five basic considerations. The first concerns the distribution of weight on the feet.

With each successive footstep, the weight of the body should be taken first by the heel and then transferred in one smooth movement along the outside border of the foot, across the forefoot, and so to the big toe, which gives a final thrust as the foot leaves the ground. In this way the foot acts like a rocking chair, so that no one part of its structure takes the entire weight of the body for more than a brief moment. This minimizes strain and eliminates the jarring that occurs with a more leaden, flat-footed gait.

During walking the kneecaps must face directly forward. This insures the correct alignment of knee and ankle and permits these joints to flex and extend easily as we walk. The ankle joint is set at a slightly oblique angle, which means that when the knees face forward, the feet turn slightly out. This natural "out-toeing" of the foot measures about 15° in bare feet and slightly less when high-heeled shoes are worn. If the feet are turned out more than this, an ungainly, flat-footed gait results that throws unnecessary strain on the ligaments spanning the inner aspects of the knees and feet.

Walking entails side-to-side shifting of the pelvis that is necessary to bring the center of gravity of the body directly over the supporting foot. This movement is more marked in women than in men because of their greater pelvic width. In both sexes, the wider apart the feet are placed, the farther the pelvis has to move, so to reduce work and to maintain an easy flowing rhythm of movement, the feet should be placed no more than an inch or two apart–just far enough to prevent the knees from knocking together. If the feet are placed wide apart, an ungainly nautical roll develops. This may be permissible when balance is difficult, as on board ship or in extreme old age, but at other times it represents a lamentable waste of energy.

At the other extreme is the exaggerated mannequin's walk. Here the feet are placed one directly in front of the other. This may look attractive, and certainly emphasizes the feminine pelvic sway, but it is equally wasteful of energy. As a technique of walking it has little to recommend it and is best limited to stage and showroom use. (The women of Papua have developed a similarly provocative walk that emphasises the vibration and sway of their buttocks. It is said that Papuan girls are taught the finer points of this vibrato technique from the age of seven or eight and use it whenever men are present, but revert to their normal gait when they are in purely female company.)

During walking the major weight masses of the body—the head, trunk, and pelvis—should all be kept in line. This facilitates balance, lessens fatigue, and prevents postural strain. Heads should not poke forward nor bottoms protrude behind. The aim should be to walk tall—to feel like a puppet being lifted up by its central string.

The final secret of good walking is that it be effortless, and relaxed. To advance from the standing position, the trunk is inlaxed. To advance from the standing position, the trunk is inclined slightly forward from the hips so that the center of gravity of the body lies just in front of the feet. In this unstable position we would fall flat on our faces but for the fact that we swing first one leg and then the other to provide temporary supports for our advancing center of gravity. There is no need to waste energy pounding the ground or pumping the body up and down. Walking is really a controlled stumble—a slight inclination of the trunk to provide the initial forward momentum and then a relaxed, rhythmical swinging of the legs to provide the necessary props to keep the body from falling.

With the application of these five principles we can learn to walk with gazelle-like grace rather than elephantine clumsiness.

Thomas Jefferson, one of the early Presidents of the United States, recommended walking "as the best possible exercise." Its easy, flowing rhythm has a tranquilizing effect. While walking, we escape the hurly-burly of the day and have an opportunity to work off tensions and ponder over unsolved problems. A Latin tag, sometimes referred to as the "tramp's philosophy," says, "Walking solves it." The philosopher Bertrand Russell was equally sure of the psychological benefits of long-distance walks. "Unhappy businessmen," he wrote, "would increase their happiness more by walking six miles a day than by any conceivable change of philosophy." The additional exercise would also help curb their middle-age spread. Studies of overweight men and women show that they walk on average less than half as far as their slim contemporaries. A half hour's brisk walking burns up approximately three hundred calories. Continued every day for a year, this would result in a loss of nearly fifteen pounds in surplus weight.

A New Jersey schoolmaster grew alarmed at the flabbiness of many of his pupils and started taking them on long cross-country hikes. Within two years they had walked just over a thousand miles, their health had improved, and he had reduced his weight from 280 pounds to 210 pounds.

Walking provides other physical benefits. It is an excellent circulatory stimulant, an established treatment for varicose veins and chilblains, and an accepted procedure now in the management of even severe cases of gangrene. This novel treatment started some years ago when an American truck-driver was admitted to a hospital with a gangrenous big toe. Instead of being confined to bed as was customary at the time, he was allowed to walk about the ward on crutches. This brought such rapid relief of the pain that he was able to dispense with his crutches and walk with a cane. On this regimen his flesh healed with unexpected rapidity and he was soon able to resume his normal energetic work. Encouraged by this success, the walking cure was repeated in a further twenty-two cases of gangrene. Only one failure was reported—a woman who responded well in hospital but failed to maintain the treatment at home. Her family thought it was cruel to expect a person to walk on black, gangrenous toes, so they put her to bed. Without regular movement to aid her circulation her condition worsened, the gangrene spread, and she had to return to the hospital, where an amputation was performed.

Many of the telltale signs of advancing age, the deteriorating circulation, the breathlessness on exertion, the stiff joints and flabby muscles, are symptoms not of aging, but of chronic lack of exercise. Research workers at Loughborough University, Leicestershire, studied the physical-fitness levels of a large number of university students, county cricketers, professional golfers, and

Olympic oarsmen and found that the fittest group was the golfers, despite the slightly higher average age of its members. This they attributed to the distances they walked every day of their working lives. Regular walking like this can be the open-sesame to the fountain of youth.

A British radio reporter, Wynford Vaughan-Thomas, covering the 1947 royal tour of South Africa, was invited to accompany Field Marshal Jan Smuts on one of his early-morning strolls. "I turned up at the appointed place," Vaughan-Thomas records in his autobiography, "to discover that the Field Marshal's idea of a morning stroll at the age of 76 was a brisk climb up the 3,500 foot Table mountain behind Cape Town. I arrived panting at the summit ten minutes behind him. 'Young man', he said smiling, 'at my age I haven't as much time as you for loitering.' " That is the way to keep young and healthy.

Dr. Harry Johnson, an American physician with a specialist interest in the health of businessmen, recommends that executives over the age of fifty should take three twenty-minute walks every day, with an additional five-mile hike each weekend. In Germany this has been encouraged by the Stiftung Spazierengehen, or "Walking Foundation." This was set up by industrialist Georg von Opel to encourage a highly mechanized nation to rediscover the health-giving pleasures of long-distance country walking. Within a short while the foundation enrolled 50,000 members. Many reported on the marked physical benefits they derived. Several said that on their walks they were inspired to compose poetry. In this they followed a long tradition. Coleridge, creator of "Kubla Khan" and the "The Ancient Mariner," walked for ten miles every day and found inspiration on his travels. So too did Wordsworth, who walked an estimated 185,000 miles during his lifetime and at sixty was said to be as fit as he was at twenty. Socrates sought the truth as he wandered through the streets of Athens, and Aristotle, the father of logic and scientific thought, walked so much that he became known as the "Peripatetic Philosopher."

There can be few activities that equal walking as a conditioner of body and mind.

Will Power

The Victorians placed great emphasis on the need for discipline and self-control. They believed that a strong will could act like an alchemist's lodestone and convert dreams into reality, failure into success. We fail to achieve our full potential in life largely because we lack adequate motivation, will power, and drive. It is a mistake to think that ability automatically insures success. Stated in mathematical terms: Achievement = Ability + Motivation and Drive. When we fail, we fail more often from lack of adequate motivation than from lack of overall ability. Will power is often the missing factor in the equation of the unsuccessful life. We need to summon up our energies to overcome the multitude of physical and mental blocks that stand between us and the realization of our goals. We need to break down the barriers between thoughts and actions, desires and satisfactions, hopes and their fulfillment. But how is this strength of will developed? Countless books have been written on the subject, but in essence their advice is this.

Set definite targets, for targets serve as a spur to action. High jumpers always leap a little higher when they have a crossbar to clear. Make sure the goal is clearly defined and single, for if there is a conflict of desires action will be paralyzed. We lie in bed on a cold winter's morning, for example, saying "I must get up." But in truth only part of us wants to rise; our alter ego wants to stay in bed continuing to enjoy its comfort and warmth. Since we cannot split ourselves in two, we vacillate between the two competing goals.

The psychologist William James made a lifelong study

of the problems of the human will. His interest stemmed from his own inadequacies, for throughout his life James was plagued by agonizing indecision. In the latter days of his career at Harvard University he tried to make up his mind whether or not to give up lecturing. One day he would write in his diary "Resign," the next day "Don't resign," and the following day "Resign." Torn by this conflict, his ability to act effectively became impaired, so that he was "not so much a person as a civil war." The goals we set, therefore, must be clear, realistic, and with a set time laid down for their execution. As New York psychotherapist Rollo May has said, "The road to Hell is paved with vague intentions." It is no good saying, "I must get down to some letter-writing." That is far too vague to pin us down: We can still avoid writing certain letters or postpone all letter-writing until tomorrow, next week, or even the following month. We must be more precise. The goal should be, say, to write a letter of condolence to Aunt Betty before lunch. Similarly, if we want to become an international-class high jumper and can now barely clear five feet, we shouldn't start by aiming to jump seven feet, but should set ourselves the more realistic task of clearing five feet six by the end of the season.

Having set definite goals we must then concentrate all our emotional energies on seeking their achievement. This involves the stimulation of desire, rather than the application of strenuous effort. When we are starving we need no act of self-discipline to motivate us in our search for food. When we are in love, however poor our memory for everyday events, we have no difficulty remembering the exact hour and place of our next meeting with the one we love. As Aristotle said: "Will moves through desire." The more passionate our desires, the more likely we are to achieve them. We don't have to coax ourselves to run when we're chased by a bull. Similarly, there is no need to make an effort of will when we are driven by strong desire. In fact employing effort is often counterproductive because it introduces an element of conflict between wish and counterwish. If I want to get out of bed in the morning on a cold winter's day and try to stir myself into action by saying, "You *must* get up," I immediately suggest to my subconscious mind the counterwish, "But it would be much nicer to stay in bed." Far better that I should say: "I must get up and see what the postman has brought," for then I avoid a conflict between wish and will. Whatever our chosen goal, we should first make it the object of our desires, and then concentrate on obtaining it with singleness of purpose, for concentration, as Ralph Waldo Emerson said, "is the secret of strength in politics, in war, in trade—in short, in all management of human affairs."

We must concentrate our energies and focus our imagination on achieving our goals. If we have chosen a realistic target, we must have faith in our ability to achieve it. Emil Coué, the father of autosuggestion, founded his therapy on the belief that "if you think you can, you will." He gave a telling illustration of the power of suggestion and faith: "Suppose that we place on the ground a plank thirty feet long by one foot wide. It is evident that everybody will be capable of going from one end of this plank [to the other] without stepping over the edge. But now change the conditions of the experiment, and imagine this plank placed at the height of a cathedral. Who then will be capable of advancing even a few feet along this narrow path? . . . Why is it, then, that you would not fall if the plank is on the ground, and why should you fall if it is raised to a height above the ground? Simply because in the first case you *imagine* that it is easy to go to the end of this plank, while in the second you imagine that you cannot do so."

Similar effects have been demonstrated under hypnosis. Men with a grip strength of 101 pounds have managed to exert a grip of 142 pounds when told they were strong, but have been reduced to weaklings able to exert a pressure of only 29 pounds when told they were weak. Such is the power of the imagination. It is useless to try to hold back the sea with an effort of the will when the tide of emotions is flowing in the opposite direction. As Coué demonstrated, "When the Imagination and the Will are in conflict the Imagination invariably gains the day."

A tennis player reaches a crucial stage in a game and thinks, "How dreadful if I serve a double fault." Time and again, with these thoughts in mind he drives consecutive balls into the net. A child learning to ride a bicycle spots a stone in the road and thinks, "I mustn't hit that stone." Invariably, like a magnet, the child is drawn toward the stone, for actions follow thoughts. If we want to serve well at tennis, we must concentrate on serving an ace, not on avoiding a double fault. We must hold only positive thoughts. Thus, if we want to be healthy we must crowd out all thoughts of sickness and fill our minds with thoughts of vitality, health, and strength. If we wish for happiness, we must flood our minds with cheerful thoughts, for "As a man thinketh in his heart, so is he."

One big obstacle still remains: the dreadful inertia that so often blocks effective action. An author desperately wanted to write. He woke up each morning feeling sure this was the day when the muse would be with him, but first of course he had to have his breakfast. Then he wanted to take a walk to clear his head. When he came back he felt he needed a brief rest, during which time he read the daily papers. Then it was time for coffee. By this time he found one or two trivial chores to do and then it was time for lunch. The same thing happened in the afternoon, and so all thoughts of writing were postponed until the following day. A wise doctor, hearing his problem, advised him to work to a set timetable: just two hours' work a day immediately after breakfast with the rest of the day free. On this far-from-arduous schedule he overcame his procrastination and completed some valuable work. Mark Twain, when asked the secret of becoming a successful writer, gave similar advice: "Apply the seat of your pants to the seat of a chair." If you dream of becoming a writer, start writing. If you want to reduce your handicap at golf, get out and start practicing. Work to a definite schedule, and start the schedule *today.* Students don't need urging to work two days before a final examination, and most people find they work best when given definite deadlines. The *first* step on the road to success is generally the most difficult one to take.

Then, having started out towards your goal, carry on. Persevere, for the more a task is repeated the easier it becomes. By repetition we can train ourselves to be quitters or stickers, sinkers or survivors, achievers or failures. As Cecil Mace, professor of psychology at the University of London, says in *The Psychology of Study:* "One of the most profound and practically important truths that the psychologist reports concerning the human will is that *what we do on any particular occasion depends not so much upon what we think and feel and desire on that occasion itself, but upon what we thought and felt and desired some time, perhaps a very long time, before that occasion*" (author's italics).

We are conditioned by the past. Our mind is like a barrel organ. The tune we play is preset and appears every time we turn the handle. Will power may be needed to call the tune initially, but after that it takes little effort to turn the handle.

Wind

The human stomach and intestine contain about 1,000 cubic centimeters of gas, consisting of nitrogen (59 percent), hydrogen (21 percent), carbon dioxide (9 percent), methane (7 percent), and oxygen (4 percent). We swallow gases—air—during the process of eating, and still more gas is produced in the large intestine as the result of bacterial action. When produced in large quantities, gas can give rise to abdominal discomfort. This happens in people who constantly gulp air, a nervous habit akin to blinking, facial tics, and obsessive knuckle-cracking. Gas production is also increased by a diet rich in vegetables such as beans, peas, and cabbage, and as a result of emotional excitement. Casanova relates in his *Memoirs* the tale of one of his paramours whose main claim to fame was that she passed large quantities of flatus whenever aroused to a state of sexual excitement.

Discomfort can also arise as a result of air travel, for atmospheric pressure is halved at an altitude of 19,000 feet, which means that without pressurization of aircraft cabins, the volume of gas in the intestine would double.

The popular schoolboy trick of setting light to gas passing from the rectum demonstrates that the intestinal gases are capable of supporting combustion, and in some areas practical use is made of this by running a series of street lamps on sewer gas. Occasionally the proportions of hydrogen, oxygen, and methane in the intestinal gases produce an explosive mixture, and explosions have been known to occur during abdominal surgery and on rare occasions when a burp has coincided with the act of lighting a cigarette. Dr. Theodor Rosebury, emeritus professor of bacteriology at Washington University, St. Louis, has suggested in view of this that "smoking might not have become popular if the evolution of mammals had not placed the anus at a good distance from the mouth."

Some of the intestinal gases are absorbed into the bloodstream, but most find outlets from the body either through the mouth or anus, sources of disposal that both present social rather than medical problems. Some people troubled with what they consider to be excessive "wind" eat charcoal biscuits or burnt toast, on the grounds that dry activated charcoal absorbs large quantities of gas, but experiments have shown that once charcoal enters the intestine and is wetted and mixed with a variety of electrolytes and colloids, it loses most of its absorptive properties and so has little therapeutic effect. Another remedy of doubtful value is the taking of bicarbonate of soda for "indigestion." This may help to bring up the gas but can also aggravate matters, for when the gastric juices act on bicarbonate of soda they produce quantities of carbon dioxide gas, which must itself find release. Furthermore, prolonged taking of sodium bicarbonate can dangerously alter both the sodium content and the acidity of the blood. Learning to relax is a more certain cure for "gas" because it improves digestion, quietens the rumblings of an overexcited gut and checks the nervous tendency to gulp air (see *Relaxation*).

Man's anxiety over the volume of wind within him is of great antiquity. One of the most potent evil spirits inhabiting the world of the ancient Babylonians was Lilith, the demon of wind, who was thought to be responsible for much human suffering. Babylonian mothers were particularly fearful lest Lilith should enter their babies during the night and give them colic. And so they sang lullabies, not simply to soothe their children to sleep, but also as a chant to keep the demon Lilith at bay; hence, it is suggested, the derivation of the word lullaby (Lili-a-bay).

Today mothers no longer believe in evil spirits, but in the West they still struggle to rid their babies of the demon wind, and many popular books on infant care continue to insist that babies should be "burped," "winded," or "bubbled" after their feeds. But what exactly does this achieve? The fact that a child draws its legs up to its stomach after a feed does not mean it is suffering from abdominal pain. This is a normal accompaniment of crying, and not a sign that the baby is suffering from "wind" or hunger pangs. Adults and children alike swallow air when they eat, but no one suggests that adults need "burping," although no doubt they too would belch convincingly if immediately after a meal they were bounced up and down and patted vigorously on the back. The comfort a child derives from the burping ritual probably stems from the close bodily contact it receives from its mother, together with the reassuring patting and rubbing on its back, comforting gestures that Desmond Morris, the eminent ethologist, has observed within ape families. Once the child is soothed, the valve at the upper end of its stomach relaxes, so that it is likely then to bring up the wind it has swallowed while crying and feeding, but it is the comforting which produces the wind, rather than the wind the comfort.

As one pediatrician has said, "We have no difficulty in recognizing fetishes in other cultures . . . we must also recognize our own fetishes, being aware that the present day obsession with bringing up the wind has become comparable with a need to get the evil spirit out of the baby."

Zest

The philosopher Bertrand Russell found it appropriate to devote an entire chapter of his book *The Conquest of Happiness* to the subject of Zest, which he described as "the secret of happiness and well being." It is the ingredient that above all others gives life its sparkle, gaiety and ebullience. It is the bubbles in a glass of champagne, the icing on a cake, the yeast that leavens a loaf. Without zest life is like a meal without relish–dull, flat and insipid. (Originally the term was used in reference to the flavor extracted from the peel of lemons, but now it has all but lost its culinary associations and is used only to describe the spice of life.)

Little that is worthwhile in life is achieved without zest. It is the charismatic quality that attracts friends and gains allies, and the dynamism we use to break down barriers and secure our goals. As Ralph Waldo Emerson says: "Nothing great was ever achieved without enthusiasm."

Yet, ironically, from childhood we are trained to "play it cool," and taught to fear the activists, even though experience shows that these are the people who are most likely to achieve success and who are most truly masters of their destiny. If we wish to attain our full potential and extract the maximum enjoyment from life, we must reject the stultifying habit of dull conformity and learn again to live with passion. "Le seule morale," said one French philosopher, "est de vivre avec ferveur." (The only principle is to live with passion.)

Health alone is not enough. This book began, appropriately, with Apathy and ends with Zest; but apathy will not be dispelled nor zest acquired simply by leafing through its pages. Zest is vitality in action. To find it we must put habits into action, banishing our timidity and setting out to seize with both hands the excitement, opportunities and challenges that life affords, living at all times as nature intended—with vigor, passion, courage, and zeal.